Exploitation and Exclusion: Race and Class in Contemporary US Society

African Discourse Series

General Editor: Abebe Zegeye

No. 1: *Forced Labour and Migration: Patterns of Movement within Africa* (eds A Zegeye & S Ishemo)

No. 2: *Repression and Resistance: Insider Accounts of Apartheid* (eds R Cohen, Y Muthien & A Zegeye)

No. 3: *Exploitation and Exclusion: Race and Class in Contemporary US Society* (eds A Zegeye, L Harris & J Maxted)

Exploitation and Exclusion:

Race and Class in Contemporary US Society

Edited by

Abebe Zegeye
Centre for Modern African Studies, University of Warwick

Leonard Harris
Department of Afro-American Studies, Purdue University

Julia Maxted
Centre for Research in Ethnic Relations, University of Warwick

Published for the Centre for Modern African Studies

University of Warwick

HANS ZELL PUBLISHERS

London • Melbourne • Munich • New York • 1991

Hans Zell Publishers
is an imprint of Bowker-Saur Ltd, a Reed International Books Company.
Borough Green, Sevenoaks, Kent, England TN15 8PH

British Library Cataloguing in Publication Data

A catalogue record for this book is available from the British Library.

Library of Congress Cataloging-in-Publication Data

Exploitation and exclusion : race and class in contemporary US society
/ edited by Abebe Zegeye, Leonard Harris, Julia Maxted.
  296p. 220cm. -- (African discourse series : no. 3)
"Published for the Centre for Modern African Studies, University of
Warwick."
Includes bibliographical references and index.
ISBN 0-905450-67-1 (alk. paper)
  1. Afro-Americans--Social conditions. 2. United States--Race relations.
3. Social classes--United States. I. Zegeye, Abebe. II. Harris, Leonard, 1948- .
III. Maxted, Julia. IV. Univeristy of Warwick. Centre for Modern African Studies.
V. Series.
E185.86.E8 1991
305.896'073--dc20   91-31148
                                                              CIP

Cover design by Robin Caira

Printed on acid-free paper.

Typeset by Selro Publishing Services, 34 Warnborough Rd. Oxford
Printed and bound in Great Britain
by Antony Rowe Ltd.
Chippenham, Wiltshire.

To Ann and Michael Dummett

Contents

Preface

The Editors

The character of race and class in the late twentieth century is complicated by the blurring of popularly accepted race and class distinctions. Such distinctions have been the popular categories through which persons have defined their identities and given meaning to their experiences in a segregated and class-divided world. The ideas of race and class as distinct natural or unnatural entities have framed critical approaches to their interrelationship. Recent arguments have contended that the ideas of race and class are constantly changing meaning according to social conditions and lack scientific validity. Concepts which have tended towards constructing a totalized world view or episteme, and which have sustained sharp distinctions between race and class, have been the subject of critical attention and revaluation. Race and class situations, and the identities associated with them, certainly reflect different life chances and cultural realities, and they influence behaviour in varying ways. While it is arguable that race and class exploitations differ fundamentally, none the less what stands behind explanations of their relationship is often a view of what is 'natural', and this view often conveys inadequate explanations.

In providing a greater degree of cogency in explaining race and class, and in countering the inadequacy of naturalist assumptions, several chapters approach and evaluate the current position of theoretical articulation of racial and class formation. In Chapter 1 Anthony Appiah argues against dependence on empirical sciences and the 'optimism of the intellect' to which it gives rise. This optimism of the intellect is the belief that empiricism can ultimately answer racist and racially divisive perspectives. He argues that rather than countering reactionary beliefs and views, too great a reliance on the utility of scientific knowledge to questions of race is itself reactionary, in that such reliance gives credence to and supports the divisions and divisiveness within forms of knowledge which allow hegemonic rule to continue undisturbed.

In addressing the problem of discrimination against black workers, Mark Gould (Chapter 7) takes issue with orthodox and non-orthodox neo-classical theories of a competitive, egalitarian economy, and the failure of these theories adequately to explain the continuing discrimination within the US labour market. He argues that an adequate model must take account of the role that power — especially in the relations between employer and employee — plays in a competitive labour market and how racist attitudes affect market discrimination. The shifts in perception such a changed model would inculcate, he concludes, would lead to a better-developed movement for structural economic change.

David Goldberg (Chapter 6) counters traditional social scientific analysis of race on the basis of its reductionism. After a description of the socio-historical grounds of racism, he distinguishes between the discursive formations of race and class, arguing for the autonomy of racist discourse. The distinction, he concludes, depends on class discourse being based on exploitation, racist discourse functioning in terms of exclusion.

Howard McGary (Chapter 2) examines the question of race and class exploitation. Marxist and conservative interpretations of the forms of exploitation are described and analysed, but are found wanting in their reduction to either material or psychological determinants. For McGary, on the other hand, the distinction between class and race exploitation revolves around the question of personhood: a status which in the case of class is granted, but in the case of race is denied.

Leonard Harris (Chapter 3) looks at theories of a simple core meaning of racism and of the concept of multiple variegated racisms. Both concepts are inadequate, he suggests, and this inadequacy is exposed by their applications in supporting either colour-blind or colour-conscious principles of justice. Rather, he argues, the contextuality and cosequentiality of racism should be considered.

Thomas Boston (Chapter 9) starts by referring to the reactions to his 1988 book, *Race, Class and Conservatism*, where the conceptualization of racial class formation and the elucidation of interactions between race and class were undertaken. He discusses the particular specification of social classes in African-American society, and focuses on the internal structures of such classes. Folllowing an abstracted definition of class, derived and modified from the definitions of Marx, Weber, Poulantzas and Giddens, the correlations between class, economic status and the strata within classes are delineated.

Howard Winant (Chapter 8) examines the concept of racial formation in social life, a formation constituent of individual, interrelational and collective identities and social structures. Of particular importance in racial formation is the process of rearticulation, whereby individual and group identities are shaped and transformed. He identifies three actors within these processes — persons, the state and social movements — and underlines the immense importance of social movements in rearticulating the formation of race.

In other contributions the areas and theoretical insights outlined above are brought to bear upon and are reflected by actual social movements and questions in contemporary US society. Lou Kushnick (Chapter 10) undertakes an extensive examination of the civil rights movement in the US, seeing it as having achieved much-needed but nevertheless limited success in the ending of legalized segregation. The limitations of the movement are associated with the development of US economic and diplomatic objectives in the post-war period (particularly with regard to domestic anti-communism and cold war relations), and Kushnick concludes by delineating the challenges still faced by both blacks and progressive whites.

Gerald McWorter et al. (Chapter 11) use the paradigm of the social movement in their analysis of the Chicago mayoral election of 1982/3. Distinguishing between the roles of political 'insiders' (from the traditional political machine and institutions) and 'outsiders' (drawn from black nationalist and radical socialist movements), the establishment of a dual leadership, its development throughout the campaign, and the particular contribution of the outsiders (especially in the early mobilization stages) are examined.

Julia Maxted and Abebe Zegeye (Chapter 12) examine the ways in which race and class have been rearticulated in the development of post-war Los Angeles. The social and spatial structures which sustained post-war Fordist consumption are becoming increasingly disengaged, giving rise to new patterns of racial subordination, amplified by gender and class.

Geneva Smitherman (Chapter 5) addresses the question of the dominant role of language in social transformation. She provides an explanatory framework independent of traditional socio-linguistic and Chomskyan models, and analyses the historical formation and development of black English in the US. Following an account of empirical research amongst black and white motorcar workers, she argues that black English is in the process of becoming a class sociolect, transformative of social relations.

Bernard Boxill (Chapter 4) examines the position of the black 'underclass' (a term contested by some of the other contributors to the volume), and analyses the deficiencies of conservative, liberal and libertarian proposals for its assimilation into mainstream US society. In conclusion, he offers suggestions of both external (governmental) and internal (within the black community) steps which can be practically taken.

Acknowledgements: The editors would like to thank Ceri Peach for his support and St Catherine's College, Oxford, for kindly providing the venue for the conference. We would also like to thank Selina Cohen for her fastidious copy-editing.

1

Social Forces, 'Natural' Kinds

Kwame Anthony Appiah

Many Western liberals are prone to a specific form of 'optimism of the intellect'. It shows up in a number of different domains, but is most striking, perhaps, in two that have preoccupied many of us recently: namely, gender and race. What I have in mind is a tendency that shows up in every case in which political reactionaries hold that invidious discrimination between groups — boys and girls, Jews and WASPS, the working classes and the middle classes, blacks and whites — is justified by an objective difference between those groups — in strength, in patriotism, in diligence, in intelligence or whatever. The specific form of optimism of the intellect I have in mind is the liberal assumption that we may win the argument with the reactionary by replying: 'There is no such difference.'

This strategy of response to the racist, the sexist, the classist, strikes me as almost always mistaken: for it concedes practically everything to the forces of reaction, while deferring the outcome in practice to an empirical investigation whose outcome is by no means assured. And it is important to be clear that the reason its outcome is not assured is that the empirical investigation of these issues is so ideologically constructed that we can confidently predict in many cases that the 'results' will depend on the initial disposition of the investigators. By the time the issue of whether black children should be educated in the same way as white children has come to depend on the outcome of Professor Shockley's investigation of 'racial' IQ differences; or the issue of whether a mathematics education for girls is worthwhile has come to depend on psychologists' investigations of innate gender differences in cognitive capacity; or the question of welfare-payments has come to depend on finding out whether the underclasses have sufficient empirical incentive to seek work; by that time, we have usually lost any chance of changing minds let alone policies.

In this chapter I want to argue that in our world we should almost never simply defer questions about the justification of discrimination to the empirical sciences (which is not to say that we should never support or learn from empirical investigations).[1] I want to argue (a) against assuming that once we turn the sciences loose on the question of difference they will usually find in our favour — against the optimism of the intellect, while reminding one of a few of the familiar arguments; and (b) against supposing that even if the facts were not as we would like, that would usually settle the issue.

Two Strategies of Argument

Let me start with (b), which is, as I say, a familiar line of thought. Optimism of the intellect urges us to suppose that, with genuinely equal education, a random assortment of boys has about the same chance as a random assortment of girls of coming to understand set-theory or the theory of monster groups.

But suppose this were not true: suppose that, with equal education, the girls would do better on average. Why should this have the consequence that we should use gender as a criterion in allocating mathematical education to children? We can state clearly why it does not follow if we allow ourselves a little terminology.

Consider any capacity, C, of which it makes sense to make comparative judgments to the effect that some individuals have more C than others. Let us say that distribution of that capacity across groups, G_1, G_2, and so on ranks G_1 above G_2 with respect to C if either (a) the median member of G_1 is more C than the median member of G_2; or (b) the modal C-value of G_1 is more C than the modal value of G_2; or (c) the mean C-value of G_1 is more C than the mean value of G_2.[2]

Let us say that a ranking with respect to C over groups G_1, G_2 etc. is *disjoint* if every member of the group that ranks highest is more C than every member of the group that ranks second-highest; and every member of the second-highest group exceeds every member of the third-highest, and so on.[3]

We can now see at least two strategies for arguing against an inference from a statistical correlation to a justification for different treatment of the groups. Strategy One, which has often been made to good effect against Shockley and his kind, is to argue that a statistical correlation between group membership and some intellectual capacity, cannot by itself justify treating every member of one group differently from every member of other groups, unless the distribution of that capacity across the groups is disjoint. Indeed, where C is almost any characteristic that is plausibly relevant to how people should be treated that has ever been offered — and this is certainly true in the case of IQ and mathematical capacity — there is almost no group that has actually been discriminated against on the basis of an alleged ranking of groups with respect to C, for which the ranking is either disjoint or almost so. Simply put, it has always been clear that there were many women and many blacks who were stronger or more intelligent than most white men.

It has not always been noticed that this observation provides the basis for arguing against discrimination between individuals because of their detectable membership of some group that has a certain statistical character, even if there is a pure Bayesian reason for treating them differently because that is all the evidence we have about them.[4] As a result of historical discrimination black-skinned people in the USA are more likely than white-skinned people to be brought up in circumstances of poverty and to be subject to greater temptations to theft. It may well be true therefore that the conditional probability that a person will rob your shop, given only that he or she is white-skinned is less than the conditional probability that someone will rob your shop, given only that she or he is black-skinned. Does it follow that shopkeepers, seeing a black-skinned person outside their door may sometimes legitimately refuse to permit them entry even though they would admit someone who was white-skinned and otherwise indistinguishable? To answer 'Yes' to this question is to allow the burden of the historical wrong to be borne disproportionately by black-skinned people; and especially by black-skinned people who have no special disposition to commit theft.[5]

A second strategy of argument — Strategy Two — however, can be conducted even where the differences between the groups *are* relevant to the discrimination *and* the rankings are disjoint. Thus, for example, suppose that the results of some test — call it an 'EQ' test — were genuinely relevant to how effectively a child could use educational resources; and consider two groups: namely, those with EQs above and those with EQs below some value. Even in such a case, where the ranking is by definition disjoint, an argument needs to be mounted for allocating educational resources unequally between members of these two groups. If, for example, each child has a right to an equal expenditure of educational resources, then the fact that the resources that my child is owed would, if added to those available for your child, make yours a much better mathematician than she now is and only slightly improve the mathematical performance of mine does not entitle anyone to reallocate my child's share.

The existence of these two familiar strategies is by itself sufficient to guarantee that even if the optimism of the intellect that I have been discussing were simply factually mistaken — even if the groups that had been the victims of invidious discrimination did in fact differ in statistically significant respects in characteristics relevant to how individuals should be treated — it would not follow that the members of those groups should be treated differently.

The Falsity of Racialism

If the points I have been making under project (b) — arguments against supposing that we need optimism of the intellect to support resistance to current forms of racial and sexual discrimination — are familiar, the points I want to make now, under project (a) — arguments against assuming that science will find in our favour — are I think, both less obvious and less well known. To make them I shall be using some familiar talk — in particular of 'knowledge and human interests' — in what I think is an unfamiliar way.[6] And to get where I am going it will help, I think, if we allow ourselves *reculer pour mieux sauter*. One particular form of my 'optimism of the intellect' holds, in the case of racism, that the racist's fundamental presupposition — that there is a biologically given category of race — has been shown empirically to be false.[7] I have argued this myself elsewhere.[8] I have argued, that is, against:

the view — which I shall call racialism — that there are heritable characteristics, possessed by members of our species, that allow us to divide them into a small set of races, in such a way that all the members of these races share certain traits and tendencies with each other that they do not share with members of any other race. These traits and tendencies characteristic of a race constitute, on the racialist view, a sort of racial essence; and it is part of the content of racialism that the essential heritable characteristics of the 'Races of Man' account for more than the visible morphological characteristics — skin colour, hair type, facial features — on the basis of which we make our informal classifications.

And I still believe that racialism, so defined, is false.

Despite this, however, talk of race — in human evolutionary biology, in physical anthropology and in all areas of medicine — persists. Doctors of science and of medicine do not normally refer to phlogiston or to animal spirits, whose official fate is the same as that of race. And the question why this is — given that such people usually know (often better than I!) the very same experimental and theoretical literature that I have argued shows that there are no races — is worthy of consideration. And it is in the course of discussing that question that ideology and interest will come into play.[9]

The Harmful Residue

The recent literature on natural kinds and the semantics of kind-terms has brought into focus the widespread belief, among philosophers and natural scientists alike, that some classifications are artificial while others 'cut nature at the joints.'

Even someone like myself who is sceptical of our entitlement to the sort of strong realism that seems to underlie such thoughts, can acknowledge that, looked at from the point of view of current theory[10] some previous theories (early nineteenth century chemistry, say) look as though they classified some things (acids and bases, say) into the right kinds, even if a lot of what they said about those things was pretty badly wrong. And our recognition of the fact that the classification was in itself an intellectual achievement is recorded in the fact that we are inclined to say that when an early nineteenth-century chemist — who could hardly be expected to have understood the notion of a proton donor — used the word *acid* he was nevertheless talking about the very proton donors we call 'acids.'

Causal theories of reference are often invoked at this sort of point: we are urged to believe that the stuffs 'out there' in the world that really accounted for the central features[11] of Davy's *acid* talk really were acids and that is what accounts for our sense that Davy was not simply talking about something else.

I confess I have never been at all happy with this as an explanation of why acid is saved and, for example, animal spirits are not. This story just gives the wrong answer to the question, 'Why do we think that Davy's term acid refers, while, say, Descartes's term animal spirit does not?' One thing that struck me when I first read Descartes's *Treatise on the Passions of the Soul* was how much of what he said would have been true had he spoken not of animal spirits but of anions and cations. And what were really out there in the nerves about which Descartes spoke — which were, of course, well-known structures in the anatomy of Descartes's day — were sodium and potassium ions and the like; they really did travel through those nerves and their passage really did, as Descartes supposed, account for many features of sensation.

Why, then, do biologists say that there are no animal spirits, rather than saying the sort of thing we say about acids: that they exist, that, in fact, they are certain ions, and that Descartes had a good many false beliefs about them? I am sceptical that the causal theories of reference allow us to answer this question. For a consistent causal theorist of reference, persuaded that there is enough of the right stuff in the use of the term animal spirits in Descartes and his contemporaries is likely, I think, to say that it is a mere prejudice that accounts for our unwillingness to allow that the term refers. And this, though consistent, is to defer the explanation of why we do not treat it as referring to somewhere else or, perhaps, to nothing at all.

I do not have the time to argue in favour of the view that animal spirit is a term that is in at least as good a shape as Davy's (or Newton's) use of the term acid. But I offer this pair of contrasting cases only because they suggest an answer to the question — 'Why does animal spirit not get treated as a referring expression?'; an answer that itself suggests an important moral for our pursuit of the reference of the term race.

That answer is that the term animal spirit belongs to a vocabulary that is simply too close to a language we nowadays think of as vitalist (at best) and religious (at worst) and that the resistance to seeing continuity between Descartes's theorizing and ours is in part a residue of the nineteenth century battle between religion and science.

This residue is, I suppose, in this case, quite trivial. But I want to suggest that an analogous residue exists in talk of race in the sciences, and that there the residue is far from harmless.

The Adequacy Condition

At last three things are required for us to allow that a past theorist who spoke of 'Ys' and was badly mistaken was nevertheless talking about something, call it 'X': first — the existence condition — we must acknowledge the existence of X; and, second — the adequacy condition — some of what was thought to be true of what 'Y' denoted must be at least approximately true of X; and third, X must be the best candidate for the job of 'Y's' referent, so that no other thing that satisfies the existence condition satisfies the adequacy condition equally well. Provided these conditions obtain we may even feel that there is not much harm in using the old term 'Y,' in a sort of self-conscious way, remarking from time to time, in case we should forget, that, of course this is not exactly right.[12]

In relation to the term race something like these three conditions are widely held to be satisfied: the notion of a population of organisms, where most mature females and males are mutually sexually fertile being the idea for which we still have a use; much of what was believed about races being, allegedly, approximately true of such populations; and there being no other candidate notion equally suited to do the job.

And on most causal theories of reference, whether or not we still talked about races, that would justify us in supposing that 'race' referred to such populations.

To see why this way of looking at things substantially distorts the real situation, it will help to borrow and then modify Habermas's notion that an area of inquiry is partially constituted by a characteristic range of interests.

Habermas accounts for the distinction that Dilthey had sought to establish between the *Naturwissenschaften* and the *Geisteswissenschaften*, by arguing that each kind of knowledge is constituted by a distinct kind of interest. The natural sciences are rooted in a 'knowledge-constitutive interest in possible technical control,'[13] while the knowledge-constitutive interest of the *Geisteswissenschaften* is 'practical.'[14] There are many problems with this line of thought: the distinction between a 'practical'

interest in mutual understanding and a 'technical' interest in
control is far from clear, for example; nor is it clear how these
differences in interest 'constitute' a field of inquiry; or that we
should seek to understand differences between domains of
knowledge at the perilous level of abstraction at which natural,
social and critical knowledge are supposed to be differentiated.
But the idea that interests play a role in the constitution of areas
of inquiry or of the institutions we call 'disciplines,' while
already less specifically Habermasian, is surely something we
can borrow.

'Interest' here should carry both its senses: the sense in which
it contrasts with disinterest and the sense in which it contrasts
with a mere lack of epistemic engagement. I shall argue in a
moment for this claim in the case of race science. But what
should immediately draw our interest is the question of what it
is for an interest — in any sense — to constitute an area of
enquiry or a kind of knowledge.

And here, I believe, we can draw on some recent work in the
philosophy of psychology and the philosophy of physics. First,
take an example from psychology. It has been argued by many
recently, both Davidson and Dennett, for example — that in understanding people as intentional systems — as having the
beliefs, desires, intentions and other propositional attitudes of
common-sense psychology — we make a certain projection of
rationality. We ascribe beliefs and desires to people in such a
way as to 'make rational' their acts. The details here are not
important for what I want to say now: the crucial point is that it
is also acknowledged that it is simply false to suppose that
agents are generally (indeed ever) rational. If this line of thought
is correct, then, our psychological theories are at best implicitly
conditional upon a false presupposition, at worst inevitably
false.

At this point it is usual to mention 'idealization.' As Fodor
has often insisted, we should not make methodological demands
of psychology that cannot be met by chemistry and physics. And
so, the argument goes, since it is clear that, for example, ideal
gas theory is still held to be usefully explanatory because
'approximately true,' why should we not hold that rational psychology is useful because roughly correct also? But the crucial
point here, one that often gets missed, is that what is being
offered is an argument in defence of a theory that is acknowledged to be false: for, if I may be permitted an aphorism,

being approximately true is just a special way of being false.

The same sort of problem arises for physics if, as Nancy Cartwright argues, most of the laws of physics are false and known to be so. Here too, idealization is common; and here, as in psychological theory, the notion of approximate truth has been driven very hard. I am sure that some notion of approximate truth is needed to handle the case of psychological theory or the theory of lasers. But, as Cartwright says apropos the idealization in physics:[15]

> in calling something an idealization it seems not so important that the contributions from omitted factors be small [gloss: so that the theory is approximately true] but that they be ones for which we know how to correct. If the idealization is to be of use, when the time comes to apply it to a real system we had better know how to add back the contributions of the factors that have been left out... either the omitted factors do not matter much or we know how to treat them.

There are thus two major sources of idealization: one is approximate truth, the other is what we can call truth under idealized assumptions. Thus, in the case of ideal gas theory, the theory may be horribly inaccurate in its handling of a case — a large molecule gas at high temperature, even though, if the explicitly counterfactual assumptions of the theory — that the gas is composed of frictionless, perfectly inelastic point-masses — were true, the theory would indeed (in some sense) give the right answer.

Now the crucial point in each of these cases, whether the issue is approximation or idealized assumptions, is that the question of whether we count the theory as false *simpliciter* or approximately true is a question of *judgment*, a question that may legitimately depend on our interests (in both senses). A chemistry whose practical focus is on the development of industrial dyes might, say, accept the idealizing assumption that filtered river-water is H_2O; a chemistry interested in energy regulation at the cellular level probably could not. And as for 'approximate truth,' 'good enough' in the theory of the laser is 'good enough to build a laser that does its job.'

So, we learn from recent philosophical psychology and philosophy of physics that our theories are best conceived of as idealizations, and that this means that they are both (in some sense) approximately true and conditional upon false assumptions that simplify the theoretical task. Interests constitute areas of inquiry in part by determining what sorts of falsehoods are tolerable. And, given that this is so, there is the inevitable possibility of a dimension of theoretical criticism that challenges not the claim of a theory as an idealization, but rather the interests by which that idealization is judged adequate. We do not need to keep hold of purely disinterested reasons for idealizing any more than we can insist on *un*interested ones. An idealization is a useful falsehood: if we manage, disinterest and uninterest will leave us simply rejecting idealization (and thus theory) altogether; useful always means 'useful for some purpose.' Which brings me back, by the roundest of roundabout routes, to *race*.

The Utility of Falsehood?

Suppose that we conceded what I am not disposed to concede in fact: that race is, as some evolutionary biologists evidently believe, a term worth hanging onto, because it allows us to refer to populations. Of course it is rooted in a theory whose presuppositions are mostly strictly false; but that, as we have seen, does not distinguish it from the theory of the laser or of anything else. Well now, it seems to me, we have a theoretical ground from which to ask: 'For what purposes is this falsehood useful?'

The Hegemony of 'Common Sense'

And the answer, I think, by and large is that, in our current conjuncture, the purpose — the interests, in the political sense — that are served by talk of race are reactionary.[16] For it seems to me that (as John Thompson argued recently in a powerful but appreciative critique of Bourdieu) it is a mistake to think of social reproduction presupposing 'some sort of consensus with regard to dominant values or norms.' Rather, the stability of today's capitalist society may require 'a pervasive *fragmentation* of the social order and a proliferation of divisions between its members.' And it is precisely this fragmentation that prevents oppositional attitudes from generating 'a coherent alternative view which would provide a basis for political action.'

> Divisions are ramified along the lines of gender, race, qualifications and so on, forming barriers which obstruct the development of movements which could threaten the *status quo*. The reproduction of the social order may depend less upon a consensus with regard

to dominant values or norms than upon a *lack of consensus* at the very point where oppositional attitudes could be translated into political action.[17]

Hegemony sets the framework. It defines the dominant system of concepts, the 'common sense,' in terms of which social and political reality will be lived. But in so doing, it does not need to be so totalizing as to enforce consensus on every central question of fact or of value. Sometimes — as those master hegemons, the Roman imperialists, knew — it is better to divide and rule.

I have suggested one way in which ideology may infiltrate the sciences, through a space left open by the necessity of idealization. But there is much more to be said on these topics; as there is, too, on the connections between them.[18]

Notes

1   As Leonard Harris has pointed out to me, what I actually argue against is deference to biology in matters of race. But I will stick with the stronger claim, noting only that further arguments would have to be made to support it.

2   We can call these 'median-ranking,' 'mode-ranking' and 'mean-ranking,' in cases where the difference between them matters.

3   I shall say that it is almost disjoint if almost every member of the first-highest group exceeds every member of the second-highest, and so on; so that 'almost disjoint' inherits the vagueness of 'almost.'

4   This fact has considerable consequences for the ethics of setting insurance premiums.

5   Thus, it seems right to say, in this case, that the correct solution is to have a legal requirement of equal access, combined with special state (i.e. police) protection against theft in places where the danger to life and limb (or the cost in property) to the shopkeeper of observing this legal requirement is high.

6   I say this only to reduce the chances of being misunderstood.

7   See, for references, Nei and Roychoudhury (1983: 1-59) and, for useful background, Nei and Roychoudhury (1972: 434-5).

8   'Racisms' in Goldberg (1989).

9   Leonard Harris has suggested to me that one might think that
        these uses of the term 'race' are just innocent ways of talking about
        morphology, and that they can go on without the essentialist
        implications of the doctrine I call 'racialism.' Well, one might
        indeed think this, but I argue in Gates (1986: 21-37) apropos Nei
        and Roychoudhury's work, that this was not so. The way they use
        the term 'race' actually sometimes presupposes that they are using
        an innocent morphological tag and at other times requires that
        they should be understood as referring to a population of which
        only some members have the defining characteristic. For example,
        a light-skinned 'Negro passing for white' would count as a Negro
        for their purposes, and thus plainly by 'Negro' they do not mean
        black-skinned. My own conclusion is: if you want to talk about
        morphology, talk about morphology; if you want to talk about
        populations, talk about populations.

10   And not, as the realist requires, from the point of view of the
        universe.

11   It has to be something that accounts for central features: otherwise
        there are too many competitors. Sometimes it is suggested that
        what we want is the stuff that accounts for most of the acid-talk;
        but without a clear notion of what is to count as more and less of
        the talk, this strikes me as unhelpful. After all, suppose that
        numerically most of Davy's acid-utterances were readings-out-
        loud of sentences about acids written by Paracelsus, with Davy
        vigorously dissenting in *foro interno* from them, because most of
        what Paracelsus says is based on the mistaken impression that
        caustic soda is an acid. That does not commit us to thinking that
        Davy was talking about caustic soda. Suppose most of what Davy
        and his chemical contemporaries said about 'acids' had been based
        on samples of caustic soda, why should we suppose that this was
        not just based on the false belief that caustic soda was an acid;
        especially if most or all of their other utterances were true or
        approximately true of acids.

12   This solution is recommended regularly for non-relativistic mass:
        of course we now know there is no such thing strictly, but what
        harm does it do to speak of the Newtonian mass of a bridge
        moving slowly with respect to the Earth.

13   Shapiro (1972: 135).

14   Ibid., p. 176.

15   Cartwright (1983: 111). The idea of ignoring factors for which we know how to account is a very old one: consider Anselm's discussion of the existence of God *remoto Christo*. Here, removing Christ from the picture is plainly not meant to be a trivial move, a move that leaves the world 'approximately' as it was. But the point of considering whether we can prove the existence of God, *remoto Christo*, is that Anselm is clear enough that he knows 'how to add back the contributions of the factor[s] that have been left out.'

16   Which is not, of course, to say that those who talk of race must be reactionary: ideological hegemony makes possible the domination of certain interests even in the thinking of those who are trying to undermine them.

17   Thompson (1984: 62-3).

18   I take up many of these issues in more detail in the first two chapters of a book now in preparation and (tentatively) entitled *In My Father's House*.

2

Race and Class Exploitation

Howard McGary, Jr

The term 'exploitation' is used to describe the condition of numerous individuals and groups. We often hear the terms class exploitation, race exploitation and the exploitation of women tossed about in discussions about equality and justice. All these uses of the term 'exploitation' are thought to denote a negative or unacceptable state of affairs, but it is not obvious that they all refer to the same thing. Some activists and social critics have assumed that to be exploited is a terrible thing and that it serves no useful purpose to attempt to distinguish between, say, class, race or sexual exploitation. For them, such efforts only prove to be divisive and contribute to the lack of solidarity exhibited by exploited groups. I disagree. A thoughtful analysis of the different forms of exploitation may serve to provide the conditions for solidarity rather than disunity. It also may put us in a better position when it comes to eliminating the causes of the different types of exploitation.

In a short chapter I cannot hope to examine all the various modifiers that have been attached to the term 'exploitation'. Instead I shall examine the concept of exploitation with an eye towards determining whether or not there are any significant differences between exploitation based upon class and exploitation based upon race. In my discussion, when I refer to racial exploitation I will mean the exploitation of people based upon claims about the distinct natures of groups of people according to supposed inherited unique mental or physical traits. These physical traits are thought to play a causal role in the formulation of the personal attributes of members of the group.

Furthermore, these traits are thought to figure largely in the shaping of cultures. However, it should be noted that the alleged scientific evidence in support of these two claims is quite suspect. There is little, if any, scientific support for biological or genetic accounts of race. None the less people from all walks of life still insist that the notion has some biological or genetic foundation. This religious-like commitment to the biological or genetic conception of race and races has strong political, psychological and sociological consequences. People are categorized, identified and oppressed because they are thought to be members of certain racial groups. It is also true that racial identification has become one of the most common means of self-identification. So, even though it is correct to emphasize that in a physical sense races do not exists, in a social sense they do because the myth of race has created a reality unto itself (Montagu 1969).

Some people argue that race, in itself, is a benign notion. It is only when some racial groups are thought to be superior to others that the problems arise (Wasserstrom 1977). Others maintain that the very existence of racial groups is harmful. I shall not enter this debate, but I mention it here because some people argue that the only way to stop race exploitation is to eliminate or down play the importance of races, while others contend that we can still classify people on the basis of race and assign importance to a person's race, but not exploit them on the basis of their race.

Before we begin, two points of clarification are in order. When I use the term race, I acknowledge that racial classifications have been employed in different ways in response to different historical, social and economic conditions. So one's group membership can be, in part, effected by these influences, but at the core there are still ontological claims about the physical nature of the being that determine racial identification. Secondly, we must be aware that members of the same racial group can exhibit 'racist-like' attitudes and behaviour against members of their own group. But we should be careful to distinguish something that is racist from something that is 'racist-like'. For example, Charles Dickens in describing the English working class employs language that is similar to the language employed by racist white Southerners to describe blacks, but I shall suggest a reason why this language and the treatment of the white working class was deplorable, but not racist. I do not intend to imply by these remarks that racial exploitation can only occur when races are defined in terms of obvious physical characteristics like a person's skin colouring. In my view it is impossible for people with the same skin colouring and national origins to divide into different racial groups and thus it is not impossible for racial exploitation to occur towards members of the subgroup.

In this chapter I focus on the relationship between blacks and whites, but I in no way intend to suggest that other racially defined groups are not exploited. Much, if not all, of what I say about the exploitation of blacks can be extended to other racially exploited groups.

In the first section I lay out what have now become standard accounts of the general concept of exploitation. These accounts are drawn from the works of both progressive and conservative authors. In the second section I construct the conservative and progressive accounts of race and class exploitation. Finally, I describe and defend my own accounts of racial and class exploitation in the light of my discussion of the standard accounts.

Standard Accounts of Racism

In this section I briefly spell out three interpretations of Marx's concept of exploitation criticized by Allen Buchanan in his book *Marx and Justice* (1982) and present Buchanan's own interpretation of Marx's notion of exploitation. I then discuss a Harvard University philosophy professor, Robert Nozick's (1975) conservative critique of the Marxist account of exploitation and the challenges he raises for a Marxist interpretation of exploitation.

Buchanan examines, and eventually rejects, three popular interpretations of Marx's concept of exploitation. He argues that these interpretations are plausible, but in the final analysis do not accurately capture the important relationship between Marx's concept of exploitation and his theory of alienation. Buchanan argues that this connection is more intimate than Marx's scholars have realized.

Now let me briefly state the three interpretations of Marx's concept of exploitation that Buchanan criticizes.

The first interpretation of Marx's concept of exploitation is based upon the wage-labour process in a capitalist mode of production. According to this interpretation, the worker in a capitalist mode of production is exploited because this labour is forced, he is deprived of the surplus value that results from his labour and does not control the product that results from his labour.

The second interpretation also focuses on the three conditions listed in interpretation (1), but claims that modes of production other than capitalism can generate these states of affairs, for example, oriental despotism, ancient slave holding societies and feudalism.

The third interpretation of Marx's account of exploitation is more general and goes beyond the wage labour process. According to this interpretation, bourgeois human relations in general are exploitative because they utilize persons as one would a tool or a natural resource. This utilization harms the person being so used, and its benefits accrue to the user rather than the person being used (Buchanan 1982, Chapter 3).

Buchanan is sympathetic to some of the reasons why scholars have interpreted Marx's concept of exploitation in the three ways described above. There is textual support for all three interpretations; they are all faithful to Marx's radical critique of capitalism and are consistent with his call for revolution by the working class. None the less, Buchanan believes that the first two interpretations are too narrow and restrictive and the third interpretation lacks content or substance because it fails to provide a systematic classification of the ways in which human beings are utilized and the specific forms of hardship that this utilization inflicts upon them.

Buchanan's own interpretation of Marx's notion of exploitation builds upon the third interpretation, but he attempts to give substance to what it means for a person to be utilized by drawing upon Marx's theory of alienation. By alienation, Marx basically meant that a person is treated as an alien being not as a fellow human being with human capacities which must be nurtured if they are to develop. Buchanan cites the following passage from *On the Jewish Question* (Marx 1976: 248) to support his contention that we cannot truly understand Marx's notion of alienation without recognizing the intimate connection between Marx's notion of exploitation and his theory of alienation: 'Selling is the practice of externalization.... Man thereby converts his nature into an alien, illusory being, so under the domination of egoistic needs he can only act practically, only practically produce objects by subordinating both his products and his

activity to the dominion of an alien being the capitalist, bestow-
ing upon them the significance of an alien entity — money.'

Buchanan recognizes that any viable interpretation of the
concept of exploitation must have a normative component.
Marx's account of exploitation is no exception. Buchanan rejects
those interpretations of Marx which conclude that he was
merely doing descriptive or 'scientific' work. Clearly he is right.
How could one give an adequate account of the notion of
exploitation that lacked an evaluative or normative component?
However, both Marxists and non Marxists face the problem of
supplying this normative content. Non Marxists have appealed
to moral or religious principles in their attempts to supply
normative content to their accounts of exploitation. Unfortunately, given the received interpretation of Marx's views on
morality and religion advanced by noted Marxists scholars like
Robert Tucker (1969) and Allen Wood (1972), consistent Marxists cannot appeal to morality or religion to give normative
content to their notions of exploitation.

How should this normative content be supplied? There
appear to be two principle strategies that Marxists might take. It
could be supplied by a theory of practical rationality that would
make it rational for agents to prefer a mode of production that
did not utilize them as alien beings over one that did or by
adopting a theory of human nature that would show that
human beings would desire as a matter of their nature relationships where they were not treated as alien beings. However,
these strategies do not explain why exploitation is wrong or
unjust. They can only give us reasons why people prefer or
desire not to be exploited. But we should remember that people
can desire or prefer things that are wrong or unjust. So even
though a capitalist society treats certain of its members as alien
beings, and these persons do not prefer or desire to be treated in
this way, we should not conclude that they are being treated
wrongly unless we a have sound argument in support of our
evaluative conclusion.

Marxists might attempt to explain why exploitation is wrong
by appealing to some utilitarian-like standards that measure the
right and the wrong in terms of the maximization or satisfaction
of undistorted individual desires or preferences. On the other
hand, they could appeal to an ideal of persons or community
that are not reducible to the undistorted desires and preferences
or standards of individual satisfaction. Buchanan believes that a

consistent Marxist account of exploitation that is able to supply the normative component will do so by appealing to a set of distinct normative ideals of persons and community. He believes that providing the support for such ideals is one of the principal task of Marxist scholarship and this work will draw Marxists scholars into some of the traditional problems in moral philosophy. So, for Buchanan, Marxists cannot define exploitation in purely descriptive or scientific terms. They must do so by an appeal to morality.

On the other end of the political spectrum, we find the supporters of individualism and the capitalist mode of production maintaining that capitalism is not an exploitative system and that the wage-labour process is not necessarily exploitative. These theorists have their own definitions of exploitation. I will not consider all the different versions of the conservative account of exploitation, but what I shall do is briefly spell out one notable and representative account. Robert Nozick argues against the Marxist account of exploitation because he believes that such an account violates the moral right that we all have to be free. In his view, the Marxist account of exploitation is incompatible with our right to individual freedom. Although capitalism may allow and even encourage persons to take advantage of the lack of insight or abilities of others, it is not unjust. Since Nozick believes that to exploit another is to do something unjust, he refuses to define capitalism as an exploitative system because he does not think that capitalism can be defined as unjust. It is important to note that, for Nozick, something can be immoral without being unjust. Capitalism may allow for certain immoral acts, but for Nozick, this is one of the acceptable consequences of respecting an individual's just right to individual freedom. Nozick refuses to define justice in terms of end-state, egalitarian, welfarist or perfectionist principles.

The concept of 'coercion' is a crucial ingredient in Nozick's and any other conservative account of exploitation. For them, one is exploited only if forced to do or refrain from doing something that one has a right to do or refrain from doing. For example, people who are captured and sold into slavery against their wills are exploited, whereas people who agree to work for a low wage because they believe it will enhance their life prospects are not exploited. Of course, there are heated debates about when a person is coerced and when a capitalist market exchange is voluntary, but my point is simply that the conservatives are unwilling to say that a person has been exploited simply because that person is down and out or that others have been able to benefit because of the free choices of individuals and others have failed to benefit by these same choices. So, if what I have said above is true, then a viable Marxist account of exploitation will rest on a theory of alienation and principles of morality, while a viable conservative account of exploitation will rest on the defence of a strong legalistic right to individual freedom and a working example of coercion, i.e. an account of when a person is forced to do something against his or her will.

Conservative and Progressive Accounts

What about race and class exploitation on these accounts? Let us first look at the Marxist response. The classical response by many Marxists has been to deny that here are any significant differences between race and class exploitation. Some Marxists have even contended that race exploitation is simply class exploitation. The supporters of this reductionist position are not simply making a claim about what is the best approach to take if one wants to eliminate all forms of exploitation, they see themselves as describing the nature of exploitation. For them racial exploitation is a species of class exploitation, but they do not believe that the converse is true. In other words, we can describe racial exploitation in terms of class exploitation, but we cannot describe class exploitation in terms of racial exploitation.

How are we to understand 'exploitation' in multiracial, gender conscious capitalist societies? According to the reductionist position above, we just have to explore more thoroughly the class analysis of such societies and by so doing will come to see that we do not have to abandon a properly worked out class analysis or amend such an analysis in fundamental ways in order to describe accurately the nature of the various other forms of exploitation experienced in multiracial, gender conscious capitalist societies like the US. Bernard Boxill correctly points out in his article 'The Race-Class Question' (1983) that supporters of such a reductionist position do not mean that we can define race in terms of class. They would admit that these two things are distinct and would require different analyses. They also do not need to contend that racial exploitation is always less objectionable than class exploitation. In fact, they could even believe that, morally speaking, things like racial and sexual prejudice are more objectionable than class prejudice, yet still maintain that race exploitation can be reduced to class exploitation. Finally, they could admit that to understand and eliminate exploitation we cannot ignore such things as a person's race or sex and yet still insist that in the final analysis other forms of exploitation are reducible to class exploitation.

What does such a reduction amount to? Bernard Boxill (1983: 108-9) interprets their position as follows: 'the claim that race is subsidiary to class means that it is the class struggle that is the cause, condition, or explanation of racial antagonisms, not racial antagonisms that are the cause, condition, or explanation of class struggle.'

Boxill thinks that if the Marxists simply mean that a theory of racial antagonism can be deduced, with the appropriate transitional principles, from a theory of Marxist class struggle, then they may be right. What Boxill objects to is the Marxist's claim that class struggle is the cause, condition and explanation of the transcendence of racial antagonisms in multiracial capitalist societies. So, his worry is not with the claim that class analysis is the more fundamental theory if we are correctly to understand exploitation in multiracial, gender conscious capitalist societies, but with the claim that class analysis is the only viable analysis for explaining how a society overcomes racial antagonisms. Perhaps Boxill has been premature in accepting the position that class analysis is more fundamental when it comes to explaining various types of exploitation. I would like to explore this possibility.

Does racial exploitation really reduce to class exploitation? Perhaps it has been thought to do so because of the belief by some that exploitation must be defined in purely economic terms. In other words, people are exploited because of their relationship to the labour process. By this reading, a person's race may be useful in helping us understand why certain people are exploited, but it cannot explain what counts as exploitation. Remember, for the Marxists, exploitation is directly related to where a person stands in the economic system. So, according to this view, there is no conceptual confusion involved in saying that someone is black but not exploited, or white and exploited. Even though the overwhelming majority of blacks are exploited on this account, it is because of where they stand in relation to the means of production and this condition is not defined in racial terms, either sociologically or genetically.

If we recall our earlier discussion, Buchanan argues that we should not understand Marx's account of exploitation solely in economic terms. Remember he rejects accounts of exploitation that are defined solely in terms of the labour process. For Buchanan, these accounts depend upon the discredited labour theory of value and thus fall prey to some of the criticism mounted against this theory. Finally, he believes that these accounts tend to treat exploitation as a purely distributive matter and, by so doing, commit Marx to a dependency upon a notion of distributive justice, something that Marx clearly rejects.

What if we move to the general account of exploitation defended by Buchanan? Does his interpretation of Marx's account of exploitation entail that class exploitation is the most fundamental form of exploitation? In answering this question, we should remember that, according to this interpretation, people can be exploited in systems with various modes of production even though they occupy positions of relative privilege within that social and economic system. On this account, slaves, serfs and workers can all be counted amongst the exploited.

Buchanan's interpretation of Marx's account of exploitation does not connect exploitation narrowly to the capitalist labour process, but this interpretation does flatly deny that persons in a capitalist system can sell their labour to other persons for wages and not be exploited. Highly skilled as well as unskilled workers are exploited according to Buchanan's interpretation of Marx's notion of exploitation. So, this account of exploitation has both a material and a psychological component. Remember that, according to Buchanan's expanded interpretation of Marx's notion of exploitation, in class societies all the members of the society are exploited because they are used as tools for the ends of others.

Conservatives define exploitation as coercing someone to serve the ends of another or as coercing someone to serve their own ends (paternalism). They deny the existence of class exploitation. In other words, they reject the view that workers are necessarily exploited by virtue of living in a class-structured society. In their view, exploitation can exist in capitalist societies, but it need not exist. But communist and socialist societies are judged to be necessarily exploitative because, according to conservatives, by definition, these societies justify coercion to achieve egalitarian, paternal or welfarist ends.

Although conservatives deny that there is any such thing as class exploitation in the Marxist sense of the term, they do recognize that there can be such a thing as race exploitation under capitalism as well as communism. However, they usually go on to point out that racial exploitation does exist, but it is not a necessary or defining ingredient of capitalist societies. So, for the conservative, racial exploitation cannot be reduced to class exploitation because class exploitation in the Marxist sense does not exists. We must be careful here and notice that the conservatives are not maintaining that only racial groups can be exploited. Their point is simply that we should not confuse a social group with a class defined in Marxist terms. Remember conservatives reject the view that classes are used as unwilling tools to satisfy the ends of others.

Conclusion

What should we conclude from this seeming impasse between the conservatives and Marxists? Are their positions mutually exclusive? I believe that we should not deny the existence of class exploitation in order to show that racial exploitation is different in a fundamental way from class exploitation.

We can discern the differences between race and class exploitation by focusing more clearly on what it means to be used as a tool or to be treated like an alien being in a society. Unfortunately, Marxists and capitalists tend to interpret racism in either strictly material or psychological terms. In other words, they focus on the material things that people are denied by virtue of their racial identification or the psychological problems they encounter relative to their self-concepts. This focus on one or the other obscures a fundamental difference between class and race exploitation. The fundamental difference, as I see it, is that when a man is treated as an alien being or used as a tool because of class membership, then he is accorded personhood even if he is deprived of the fruits of his labour with all that this entails. But when a person is used as a tool by virtue of his race, he is thought by the prevailing ideology of the society to be less than a person and treated accordingly. The denial of personhood means a lack membership in the moral community rather than a lack of full membership. We should note that the denial of membership all together or the denial of full membership does not always entail material deprivation. Even when those who are conceived of as non members or less than full members are afforded the things they need or want, this is still compatible with their not having full membership in the moral community. Some domestic pets and plants live quite comfortable existences without being accorded the status of full members.

An important part of racial exploitation (defined here as treating persons as non-person tools) is the fact that members of the racially exploited groups are thought to be naturally incapable of satisfying the conditions of personhood. Racists believe that a biological or genetic barrier prevents these beings from ever becoming persons, even though they may be capable of doing the things that would normally qualify people for personhood. The evidence is always discounted for what are often the most rationally unconvincing reasons. However, it may be presumptuous to expect that rationality would always force the racist to abandon his racist views. Racists are strongly driven by their emotions or sentiments even though they may employ ingenious schemes for rationalizing their feelings and sentiments about certain groups. The Scottish philosopher and famous sceptic, David Hume, was a classic example of a well educated person who took great pride in being rational, but who none the less held and expounded racist views about members of certain racial groups (see Popkin 1977/8, 1984). He did this in spite of obvious counter examples to the rationalizations he used to support his position.

Much of my argument about the differences between race and class exploitation hinges on my being able to draw a meaningful distinction between less than full membership and lack of membership in the moral community. Ralph Ellison (1953) draws graphic attention to what it means not to be seen as a bona fide member of a community. He describes the phenomenon for blacks in terms of invisibility. In other words, he described how blacks in America were beings who were not seen as authentic human beings with all that this implies.

We also find Cornel West, in his book *Prophesy Deliverance: An Afro-American Revolutionary Christianity* (1982, Chapter 2), contending that regarding black people as human beings is a relatively new discovery in the modern West. He asserts that 'the modern world has been shaped first and foremost by the doctrine of white supremacy, which is embodied in institutional practices and enacted in everyday folkways under varying circumstances and evolving conditions.' In a similar vain, Richard Popkin (1977/8, 1984) in an excellent series of articles, clearly demonstrates that the 18th century was the watershed of modern racial theories that saw blacks and American Indians as inferior human beings. However, none of these authors clearly assert that blacks were perceived by whites not to have any moral status, though it is clear that they believe that blacks were not assigned full moral status with whites. By full moral status, I mean acknowledging and treating a being as having a natural right to having intrinsic value assigned to his or her well-being and freedom (see Williams 1962; Vlastos 1970; Wasserstrom 1970). Furthermore, this being is entitled to demand to be conceived of and treated accordingly. So, in my view, having less than full membership means that you do not have a right to have intrinsic value assigned to your well-being and freedom, though your well-being and freedom is not seen as unimportant, for example, cats and dogs. Non membership in the moral community means that your pain and well-being are unimportant and do not have to be considered, for example, weeds or insects. This is tantamount to treating beings as objects. The denial of personhood to certain groups and the rationalizations that accompany them are fuelled by the difficulty encountered when one attempts to give clear, necessary and sufficient conditions for personhood. We all think that we know what it means to be a person, but our knowledge is called into question when we are forced to explain what we mean exactly by the concept.

In writing on the morality of abortion, Mary Ann Warren (1985) offers the following traits as central to the concept of personhood: consciousness, reasoning, self-motivated activity, the capacity to communicate, and the presence of self-concepts. However, she is quick to admit that there are numerous problems involved in formulating precise definitions of these criteria for personhood, let alone in developing sound behaviour criteria for deciding when they apply. I think that she is right and racists who seek to rationalize their racist beliefs and deeds take great comfort in this uncertainty about the exact nature of personhood. By these remarks I do not mean to imply that this gives validity to their rationalizations, but it is a way of masking the inconsistency of their views about why members of one group should be treated differently from those of another group by virtue of their group membership.

American chattel slavery is a clear example of the treatment of persons as non persons; some people have objected to slavery on the grounds that it singled people out for such treatment. Slavery was not abhorrent because it singled out blacks for such treatment, however, but because it treated persons as non persons. It is not just that some persons were treated in ways that other persons were not. Slavery was wrong even if the slave master was an equal opportunity enslaver. Of course, one might object that at one time in American history this view about blacks might have prevailed, but surely it does not still obtain in the 20th century?

It is tempting to accept such an objection until we recognize that we should not confuse law with morality and theory with practice. There is a good case to be made that laws in the US acknowledge the personhood of blacks and other racial minorities, but even if this is true, it does not follow that the moral outlook in the US is one that accords the status of persons to blacks. There is still plenty of room in everyday practice for blacks to be used as non person-like tools even if formally the law prohibits such treatment in certain defined areas.

Another objection to this position is that surely in our everyday lives we have come to accept people of all races as fellow human beings and, as such, persons. Unfortunately, even if we agree that people have come to recognize each other as genetic human beings, it does not follow that they acknowledge all genetic human beings as persons. Moral debates over abortion and euthanasia have shown us that being genetically human does not imply personhood and that there is considerable dispute about the conditions that constitute personhood.

By maintaining that white workers are not treated as non persons, I do not mean to suggest they are allowed to achieve their full human potential. I firmly believe that they are not. Being conceived of as a person, but treated like a tool is a serious affront. However, when one is conceived of as a non person by the prevailing ideology of a society and treated like a tool, then it is more difficult to cut through the false consciousness created by such a powerful mythology. Nor do I want to rule out that, conceptually, white workers can be defined and treated as an inferior racial group. My point is simply that they were not because it was believed that it was possible, even if highly unlikely, that white workers could become the owners of the means of production and thereby a member of the superior group. If not obvious already, I should point out that by racism I mean something more than racial prejudice. In order to be a racist, one must be in a position to put ones overarching negative beliefs into practice. One must have power over the groups that stand to be victimized if these negative beliefs make their way into practice. However, this power does not only accrue to those who have wealth or prestige, it can occur by virtue of being accorded certain benefits, or at least from being exempt from certain societal disadvantages.

My position does not commit us to the view that people must organize on the basis of race to eliminate racial exploitation. Nor does it imply that some whites do not conceive of blacks as persons. Oddly enough, it even allows for some members of the same group to consider a subset of their group as inferior. We must remember that no group or individual is immune to racist ideology in a racist society. There needs to be a great deal more work done on the psychology and sociology of racism. This work must be accorded the highest priority because racism is still a far reaching personal and social evil.

3

Justice and the Concept of Racism

Leonard Harris

The belief that races exist, on some accounts, is the core meaning of racism. The core meaning provides a common thread for what counts as uniquely racist. I argue against this view. The meaning of racism is also not captured, I argue, by the concept of racisms, i.e. an amalgam of variegated forms of discrimination such as prejudice, ethnic chauvinism, caste oppression using racial distinctions, or the unintended consequences of institutional rules. This meaning suggests that there is a wide variety of types of oppression by race in different social situations which can be roughly grouped together, not reduced to a single definition. Each meaning, I contend, is inadequate. They are inadequate because a social reality that uses racial identity to deny the intrinsic worth of persons through a praxis which normalizes and reproduces racial identities and material disparities is both common across different social situations and simultaneously variegated. One implication of this view, I argue, is that the reasons usually offered to support either colour-blind or colour-conscious principles of justice are undermined.

Racialism is the view that human beings consist of naturally different kinds, categorized as separate races. Differences between races are explained by reference to different heritable characteristics. Differences may include personalities, skills, potentials, intelligence, and moral virtues determined by the unique heritable. The prejudicial evaluation of differences provides the concept of racism simplex with plausibility as the core of various prejudicial beliefs.

28

The concept of racism simplex is referential — it refers to the belief that races exist. That is, it treats 'racism' as a rigid designator. The word 'racism' is meant to pick out or point to a specific belief, such that that belief is referenced by it and it alone. No other word picks out that belief and no other word picks out as well the corpus of ills associated with it. Legally segregated housing, the exclusion of citizens of a certain race from holding office or gaining full citizenship rights, for example, are situations historically justified explicitly or implicitly by the unnecessary differentiation of race. The use of racial distinctions is the use of a factor irrelevant to a person's character. In addition, distinguishing by race supports a myriad of social ills and morally unjust practices. When racism is conceived of as racism simplex, the existence and use of distinctions considered racial are unjust.

The concept of racisms is distinct from that of racism simplex because it insists that there are a variety of beliefs and practices which are not captured by the belief that races exist. Racists' views may include claims about human biology (for example, that people are properly classified by race because of differentiated features of their heritable structures); claims about human nature (for example, that it is in the nature of things or human psychology that groups of persons are or should be separate); normative claims (for example, that there is a hierarchical ranking of kinds of persons in terms of superior and inferior types); teleological claims (for example, that the future of groups fundamentally differ); and valuative claims (for example, that virtuous or morally appealing characteristics are subject to be manifested differently according to race). These various views may be considered more or less central to the nature of racism by a given author or more or less operative in a given society. Consequently, the idea that there are racisms, rather than a racism simplex, has gained appeal. It gains additional appeal because it allows the use of colour-conscious principles of justice. That is, it allows the distribution of goods and services according to race for the purpose of redressing imbalances caused by the history of segregation, discrimination, and apartheid. So doing would not be a form of injustice because it tenders race specific awards.

I first consider problems that affect both the concept of racism simplex and the concept of racisms. I then consider the way colour-blind and colour-conscious principles of justice are undermined because of their association with untenable views of racism.

The Problem of Enunciation

The problem of enunciation affects how we talk about persons, and this problem affects both the concept of racism simplex and the racisms. The problem of enunciation is this: How can a critique of the totalization of reasons proceed except through the use of that very reason, a move which could only reproduce domination? This is a problem addressed by Derrida, Foucault, Althusser, and Jameson, to name a few. The idea is that a critique of Kantian rationality usually involves the use of the same techniques of reasoning that the critique is intended to show unwarranted; and that Kantian rationality presupposes the possibility of arguments that do not rest on unstated assumptions but, when examined, rest on a host of epistemological assumptions. One way the critique of Kantian reason (and the unstated forms of ideological domination it warrants) has proceeded is by decoding and laying out unstated assumptions of arguments presented as rational.

Analogously, how is it possible to speak against racism simplex or racisms in a world in which language (the tool through which and of which the speaking occurs) is encoded with attributing worth to peoples according to colours (black, brown, yellow, white) and types (mongoloid, caucasoid, negroid)? How is it possible to do so when geographical regions have already been associated with types of persons (Asia, Latin America, Europe, Africa) and stereotyped character traits of persons from those regions, for example, emotive (African), dramaturgical (Asian), rational (European), sensationalist (Latin), and fanatical (Arabic)?

The common noun, African, predicates being. It names a place that exists. It also names a set of states and peoples. It connotes a culture. It connotes a character type of person, normally black and in some way connected to traditional folkways. The word African does not necessarily carry all these connotations. However, if it is to function as a common noun in English, then it predicates being of some sort. Given the history of the images of Africa, at least the demeaning images that the term has been used to connote, it is a small step to predicating ontological racial being to the people who are African. That is, as

a noun, Africa names and naming presupposes a stayed existence — an existence of a place and a people, undifferentiated.
The same is true of European, Asian, and Hispanic. Changing
the connotative import of African thus includes changing not
only stereotypical images, but changing the small step of predicating ontological racial being to African people. Changing the
way nouns that name places in English in this way entail
changing the linguistic practice of associating places with
peoples and ascribing to peoples an ontological undifferentiated
being. Making such a change involves more than rejecting the
belief that races exist; it requires at least focusing on the same
type of linguistic practice common across different social situations.

Another analogy representing the problem of enunciation is
this: How is it possible to speak against racism simplex or the
racisms when, paradoxically, international capital has made
racist distinctions mute; for example, when the barons of capital,
whether European, African, Asian, Arabic or some combination
thereof, associate with one another according to perceived or
actual economic common interest in pursuit of profit and yet,
the economics of race are integral to maintaining the bastion of
international capital? How can we speak against racism simplex
when the universalization of capital has both destroyed artificial
barriers between peoples and yet enlivened new forms of
ethnogenesis by destroying old realms of identity and replacing
them with new identities constituted by larger and more
ominous groupings? Instead of a thousand different languages
and races falling under the rubric of European, there is a united
Europe with a vested interest in the gold mines of South Africa
and the ethnocide in Sri Lanka; instead of a single USSR
centrally controlled, there are numerous ethnic conflicts and
endeavours to form separate nations. The already paltry
provision of health care, education and investment in neighbourhoods dominated by Africans, combined with liberal
immigration for Europeans and the African population of Brazil,
has radically declined without the use of formal racial distinctions — how capital was used and the liberties granted persons
with capital was sufficient. The way nouns imply being is not,
by itself, racist; however, conjoined with other features of
language, it can function as racist.

Language is bounded by, among other features, its syntax
and mode of predicating and implicating. A universal language

would be so bounded. What cannot be said, at least because it lies outside the bounds of the syntax and mode of predication, is as important as what lies inside. What lies outside is at best an abstraction, an imagined place of potential codes. What lies inside is the stuff of everyday life. It is the fork, plate, bowl, goblet, urn, and coconut shell of what shapes our sense of self location in, or identical with, a community of being. But if the above example of the way the noun 'African' implies and connotes is appropriate, then what has racial import cannot be restricted to a rigidly designated meaning. Modern forms of oppression by race do not require that we believe persons are, or should be, by nature different or that there are biologically or naturally different races which are endowed with superior and inferior qualities.

Another way to see this is by considering the recent research on what has been described as the 'new racism'. On one account, 'the prevalence of a definition of racism in terms of superior/inferior has helped conceal how common is a form of racism that does not need to make such assertions — indeed, can make a positive virtue out of not making them. It is indeed, a myth about the past that racism has generally been of the superiority/inferiority kind.'[1] Referring to West Indians or Indian citizens of England as 'aliens' imputes a character to them as strange, foreign, suspicious, unknown, threatening, and fundamentally or naturally different. The term implicitly supposes that there is a natural barrier between 'us', who are normal, natural, the real citizens, the bearers of an appropriate way of life, and the 'others', who are a threat to our being. The conservatives who refer to black immigrants or citizens as 'alien' have not characteristically argued that the English are biologically superior, or that nature has ordained a separation of the races. On the contrary, they deny holding such beliefs, but regularly refer to non-whites as aliens. The way in which its arguable that this way of referring to non-whites is racist is by implication. That is, it is what the word alien implies, and the way these implications set a context of meaning that generates pernicious meaning. There is another feature of the new racism that involves considering the consequences of words and actions, not just their implications.

The new racism contends that there are beliefs and arguments about cultures which are not avowed by their promoters as racists' beliefs and are not, at least ostensibly, the sorts of beliefs and arguments normally associated with racial discrimination. Arguing that a group of people has an entitlement to preserve its language, for example, is not by itself racist. Believing that a group has such an entitlement may not entail believing that its language is superior to others or that its native speakers are superior to others. The argument for an entitlement to language maintenance functions in a racist fashion if it turns out that maintaining the language either prevents persons from having access to a larger community or ghettoizes them in a way that perpetuates subordination and differentiation. If native Welsh speakers are prevented from learning other languages, are unable to initiate new enterprises or are confined to those controlled by foreign language speakers, and if Welsh speakers are ghettoized as a separate type or kind of race, then the argument for maintaining the language has import independent of language entitlement claims. Whether a group has an entitlement to assure the continuation of its language is not defeated because of the auxiliary ways in which the argument functions. Rather, the context within which the argument exists is in need of change. The context has totalized the denial of the intrinsic worth of persons.

An emphasis on the results and contexts of arguments is a consequentialist picture of racism; a picture rather different from the one painted by racism simplex but closely associated with the concept of racisms. The consequentialist picture focuses on the way words, arguments, and acts have the consequence of, or function to, support the belief that people are naturally different. That is, people do not need to avow the beliefs traditionally defined as racists, rather, a set of codes, practices, and preferences replace the old beliefs.

It takes a special argument, for example, to show that 'alien' implies a belief about the natural separateness of persons. We must show an implicit or causal connection. Even if no implied or causal connection exists, however, alien fits a conceptual context that legitimizes racial disparities. Analogously, even if poor whites in southern America usually score significantly lower on standardized tests than middle class southern blacks, that is no reason to deny poor whites any rights or to stereotype them as inferior, whether there is or is not a causal connection between class status and performance on standardized tests. The use of standardized test scores to tell us what people are worth, like using alien to describe people, fits a context that already gives legitimacy to evaluating human worth. The implications involved in using nouns to predicate being, using descriptors that entail pernicious evaluations, and the consequences of words and practices suggests that the import of what counts as racist should not be restricted to racism simplex. If the concept of racisms allows us to take into account these various features of racial discourse, as I argue later, it fails to allow for a coherent meaning or defensible view of the injustices roughly grouped together under racisms.

Colour-Blind Principles and Racism Simplex

Colour-blind principles of justice hold one or more of the following views: 'that no law or public policy be designated to treat people differently because they are of a different colour;'[2] that the use of colour as a basis for distributing goods and opportunities is unjust in itself because so doing uses colour 'which the individual has not done, and can do nothing about; we are (or would be) treating people differently in ways that profoundly affect their lives because of differences for which they have no responsibility.'[3]

The idea is that differentiating by race is itself morally wrong. It is certain that social differentiations by race are misguided if such differentiations are purported to rest on cogent biological categories corresponding to significant cultural behaviour. There are numerous reasons supportive of colour-blind principles that give currency to the intuitively appealing idea that heightening social awareness of racial differences is inherently wrong. It is arguable, for example, that every person should be treated as an individual, and not treated as a member of some racial or ethnic group. Membership in such groups is arguably irrelevant to rights and entitlements they hold as individual persons. In addition, race is not necessarily a crucial part of one's identity but designating people for different treatment according to their race makes it seem so. So doing treats persons as group members and not as individuals with unique characters and interests. Racial membership is also an irrelevant feature of persons in the sense that their skills, abilities, desires, and character are in no way inferable from their race. To the extent that a race and a culture are codeterminant, unfounded presumptions about any particular individual's cultural needs may contribute to racial stereotyping. It is further arguable that affirmative-action programmes based on differentiating persons by race, particularly when resources such as jobs are scarce, penalizes people excluded form competition for such resources because of a characteristic they could not help but have. Such distributions, moreover, lend legitimacy to awarding benefits to persons who may not deserve them. If differential treatment is intended to correct past discriminations, for example, then so treating them would seem to miss the mark. A man's white skin may not be a reliable sign that he has benefited from past discrimination, nor is a black skin necessarily a reliable indication that he has been effected by past discrimination. What benefits whites can be said to inherit from past discrimination, it has been claimed, are not so weighty as to warrant a harm to them. (See Eastland and Bennett 1979; Sowell 1981a, 1971.)

Whether colour-blind principles of justice would, under optimal conditions, abate racism depends on whether we restrict the conception of racism to distinguishing persons by race. But such a restriction is untenable. If colour-blind principles are preferred because they do not differentiate people on the basis of race, it does not follow that race-blindness is a way of preventing, decreasing, or ending harms not caused or explainable by race but which effect a given race. (For arguments in favour of a colour-blind society, see Wasserstrom 1980: 24-5; and Gross 1977.)

One feature of economic interest theories and institutional accounts of racism is that they depict how one race oppresses another through non-race or colour-specific policies. Rules might, for example, give priority to persons with certain educational backgrounds, extra-school activities and certain achievement awards. These might be used as the criteria by which to distribute opportunities. If the educational backgrounds, activities and awards were almost certainly the ones possessed by a given group, then the colour-blind rules would favour that group over others. It is not the existence of race designation as such that maintains disadvantages, but the seemingly honourable intentions, fair procedures and heinous consequences of the rules that do so. That is, racial differentiation as such can be relatively unimportant as a social dynamic either causing or sustaining maldistribution and treatment of constituted groups. The fact that toxic waste disposal areas are primarily located in African-American communities, for example, is not a function of segregation laws directing the location of disposal areas. In another vein, if it is in the economic interest of a ruling class to perpetuate conflicts between races, and if that class is successful in prosecuting its interests, its interest is not itself racist. That is, a capitalist may not believe that races actually exist or rank them hierarchically in order to use existing distinctions to enhance profits. Such a capitalist would function as a racist, but need not hold the requisite beliefs. If for some mystical reason no one distinguished persons by race, the already existing poverty of the least well off by race could be an obvious sign and basis to begin anew to distinguish them as a race.

The fact that a policy is colour blind does not mean that it is race neutral — that depends on how it fits within the context of other policies and its identifiable consequences. It is arguable, for example, that affirmative-action programmes using racial designations to distribute goods use a reprehensible method. Racial designation, however, is consequentially neutral, i.e. its use may or may not heighten colour awareness or function to achieve racial separation or equity. If affirmative-action programmes are reprehensible it would be for reasons associated with the way they are used and the ends for which they are inclined. Colour-blind principles of justice therefore gain little support from the concept of racism simplex. This follows because even if a situation were not racist on the racism simplex account, i.e. with no one perceiving others as members of a different race, it is theoretically possible that the morally odious consequences associated with traditional views of racism could exist, although not caused by racial differentiation.

Racial differentiation can be a cause, particularly in the sense that it is referenced as a sufficient or necessary reason for an action or policy. In this sense, racial difference is reified and used as a living social dichotomy. American laws of segregation, for example, reified racial identity and racial difference such that white identity or black identity was a sufficient reason to harm blacks and benefit whites solely on grounds of racial identity. Any human characteristic can be reified and used to legitimate oppression. Language, hair colour, weight and eye shapes have all been used at various times in various countries as distinguishing marks to justify group oppression. It is arguable that social differentiation by race is a type of false consciousness. (For discussions of the concept of race and its role in social thought, see DuBois 1966: 203-31; Toll 1979; Montague 1980,

1969a; Demarco 1972: 227-42; Singer 1978: 153-83; Fortney 1977: 35-54; and Bracken 1978: 241-60.)

However, it cannot be the sheer recognition of difference that is the engine behind discrimination; rather, how the differences are used and justified must significantly figure in an adequate account of the cause or character of differentiation by race.

The central difficulty with colour-blind principle of justice, in terms of the way racism simplex implies what is wrong with differentiating by race (referencing an irrelevant feature of persons), is that arguments for colour-blind principles presuppose that this necessarily has something to do with other features we associate with racism. We would be hard pressed, for example, to show that differentiating by race requires believing that some persons are inherently inferior and others superior or that using irrelevant features of character (such as a person's state of origin) is necessarily a harmful way of distributing goods such as state scholarships. Origin of birth, language, or hair types are not chosen by individuals, for example, but may be of utmost importance in rendering an appropriate distribution of goods. If the transgression is in distinguishing persons by these, the greater harm is to do so in a prejudicial way. The distinction is banal if not acted on, but the discrimination is a felt reprehensible harm, whether or not it is motivated out of discriminatory beliefs.

Colour-Conscious Principles and the Racisms

Colour-conscious principles of justice, contrary to colour-blind principles, recommend a different attitude toward principles and methods of distributing goods. Colour-conscious principles warrant the use of race and the distribution of scarce resources according to race. So doing may be justified, according to arguments for colour-conscious principles of justice, for one or more of the following reasons: granting of reparations, compensating a group for past wrongs it has suffered, assuring cross-cultural contact, redistributing existing wealth, or creating a future society without racial inequities.[4] An affirmative-action programme would not be perceived as an unfortunate temporary tool on such accounts of justice, but as a method itself compatible with justice.

Colour-conscious principles are intuitively appealing, particularly when they are tendered as principles we should use to correct a past wrong or provide for a future colour-blind world. It is arguable, for example, that being black warrants preferential treatment because of the history of slavery and racism which placed blacks, as a people, in a disadvantageous position. Blackness on such an account functions like one's place of origin, gender, or physical disability; preferential treatment is granted to redress some imbalance or wrong. However, there are also reasons to be suspicious of colour-conscious principles.

Distributing scarce resources differently according to group membership arguably penalizes. Granting preferential treatment to blacks to redress a college's history of racial exclusion and to create a racially balanced college, for example, can be said to penalize whites. It is arguable that to use race to distribute goods not only uses an arbitrary feature of persons, but also actually fails to benefit. If a black man is wealthy, it can be claimed that he has not been harmed by a college's history of racism; and if he is poor, he may be poor for reasons having nothing to do with either racism or a college's history of racial exclusion. There are several defences of colour-conscious principles. I mention a few of these and then address the inadequacy of colour-conscious principles in the way I considered the inadequacy of colour-blind principles.

Awareness of racial disparities is a condition for fighting discrimination, and colour-blind principles cannot serve the function of explicitly addressing discrimination. Given that race is an arbitrary feature of personhood, it does not follow that it should not be used to distribute goods. It is hard to show that anyone has a right, or entitlement, to admission to a college or particular job independent of numerous criteria for which they are not responsible. In order to assure an adequate supply of doctors to rural areas, for example, we may prefer to select applicants for medical school from rural areas in the hope that they will return to such areas. Persons otherwise qualified to attend medical school from rural areas are not responsible for their place of birth, nor are urban qualified persons said to be penalized.

Even if a black man is wealthy, his claim to preferential treatment is not thereby defeated. If compensation for past wrongs is due, that is not a function of current income or status. Moreover, if a wealthy black man's participation helps redress imbalances or helps create fewer disproportions, then his claim to preferential treatment is further warranted (see Dworkin

1977; Boxill 1984). The above sketch of arguments in favour of colour-conscious principles is not comprehensive, but it does highlight major reasons supportive of such principles. The problem, however, lies elsewhere.

Colour-conscious principles can heighten social awareness of the need to fight racism, but it does not follow that social awareness is a positive good to help impel an abatement of racial discrimination. One feature of psychology based interest theories of racism is the depiction of the ways persons pursue social status and emotive senses of self worth through holding racist beliefs. Moreover, even if a person is not knowingly a racist, there are benefits associated with being a member of an oppressor group, which enhance a person's sense of self worth. Whether the battle against racism is done with the actual interest of the oppressed race infused in praxis, or whether the battle is but a ruse for the perpetuation of the oppressing group may turn on the deep psychological structure of those engaged in the battle. The hope of heightening social awareness of the need to battle against racism is not an assurance that the battle will be properly directed.

Assuming that colour-conscious principles are effectively used to distribute goods justly, such distributions may not affect the distribution of honour or the utility of stereotypical images. The granting of honour and deference is not a legal requirement in most political systems. Persons of Chinese ethnicity, for example, were the wealthiest persons in Malaya, but up until recently they were legally excluded from holding political office. The wealthiest blacks have almost always lived in, or were from, southern states — states with heinous histories of racial segregation. Who has access to what spheres of honour and deference-generating positions may not have a great deal to do with legal policies or with who holds wealth at a given point in history. The existence of social policies intended to help reshape society may be frustrated, not because they do not substantively redistribute benefits and opportunities which affect how well individuals flourish, but because some goods, such as self respect, honour, deference, or information are not redistributable through social policies.

If internal colony theories of racism are cogent, then the existence of colour-conscious policies and principles condition racial disparities. According to these accounts, the separation between races and differential treatment makes racial separation seem normal. The distinguishing features of the oppressed by race are used to justify their exploitation. They are blamed for their abject condition and oppressors characteristically praise themselves as benevolent saviours and redeemers of the oppressed. The relationship between the two requires accepting precisely what colour-conscious principles of justice warrant — the designation of individuals by race and differential treatment thereby.

Whether or not a set of policies and practices in fact benefits the oppressed is a matter of controversy, but the separation of persons is a point of concordance between those in favour of colour-conscious principles and racial segregation. Arguments in favour of colour-conscious principles lose appeal when we consider that the consequences of their use may not actually be directed toward an equitable society, but intentionally or unintentionally directed toward the formation or maintenance of an internal colony.

If colour-conscious principles of justice can be universalized, then either they are not principles of justice or they are not justifiable. One way in which colour-conscious principles are not justifiable is when they are used as permanent, fixed features of institutional rules. If preferential treatment is justified for blacks, for example, after the injustice has been redressed then the principles that warranted the preferential treatment should be rescinded. Continuation of preferential treatment would be unjust. However, temporary rules are normally conceived of as policies and not as principles of justice.

Colour-conscious principles are flexible, allowing a myriad of distributions according to what group arguably is due what at a given point in time. They are thereby unstable guides. That is, it cannot be clear what counts as justice across different cultural situations because there is no yardstick or bedrock criteria by which to evaluate justice. Distributions according to race, for example, intuitively give those who benefit an interest in the mode of distribution — inclusive of an interest in the fetishization of race. Colour-conscious principles cannot outlaw making race a fetish because the principles use, and make it appropriate to identify by, race. The variegated forms of racial oppression, if attacked by use of colour-conscious principles of justice, cannot be said to function as a powerful tool for ending differentiation by race. Colour-conscious principles fail to allow for a coherent view of injustice. This is because the psychological risks of warranting differentiations by race, or even differentiating by race itself and thereby rendering disadvantages, are allowed without making clear what is common about justice or racisms (the object of which the principles are directed) across social situations.

What Counts as Racism?

The consequentialist feature of the concept of racisms, I believe, is defensible; defensible because it provides a way of seeing commonalities across different social situations. Although consequentialism is defended, I reject the view that a composite definition is untenable.

Imagine a robot being responsible for all social arrangements. It manipulates the collective situation and relationships of all groups, monitors their activities and makes changes in situations to assure certain outcomes. Suppose that many of the consequences normally associated with racism existed, for example, patterns of social isolation, few public services systematically available to the oppressed group, the regular execution of rebels by coercive police and military powers, the exploitation of one race for the benefit of another, the delimiting of flourishing by crippling access to spheres of material control, a radical disparity of health care between races, and the promotion of distrust and lack of confidence in the cleanliness and reliability of individuals considered to be members of an oppressed race. Imagine further that humans still had some degree of free will. Imagine also that if everyone saved 20 per cent of their income, the robot's master programme would self destruct and full human self control would return. However, one group with an over representation of poor persons, does not regularly save 20 per cent of its income. The reasons for its failure to do so involve cultural factors, such as family structures that emphasize early marriages, child bearing, or spending for immediate gratification. The robot's programming is consequently not solely responsible. It follows that the cultural arrangements of the least well off, involving factors arranged neither by virtue of a given person or group's intention nor necessarily for the benefit of the most well off, functions to immiserate.

If altering the cultural factors that perpetuate poor savings habits (both intrinsically in terms of the group's own activities and extrinsically in terms of the distribution of resources by other groups to assure that the least well off acquire the needed savings results) does not occur, then an omission has occurred. This omission may not be reprehensible in the sense that an individual's promotion of racist beliefs is reprehensible, nor may we be able to blame an individual or group for intentionally perpetuating the situation. Rather, the intentional omission by the robot and omissions by the rest of society are reprehensible in the sense in which a corporation is responsible for heinous and avoidable omissions.

The consequentialist picture of racism raises an important issue: If a phenomenon is not caused by racism simplex, prejudicial beliefs, rules, intentions and interests, is it properly identified as racist?

There are several reasons to accept the consequentialist picture, which are conveyed by the following analogy. A rose, it is arguable, is not a rose by any other name. Its name has become a part of our understanding of what it is. Calling a rose a lily elicits a different picture of beauty than that of a rose. Fullness of body and oval petals are not conveyed by the name lily. The objective phenomenon may be the same in the sense that a photograph of a rose is that regardless of its name. If we find a new flower that fits the generic structure of a rose and looks like a rose we are warranted in calling it a rose, even though it may have characteristics new to the genus. If the new flower is sufficiently close to the ones we are used to, we have warrant to call it a rose, though our understanding of what counts as a rose is thereby altered. Intentionally distinguishing persons by race is less (if at all) central to the consequentialist picture of racism because such differentiations may not be the cause or explanation of racist consequences. In other words, the objective reality of the modern cornucopia of racisms may have a variety of causes, supports and aids.

The consequentialist view does not refer in a logical positivist sense, i.e. its parameters are not tightly bounded by a limited set of definitions. It does not refer, like racism simplex, to a necessary set of core beliefs. It is simply not bounded by other than the myriad of ways people are subjugated by race.

Enunciation within a Totalized World

The totalization of race in the modern world is exemplified by the way in which language predicates and attributes an ontological being to peoples and the way existing systems produce and reproduce radical disparities by following either colour-conscious or colour-blind principles of justice. In other words, neither colour-blind nor colour-conscious principles of justice exist outside a world that uses both the existence and non-existence of colour consciousness to perpetuate the conditions most readily understood as race based. Moreover, given that the world is already enmeshed in differentiating peoples, and attributing characteristics and worth to them, we may not be able to engage in enunciations that are outside this context. The negation of racial identity by ending the use of differentiations of race (racism simplex) and the use of colour-conscious principles of justice, are therefore not nearly radical enough.

By rigidly designating specific beliefs as defining what counts as racism, treating the definitions as themselves the conceptual parameters, we allow totalization. We allow the world of codes, signs and symbols to exist as somehow separate from the codes, signs and symbols that imply, connote and suggest that existing reality is normal. We must then show a connection between 'alien', its frequent demeaning application to certain physically or culturally distinguishable groups, and the belief that such groups are, by nature, different when 'alien' is already encased in a context of stereotyping differences. However, it does not follow that existing differences are permanent. The fetishization of racial identity (in the form of colour-conscious principles of justice) is tantamount to the national phobia of ethnocentricism, the essentialism of vulgar negritude, and the schizophrenic madness and irrationality of apartheid. By capitulating to the idea that there are no common features of social life across different situations that afford a coherent (but not simplistic) view of racism, it is unclear what counts as one of the racisms or the criteria for evaluating injustice.

Racism is a social reality that denies the intrinsic worth of persons through a praxis which normalizes and reproduces racial identities and material disparities; a phenomenon that is both common across different social situations and simultaneously variegated. Contrary to the concept of the racisms, commonalities give the term racism its meaning, and that meaning is always subject to revisions — particularly because the seemingly robotic actions of a totalized system of oppression and the commissions and omissions of individuals and groups are always changing. Greater value should be placed on conceiving racism consequentially and contextually. So doing would focus attention on the way racial disparities between peoples is normalized through policies of commission and omission; unintentional robotic actions and intentional consequences.

Notes

1 Barker (1981: 4). Also see Thurow (1980, 1969); Noel (1972); Becker (1971); Malvaeaux (1985: 5-28). For a general review of theories of racism (economic, psychological, internal colony), see Prager (1972/3: 117-50); Bowser (1985: 307-24).

2 Boxill (1984: 10). This book is an extensive review and critique of colour-blind principles of justice.

3 Frankena (1970: 49). For the idea of racism simplex, see the above and also Feinberg (1973); Hook (1977: 88-96); and Sowell (1977: 113-31).

4 See Boxill (1979); McGary (1977/8: 250-263); Huges 1975; Baier (1978: 121-51); Newton (1973: 308-12) Goldman (1977: 17-28); McGary (1984: 15-26). It should be noted that race and ethnicity are two distinct, though related, social categories. See Grove (1974).

4

Human Rights: The Dispute about the Underclass

Bernard R. Boxill

The black underclass is by far the worst-off class in American society. Its members are poor, uneducated, chronically unemployed and dependent on welfare; not surprisingly many engage in violent criminal activity. Living in the heart of the nation's great cities, its members are highly visible and help sustain negative black stereotypes which affect all black people. The black working and middle classes will continue to exist.

Something must be done to assimilate the black underclass into the larger society. It will not do so spontaneously. It is self-perpetuating and, indeed, increasing in size. Unfortunately there is wide disagreement over how to assimilate the underclass into the larger society. I distinguish three main positions.

First, the conservatives: Conservatives maintain that the fundamental explanation for the existence of the black underclass is that its members lack the values necessary for success in a modern industrial society. They deny, in particular, that those in the underclass lack opportunities. They insist that the opportunities are there, but that the members of the underclass fail to take advantage of these opportunities because they are lazy, lack patience and discipline, and are motivated only by the prospect of immediate gratification. Some conservatives attribute this to social welfare programmes which demand nothing in return for benefits. They complain that these programmes do not require and accustom recipients to behave according to the norms of the wider society, such as working, obeying the law, and finishing school. Other conservatives place more of the blame on the

45

legacy of slavery and past racial discrimination. Accordingly, conservatives differ on how they propose to assimilate the underclass. Those who blame the underclass for the way in which welfare programmes are administered tend to urge that these programmes be administered differently — instead of welfare, for example, there should be workfare (Mead 1986). Those who argue that the dysfunctional values of the underclass are a legacy of slavery and past racial discrimination tend to urge a different remedy. Particularly interesting is the view that the black middle class must assume moral leadership of the black community and accept its obligation to criticize and change the values of blacks in the underclass (Lowry 1984).

Most strongly opposed to conservatism is liberalism. Liberals reject the conservative view that underclass values are significantly different from mainstream values. They admit that people in the underclass do not generally behave like people in the mainstream. But they reject the inference that people in the underclass must therefore have different values from people in the mainstream and, accordingly, they deny that people are in the underclass because of their values. Liberals insist that people are in the underclass primarily because they lack decent job opportunities. They further insist that black people in the underclass do not lack decent job opportunities because of *current* racial discrimination, but because of recent, deeper, impersonal developments which have nothing to do with race. Prominent among these developments are a stagnating economy and slack labour market; the contraction of the manufacturing sector in which a disproportionate number of blacks traditionally found employment; the entry of immigrants and white women into the labour force; and the shift of employment opportunities from the inner cities to the suburbs. Liberals believe that the effects of these trends can be reversed, and the underclass set on its way to join the mainstream by a comprehensive governmental programme to stimulate economic growth, generate a tight labour market, and create employment opportunities for the underclass (Wilson 1987).

Between the conservatives and liberals are the libertarians. Libertarians are in agreement with the conservatives that the values of those in the underclass are dysfunctional and different from the values of those in the mainstream. Indeed, certain libertarians are notorious for proclaiming that the underclass is in the grip of a 'culture of poverty.' But, unlike the conservatives, the libertarians do not believe that people are in the underclass mainly because of their values. They side with liberals in maintaining that people are in the underclass mainly because they lack employment opportunities. But they reject the liberal remedy for this, i.e. that government manage the economy to create employment opportunities for the underclass, arguing that this has helped to cause the dearth of employment opportunities for those in the underclass. And they reject the conservative remedy that values of the underclass be changed by black middle-class criticism, or workfare. Their remedy is the free market. They maintain that the free market will both create the job opportunities the members of the underclass need and, by its discipline, help them acquire the values they must have to succeed in a modern industrial society (Williams 1982a; Sowell 1975).

These conflicting accounts give the impression that the fundamental issues in the dispute about the underclass are empirical. First, do the members of the underclass have opportunities and is a lack of opportunity the cause of their being in the underclass? Second, do the members of the underclass have different values from those in the larger society and are their values dysfunctional and the cause of their being in the underclass? But the impression is misleading. Closer attention to conceptual matters suggests that the empirical issues are less controversial than they seem. And, as I argue, this further suggests that the dispute about the underclass is less about facts than about morals.

Consider the dispute over the opportunities of those in the underclass. Liberals say they lack opportunities, conservatives and libertarians that they do not. The liberals seem clearly wrong, the conservatives and libertarians clearly right. Those in the underclass do not lack opportunities. They cannot lack opportunities because some of them escape the underclass. They could not escape the underclass had they no opportunity to do so. But the issue is not about whether they lack opportunities, or whether their opportunities are equal to the opportunities of those in the mainstream. They clearly are not. The issue is about whether justice demands that members of a society have equal opportunities. Liberals maintain that it does. Libertarians and conservatives, on the other hand, either reject the principle of equal opportunity outright, or argue that it is demanded by justice only if it is understood differently from the way liberals understand it. They point out that liberals understand it to mean that provisions should be made to equalize the life chances of those who are equally well-endowed, but they complain that when government attempts to secure such provisions it often has to act unjustly. They maintain that the principle of equal opportunity is a principle of justice only if it is interpreted as simply requiring that no law bar anyone from the favoured positions in society.

The apparently factual dispute over the opportunities of those in the underclass thus dissolves into a dispute over conceptual and moral issues. The same is true of the apparently factual dispute over the values of the underclass, though this will take longer to show.

Conservatives and libertarians maintain that the values of the underclass are dysfunctional and different from those of the mainstream. Liberal critics object to the view that it is hazardous to deduce differences in values from differences in behaviour (Simpson 1987: 165). They point out that people with the same values can behave very differently if their circumstances are suitably different; for example, two people may be equally opposed to stealing, but one may steal while the other does not, because one has to steal to stay alive while the other is comfortably situated. This argument is sound. But it does not bar inferences from underclass behaviour to underclass values.

The argument says that people with the same values can behave very differently if their circumstances are very different. It says nothing about the values of people who behave differently in similar circumstances. Indeed, if people in similar circumstances behave differently, it seems reasonable to infer that their values are different. If, for example, only one or two affluent people steal, it seems reasonable to infer that in some general way they feel differently about stealing, i.e their values are, on this point, different. And this is what we should expect. Values guide behaviour. This is part of their meaning.

Now, not everyone in the underclass behaves the same. If, for example, many seem to avoid working, some do not. But all are in roughly similar circumstances. Consequently, if the argument in the preceding paragraph is sound, the values of those in the underclass who avoid work, are probably different from the values those in the underclass who do not avoid work. Further, as I noted earlier, it is a well-acknowledged fact that some members of the underclass escape from it, and become integrated into the mainstream. If these escapees are drawn from the ranks of those in the underclass who do not avoid work, it seems a reasonable inference that their values have something to do with their escaping the underclass, and can, from this point of view, be termed functional; similarly, if those who do avoid work rarely escape the underclass it seems a reasonable inference that their values have something to do with their remaining in the underclass, and can, from this point of view be termed dysfunctional.

One of its premises in the above argument is that people who behave differently in the same circumstances tend to have different values. Critics may point out that even in the same circumstances people with the same values can behave differently if they 'perceive' their situations as suitably different. The favoured example here is the unwillingness of poor black children to forgo a prize in the present in order to receive a greater prize in the future. The argument is that this is not clear evidence that the values of these children differ from the values of well-to-do children who do presumably forego present prizes in order to receive greater prizes in the future; it may be evidence that the poor children perceive the situation differently from well-to-do children. For example, the poor children may have good reason to believe that promises of prizes in the future are rarely kept (Simpson 1987: 165).

I concede that people with the same values in the same circumstances, may behave differently because they have different beliefs about their circumstances. In particular, if affluent children defer gratification in circumstances in which poor black children do not, probably the most we should conclude is that the two groups of children perceive their circumstances differently. Occam's razor forbids the further inference that their values are different. But the relevant comparison is not between affluent children and poor black children. Where a minority of poor black children defer gratification and the majority do not, we cannot as easily put this down to a difference in what the children believe about the world; the further inference that the children have different values seems justified.

Further, even if the children do have different factual beliefs about the world, it may be because they have different values. By assumption, the children are equally poor and black; the minority have the same facts before them as the majority. If the majority use these facts to draw the factual conclusion that promises of prizes in the future should not be trusted, why does the minority not draw the same conclusion? It may be, of course, that the majority is simply better than the minority at drawing logically justified conclusions. But, this possibility is arbitrary. A more plausible possibility is that the majority's conclusion is not based only on the facts before it, but is also based, at least partly, on its values. Human beings are not automata, they do not impersonally register all the facts before them, or use these facts in the same way to draw conclusions. Our values, our ideas of good and bad, and right and wrong, help determine both what facts we notice and what conclusions we are prepared to draw.

It may be objected that the circumstances of the children are similar only in a most general way; that, in particular, if we examine their early life histories carefully we are certain to find that their experiences are different and, consequently, that the facts on which they base their conclusions about the world are different. I cannot, of course, deny that the life histories of the children are different. And I do not deny that this helps to explain why they draw different conclusions about the world. But I do deny that it does so because it entails that they base their conclusions on the different facts of their life histories. I submit that the different life histories of the children may help cause them to have different values and, in this way, may help explain why they draw different conclusions about the world. There is an interdependence of fact and value which the objection overlooks. Earlier I noted that our values help to determine the facts we notice and the inferences we make. The point now is that our experiences help to determine the values we have. This seems difficult to deny. It is assumed by every theory of education and individual development. If it were false, it would not matter how we are brought up: however we were brought up we would have the same values. But this is absurd.

There is a way to deny this. It may be argued that, although our upbringing helps determine how we behave, it does so, not by determining our values, but by determining how we draw our factual conclusions about the world. But this is a desperate and implausible move, motivated only by the desire to cling to the claim that the values of the underclass are similar to those of the general society. Notice that it cannot be justified by occam's razor. Occam's razor tells us that explanations should be based on as few and as plausible assumptions as are necessary. But the proposal in question requires that we make elaborate and implausible assumptions. It requires, for example, that we assume that people's values are not in any way determined by their experiences and that these values are always the same. But from where then do people get their values and why must these values be assumed to be the same? Are they innate? Theories that our values are innate, and remain constant, whatever our experiences, are more elaborate and conjectural than theories that our values are at least partly determined by our experiences.

Further, the proposal does not soften the implications of either the conservative or the libertarian thesis. According to the conservative thesis, those in the underclass cannot be saved by being offered opportunities; they will not take advantage of them even if they are offered to them; their values prevent them from doing so; to be saved, their values, a durable aspect of their characters and personalities, must first be changed by 'workfare' or the tutelage of the black middle class. The present proposal does not offer hope of a less radical remedy. It maintains that underclass behaviour is explained by underclass beliefs about the world which are fixed and determined by the early underclass life histories. This suggests that underclass behaviour is explained by underclass beliefs about the world, which are fixed and determined by early underclass life histories. This suggests that the underclass will be as slow to take advantage of opportunities as the conservatives warn. Or take the libertarian thesis. Libertarians maintain that underclass *values* will be changed for the better if its members are exposed to the discipline of the market. But it seems equally easy and legitimate for them to maintain that underclass *beliefs* about the world will be changed for the better if its members are exposed to the discipline of the market.

These considerations appear to favour the conservative thesis that underclass values are different from mainstream values and dysfunctional. But the appearance is misleading because the term 'values' is ambiguous. It may be used to refer to what principles of right and wrong a person accepts; to his or her conception of a good and happy life; or, again, to the qualities of character and personality he or she has or admires. Further, people may have similar conceptions of what is good, but dissimilar conceptions of what is right, and dissimilar views of what character and personality traits are desirable. Utilitarians, for example, allow that people may agree that the good is pleasure, but be justified in having different ideas about what kinds of action are right and about what character and personality traits are desirable. Or consider the social contract theory of John Rawls. This theory reverses the logical order of the good and right in utilitarian theory and makes the right logically prior to the good. But it also preserves the relative independence of the right and the good. Indeed, it is explicitly designed to show that people may agree on principles of justice but may, within broad limits, consistently disagree on the good.

Now, when conservatives and libertarians claim that underclass values differ from mainstream values, they apparently mean, and are naturally taken to mean, that those in the underclass differ from those in the mainstream in all three things to which the term values may refer. And, when liberals insist that underclass values are the same as mainstream values, they apparently mean, and are naturally taken to mean, that those in the underclass agree with those in the mainstream on all three things to which the term values may refer. But both positions are highly implausible.

Consider the conservative/libertarian position. The chief empirical point in its favour is that some people escape the underclass. But this does not only support the strong claim noted above. It also supports the weaker claim that underclass and mainstream agree on the good and the right, but differ in the qualities of character and personality that enable and dispose them to pursue and achieve the good and live according to the right. Moreover, this seems to be the interpretation we should adopt. Occam's razor eliminates the stronger claim.

The liberals' position is equally implausible. Their favourite positive argument for it is based on Elliot Liebow's classic study of the underclass, *Tally's Corner* (1967). Liebow strongly rejects the idea that the underclass has distinctive values. He maintains that it has the same values as the mainstream. He does admit that its members behave differently from those in the mainstream, but denies that this difference is explained by a difference in values. It is explained, he argues, by the profound sense of failure experienced by those in the underclass who fail in their attempts to achieve the conventional goals they share with the rest of society; according to Liebow they try to conceal their failure by engaging in the well-advertised underclass behaviour. But, he continues (Liebow 1967: 222), they would not experience a sense of failure unless they shared the conventional goals of the society. Liebow's arguments are well taken. But, they do not support the strong liberal claim that those in the underclass and mainstream agree on the good and the right, and have the same character and personality traits. They are consistent with the weaker claim that the underclass and mainstream agree on what they conceive of as the good and the right, but differ in the character and personality traits that enable and dispose them to pursue, achieve and live according to the conceptions of good and right on which they agree. Indeed, a sense of failure may be precisely one of these qualities of personality or character that undermine the ability and disposition to pursue and achieve what one conceives to be good and to live according to what one believes to be right. More generally, given that those in the underclass fail so consistently to achieve their goals, it would be unreasonable to expect them to have the same optimism, faith, discipline and tenacity (i.e. qualities of character and personality) as those whose experiences are more encouraging.

So, conservatives and libertarians, and liberals, are both right and both wrong. The conservatives and libertarians are right in so far as they maintain that those in the underclass are less able to and less disposed towards pursuing and achieving their goals than those in the mainstream: but wrong in so far as they imply that these goals differ from the goals of those in the mainstream. The liberals are right in so far as they maintain that those in the mainstream have the same goals as those in the underclass; but wrong in so far as they imply that the experiences of the latter have not undermined the qualities they need to pursue and achieve their goals.

Now conservatives, libertarians and liberals must insist on the weakened versions of their claims about underclass values if they are to be able to urge their characteristic recommendations. For example, it is practically, and perhaps conceptually, impossible to compare opportunities for radically different ends. Thus, to complain that the underclass and mainstream have unequal opportunities and to urge that these opportunities be made more equal, liberals must insist that the underclass and mainstream have similar ends. Similarly, the retrenched conservative/libertarian claim is necessary if conservatives and libertarians are to be in a position to make their characteristic recommendations. If the underclass and mainstream had similar character and personality traits, conservatives could not as plausible maintain that the underclass had to change its values before it could be integrated into the mainstream. But, though necessary for liberals, libertarians and conservatives to make their characteristic recommendations, the weakened versions of the claims about underclass values are mutually consistent. To insist that the mainstream and underclass have similar conceptions of the good life is not to deny that they have dissimilar character and personality traits; and, to insist that the mainstream and underclass have dissimilar character and personality traits is not to deny that they have similar conceptions of the good life.

Accordingly, the general point I made about the dispute over underclass opportunities applies to the dispute over underclass values. The empirical issues are less controversial than they may at first seem; the really controversial issues, the ones that animate the dispute, are moral. There appear to be three of these. First, is the principle of fair equality of opportunity a principle of justice? Second, does government have an obligation to cultivate the virtue of citizens and the qualities they need to succeed? Third, does the black middle class have a special obligation to assume moral leadership of the black community and, by its criticism and example, to help the black underclass escape its predicament?

These positions are not as opposed as they might seem. Specifically, the liberal argument for fair equality of opportunity concedes the conservative argument that government has a responsibility to help cultivate certain traits in citizens.

One of the important considerations weighing in favour of a set of moral principles is that it contributes to human flourishing. Since the personal qualities people develop decisively affect human flourishing, this implies that to arrive at adequate principles of social justice, we must consider not only how these principles distribute benefits and burdens, but also how they affect the personal qualities people tend to develop. If, for example, a set of principles tends to sap the self-confidence and self-respect of those who adopt and try to live by it, this weighs against accepting it. Diminished self-confidence and self-respect tend to diminish human flourishing. If, on the other hand, a set of principles tends to increase the self-confidence and self-respect of those who adopt and try to live by it, this weighs in favour of accepting it. Enhanced self-confidence and self-respect tend to enhance human flourishing. Further, if adopting and trying to live by a set of principles is self-reinforcing, i.e. if it tends to dispose its adherents towards accepting and living by it, this weighs in favour of the set of principles. On the other hand, if adopting a set of principles disposes its adherents to abandon it, or to doubt is validity, this weighs against the set of principles. Self-reinforcing principles contribute to, and self-stultifying principles detract from, social stability; and social stability is one of the conditions of human flourishing.

Liberals maintain that considerations such as these are an integral part of the justification of fair equality of opportunity. They argue that where this principle is securely established citizens generally have enhanced self-confidence and self-respect, are therefore more likely to take advantage of their opportunities, and that this naturally widens and deepens human flourishing. They also argue that fair equality of opportunity tends to be more strongly self-reinforcing than deviations from it. Now self-confidence and self-respect are clearly among the most important personal qualities people need to succeed, and if the case for fair equality of opportunity is sound, the sentiments and attitudes which tend to sustain it are the same as, or at least part of, the sense of justice. Consequently, the liberal case for fair equality of opportunity concedes the general conservative position that government has a responsibility to cultivate the virtue of citizens, and the qualities they need to succeed.

But this concession gives no support to the specific conservative proposals. The liberal account is that government must help cultivate useful traits and virtues in citizens by establishing and securing certain fundamental institutions of society, including especially fair equality of opportunity. This does not justify government failing to secure these institutions, especially fair equality of opportunity, and then trying to cultivate the traits by other means, for example, workfare. Further, if the liberal argument for fair equality of opportunity is sound, these other means are unlikely to be successful. According to that argument, establishing and securing fair equality of opportunity is the most effective thing government can do to help citizens develop the traits in question. This suggests that a government that fails to establish and secure fair equality of opportunity, but claims to want to cultivate the traits and virtues it best generates, fails to adopt the most effective means towards attaining its avowed ends and invites citizens to view the means it does adopt as having an ulterior purpose, and the traits it really wants them to develop as traits suitable for dupes. I suspect that this is exactly the feeling programmes like workfare provoke.

What about the other conservative proposal that the black middle class has a special responsibility to take on the moral leadership of the black community to help change its values. It is not ruled out by my previous discussion. If government fails to accept its responsibilities, some of these may shift to other shoulders. Further, the black middle class may succeed where government fails. I cannot hold out much hope for the latter suggestion. Clearly, if fair equality of opportunity is normally the best way to generate these traits and virtues, it cannot be very plausible. But we must distinguish the useful traits and virtues best generated by fair equality of opportunity from the useful traits and virtues that can be generated by other means. It is possible, for example, that even in the absence of fair equality of opportunity, the black middle class may persuade the underclass to be more hard-working, enterprising, far-sighted and courageous. It is even possible that government sponsored programmes like workfare can have this result. But, neither of these concessions means that liberals will relax their insistence on fair equality of opportunity. Again, the issue is not so much factual as moral.

Liberals maintain that fair equality of opportunity is generally necessary if citizens are to develop the fullest complement of desirable traits. If they are right, though the government or the black middle class may, in the absence of fair equality of opportunity, possible teach the underclass how to be more successful, neither is likely to teach the underclass to be as moral as it can be. It is even unclear whether they can teach the underclass to be moral in any sense. The difficulty is an old one. As David Hume (1985: 102, 103) admitted, when he confessed himself unable to persuade the 'sensible knave' not to act unjustly when it was to his advantage, no attempt at such persuasion can be successful if a person fails to appreciate the satisfactions of society when it is invidiously denied the opportunities the mainstream takes for granted.

Consider next the suggestion that the black middle class has an obligation to assume moral leadership of the black community and to teach values to the underclass. Every human being has an obligation to help other human beings if they need help and if he or she can give it. And, somewhat more controversially, every citizen has a special obligation to help his or her fellow citizens if they need help and if he or she can give it.

Thus, because the members of the black middle class and underclass are fellow human beings and fellow citizens, the black middle class has a general (and may have a special) obligation to help the black underclass. But these obligations we can now take for granted. Neither is the obligation at issue. That obligation does not appeal to the common humanity or citizenship of the black middle and underclass. It appeals to a more special bond between these classes, which is allegedly derived from, though not identical to, their common race. The black middle class owes that obligation *only* to the black underclass; and no other class owes that obligation to the black underclass.

That special bond is not their common race. People acquire special obligations because of their voluntary actions. That is why it is controversial that fellow citizenship creates special obligations. But people do not have the same race because of their voluntary actions. They are simply born into the same race. Consequently, they cannot have special obligations to one another because of their common race. We can similarly dismiss the special bonds of a common tradition and culture, to which nationalist often appeal. People are simply born into a common tradition and culture.

Glenn Lowry proposes a special bond between the black middle and underclass which satisfies the conditions derived from voluntary action. According to Lowry (1984), the black middle class profits from the misery of the black underclass; it uses the black underclass as a 'constant reminder to many Americans of an historic debt owed to the black community.' In this way the black middle class is able to sustain public support for race-specific programmes, like affirmative action, and minority business 'set asides'; but the benefits of such programmes accrue to the black middle class and not to the black poor, though the benefits are extracted in their name. Further, the black poor faithfully vote for black political leaders, and get them elected and into positions of power. These are, Lowry affirms, compelling moral reasons why blacks who have achieved some security and success have obligations to assist in the long task of eradicating black poverty.

The force of this argument depends on how much of the black middle class depends for its position on the black underclass. If the black poor put black politicians in office, these politicos have obligations to the black poor. This is indisputable. It also does not go very far. Black politicians are only a tiny fraction of the black middle class. Further, not all race-specific programmes need be based on an appeal to the condition of the black poor. The black poor are not the only victims of American racism. So also is the black middle class. It may deserve special treatment independently of the condition of the black poor. Finally, even where race-specific programmes are based on an appeal to the condition of the black poor, we cannot conclude that all blacks who benefit from such programmes therefore have special obligations to the black poor. Only those who seek out, accept, or voluntarily receive the benefits, have such obligations. Those who receive benefits only because they cannot reasonably avoid doing so incur no obligations. And, of course, much of the black middle class does not owe its success to race-specific programmes. After all, the black middle class did not materialize only after these programmes were implemented. It existed in the time of slavery. Far from conducing to the success of these less recent additions to the black middle class, the black underclass may have retarded its success by helping to preserve black stereotypes.

A deeper problem with Lowry's suggestion is that it faces a dilemma. Lowry maintains that the black middle class must fulfil its obligation to the black lower class by convincing the black lower class of the advantages of hard work, discipline and the possibility, indeed moral necessity, of achieving success without special governmental intervention. According to Lowry (1985) the black middle class is in an especially advantageous position to do this because it can point to its own success and achievements which were won by hard work and discipline and without government intervention. This is one of the reasons he opposes affirmative action; affirmation action, he complains, prevents the black middle class from playing its didactic role. But this complaint implies that Lowry's position faces a dilemma. Either the black middle class owes its success to race-specific programmes based on the misery of the black under-class, or it does not. If it does, it cannot, by Lowry's account, honestly play its didactic role with respect to the black under-class. If it does not, it cannot, again by Lowry's account, have a special obligation to play that didactic role. My own view, which I cannot develop here, is that if the black middle class has obligations to the black underclass, they are based not on the receipt of benefits, but on a special ability to help.

If these considerations are persuasive, the specific conservative proposals must be rejected and the general conservative thesis collapses into the liberal claim for fair equality of opportunity. But it does not follow that the specific liberal proposals are adequate. They are inadequate because they fail to secure fair equality of opportunity. To secure fair equality of opportunity they must be supplemented by certain of the conservative proposals.

Wilson's solution for the underclass requires the government to stimulate non-inflationary growth, to generate a tight labour market and to increase the competitiveness of American goods on international markets. I dare say that if the government succeeded in doing these things, most of the underclass would, in time, get jobs. If the demand for labour is high enough, employers will offer practically everyone jobs; and if the economy is growing fast enough, these jobs will pay enough to induce practically everyone to take a job. But what if government cannot, or does not, succeed in bringing about the economic conditions required by Wilson's proposals? Wilson refers airily to these conditions, as if the government were able to make them happen at will or by edict. But what if these conditions are more difficult to secure than he seems to think?[1] Wilson is silent about what would have to be done in this grimmer scenario. I submit that this is because it would compel him to confront a fact that he denies and seems anxious to avoid — the continuing racism of society. If the government succeeds in securing the economic conditions Wilson proposes, this fact will not have to be faced. If the demand for labour is high enough, employers will hire and promote blacks; those who do not will find themselves out of business. And, if the economy is growing so fast that everyone is getting better off, whites will in general not resent black economic gains. But it does not follow that employers will not avoid hiring and promoting blacks if they can hire and promote whites instead; nor does it follow that whites will in general not resent black advances if they are not also advancing.

It may be objected that I beg the question by assuming that the favourable economic conditions Wilson's proposals depend on only camouflage racism; that, in other words, I have given no reason to believe that racism is there to be camouflaged. But, this is not so.

Wilson (1987: 153, 154) claims to be 'recommending a fundamental shift from the traditional race-specific approach.'

But, while he does stress broad-based, universal, colour-blind programmes, his detailed recommendations also include 'race-specific' programmes. This is his strategy of a 'hidden agenda' for liberal policy makers (ibid. 163). This hidden agenda is to make the required 'race-specific' programmes 'less visible' by combining them with the universal programmes (ibid.). I have no quarrel with the strategy. It is good politics. But, it admits the continued salience of racism.

Presumably, the race-specific programmes Wilson thinks necessary must be made 'less visible' because, otherwise, the public will reject them. But why will the public reject them? The answer depends on what Wilson means by 'less visible.' He does not, I think, mean simply less noticeable. He means that the public will not tolerate race-specific programmes, i.e programmes providing benefits specifically for blacks, if they are not combined with programmes to provide benefits for whites too.

This cannot be because the public is opposed to governmental intervention in the economy to benefit citizens generally. If it were, combining race-specific programmes with universal programmes would not help to get race-specific programmes passed. The public would also oppose the universal programmes. Consequently, it must be because the public opposes race-specific programmes. Now it may be argued that this does not show that the public has racist attitudes. It may be argued that it only shows that the public is opposed to special governmental help being given to any specific group of citizens. But this cannot be true. The public is not opposed to special governmental help being given to specific groups of citizens. It is not opposed to special governmental help being given to victims of natural disasters, to the young, the aged, home owners, farmers and veterans. And its attitude is justifiable. Special help is due to those who, because of their special circumstances, have special needs. But no one, least of all Wilson, denies that the black underclass has special circumstances and special needs. Consequently, the public's opposition to race-specific programmes cannot be because it is generally opposed to special governmental help being given to specific groups of citizens.

It still does not absolutely follow that the public's opposition to special programmes for the black underclass is based on racism. The public may hold that the disadvantages of the black underclass, though real enough, do not qualify it for special help. Wilson, of course, cannot and does not say this. He admits that the black underclass exists because of past racism and deserves special help. Why can't the white public see this? We should note that the issue here is not special programmes for middle-class blacks. On this there is room for honest disagreement. Many philosophers have urged that such programmes are unnecessary and, indeed, unjust. Whether or not these arguments are sound, they do not apply here. The issue here is special programmes for underclass blacks. I must admit that I cannot see any opposition to such programmes that is sustained by racist attitudes.

Nor is this verdict softened by the possibility (on which Wilson's strategy is based) that the public will tolerate race-specific programmes if they are combined with universal programmes that help all classes. This only shows that the white public is prepared to tolerate black gains only if it is also gaining so fast that its advantage over blacks widens, or at least remains constant. I noted that this suggested that the white public still had racist attitudes. Now, I suggest further, that the sociological consequences of Wilson's strategy are likely to perpetuate that racism. For these consequences are that the gap between whites and blacks widens or remains constant — even if all blacks in the underclass become gainfully employed. But this coincidence of race and class, whites in the upper classes, blacks in the lower classes, is likely to sustain racist attitudes. These attitudes are caused and sustained by the perception that race — in itself insignificant — is strongly correlated with something significant like high or low income, or status. Thus, while economic integration of the races is unlikely by itself to cause racism to disappear, economic stratification of the races is also certain to sustain, or even cause, racist attitudes.

This, by itself, should give pause to those who aspire towards and would like to plan for a racially harmonious society. But some think that this ideal is utopian and to these I point out that Wilson's strategy has another more practical problem. It implies, as I have pointed out, that even if blacks become gainfully employed, they are likely to remain at the bottom of the economic ladder. Apart from sustaining racist attitudes, these blacks are in constant danger of again being propelled into the underclass. As Wilson himself argues, the underclass is composed chiefly of those who, even in favourable economic conditions, hold the least skilled and least well paid jobs in society. Their position makes them especially vulnerable to down turns in the economy. This is how he explains the disproportionately large number of blacks in the underclass. Racism had confined them to the least skilled, and least well paid jobs in society. But this reveals the weakness in his strategy. As long as economic growth and a tight labour market continue, they may lift blacks out of the underclass. But it is unrealistic to expect that these favourable conditions can be maintained indefinitely without serious interruption. On Wilson's own account, as soon as they stop or are interrupted, we can expect a reconstitution of a black underclass — even if his strategy has been completely successful.

These weaknesses in Wilson's strategy reveal the insufficiency of his controlling premise that providing jobs is not only necessary, but enough, to dissolve the underclass. It impels him, incidentally, to ignore some of the policies Western European democracies, like Germany, use to preclude the emergence of underclasses. Wilson describes these policies as essentially maintaining a tight labour market. But, apparently, this is not the whole story. In addition to maintaining full employment, through a combination of compulsory vocational training and compulsory apprenticeship for all school leavers till they reach the age of 18, Germany has kept youth unemployment down to a rate close to that of adults (Lewis 1985: 69, 70). In other words, policies similar to some conservative proposals — which Wilson dismisses — seem to be responsible for the absence of an underclass in the very countries Wilson cites as his model for helping to solve the underclass in the US.

Accordingly Wilson's strategy is likely to leave America racially stratified and, consequently, racism intact and blacks in perpetual danger of being kicked back down into the underclass, even if government can produce the favourable economic conditions he calls for, and even if his strategy works. Thus, even in the most optimistic scenario we can imagine for Wilson's strategy, it has to be supplemented with the very policies his economic determinism moves him to dismiss. The first of these is integration.

There are objections to government acting to secure integration. De facto segregation, it is often argued, may be the result of people exercising their right to freedom of association. But, if so, government acts wrongly if it does anything to secure integration, for this implies that it interferes with freedom of association. This argument does not deny that people may use this freedom to practice racial discrimination and that, in so using their freedom, they act wrongly. But it insists that even if they act wrongly, government cannot legitimately use the law to alter their behaviour. White people may, for example, move out of a neighbourhood because blacks move in; or they may take their children out of a school which becomes 'too' integrated; and they may act wrongly when they behave in this way; but, because they act within their rights when they do these things, government cannot pass laws to prevent them from doing these things.

The conservative Glenn Lowry (1985) places great reliance on this argument. He maintains that the racial discrimination involved has great economic consequences. Yet, because it appears to be protected from legal remedy by the right to freedom of association and other basic liberties, he insists that the government cannot introduce civil rights legislation to offset its deleterious effects.

Consider, first, the use of this argument to oppose busing. As I have argued elsewhere (Boxill 1984: 106-8), parents do not have a natural or pre-legal right to place their children in any school they please. Children are not their parents' property to do with as they will. Children are human beings with rights to the kind of schooling that will enable them to grow up to be fair-minded adults. Normally, the state has overweeningly good reasons for not interfering with how parents bring up their children and accords them broad legal rights to choose their children's schooling. It is the ultimate protector of the rights of its citizens, especially the rights of its child citizens, but it recognizes that in many circumstances it is best to delegate some of its responsibilities. In particular, it recognizes that to protect the rights of its child citizens, it is normally best to delegate this responsibility to their parents and, thus, to give parents the legal right to determine their children's schooling. But if parents use this rights to give their children the kind of schooling that turns them into narrow-minded bigots, the state may fairly withdraw these rights.

If this argument is sound, parents have no basic or inviolable liberty to withdraw their children from schools just because these schools become 'too' integrated; and civil rights laws may, without contradicting any basic law or principle of morality, frustrate these ways of subverting busing strategies to improve the education of black and white children.

Even if this conclusion is justified, it leaves most of Lowry's argument intact; it does not deny, for example, that people have a liberty, which ought not to be subverted by any civil rights legislation, to move out of neighbourhoods when blacks move in; or that businesses have a legally protected right to move out of (or to avoid moving into) ghettos, even if this leaves many people without a chance of employment. How can civil rights legislation avoid violating these and other liberties and yet still prevent them from having deleterious effects?

One possibility is to offer economic incentives not to flee from neighbourhoods merely because black people buy houses there. Generous tax breaks may be given to those who elect to stay; the neighbourhood can be made more attractive; and schools may be improved and refurbished. Similarly, tax breaks and other incentives could be used to persuade businesses to locate in ghettos or not to move out of them. If these strategies were successful in integrating schools, neighbourhoods and businesses and, if a rich source of the economic disparity between the races is the absence of this integration, it seems that civil rights legislation to implement these strategies could in future play a considerable role in the black struggle for equality. Yet, such legislation would not violate the various freedoms of association. It would be a violation of these freedoms to compel people not to move out of a neighbourhood, or to compel businesses to locate in ghettos. It is not a violation of these freedoms to make a neighbourhood sufficiently attractive so that people choose not to move out because some black family buys a house in it; nor is it a violation of these freedoms to offer a business economic incentives to stay, or to locate in a ghetto.

But there may be an objection on the grounds that, in the absence of general economic growth and full employment, moving blacks to the suburbs, or industry to the black ghettos, would only increase white unemployment rates. Consequently the public will resist it. Taking jobs away from whites to give to blacks would inflame racist passions, which is why Wilson calls for economic growth and full employment. If these are secured, black advance is not a zero-sum game. But if they cannot be secured, something still has to be done about the underclass.

Both in that case and in the happier case in which economic growth and full employment are secured, certain of the conservatives proposals are necessary. I cannot go so far as to endorse

Lawrence Mead's recommendations for 'workfare', but there is nothing objectionable about the German policy of compulsory vocational training and compulsory apprenticeship. Beyond punishing criminals, it is wrong for governments to try to make adults more disciplined and persistent. But it is right for governments to do this for children. This is especially important for the black underclass. Because of the break-up of the black family, black children depend more on the public schools, but the public schools they attend are getting worse (Lewis 1985: 68, 69). The problem is that the government has done very little to improve ghetto schooling and busing has been unsuccessful. Here the conservative proposal that the black middle class has a special obligation to the underclass may be especially important. Perhaps the black middle class with its experience of overcoming the obstacles of racism and poverty may succeed where government has failed. I have argued that the grounds for their obligation to help are unclear. It does not follow, however, that the black middle class does not have prudential reasons to help assimilate the underclass. Indeed, I think that it clearly does. As I noted at the beginning of this chapter, the black middle class will continue to bear the burden of race as long as the black underclass continues to exist.

Notes

1   Significantly, W. A. Lewis (1985: 121), who also argues that the integration of the underclass depends on a 'fast growth of the economy,' is more cautious than Wilson. 'The prospect for economic growth is,' he allows, 'obscure.'

5

A New Way of Talkin': Language, Social Change and Political Theory

Geneva Smitherman

Introduction

Let us begin with a traditional black gospel song, as writer Amiri Baraka's would say, 'in the Tradition.'

I looked at my hands and they looked new
I looked at my feet and they did too
I got a new way of walkin.
And a new way of talkin.

In traditional black Church theology, a person who has been 'saved' is one whom God has rescued from the travails of sin and transformed into a new being. This transformation involves a revolutionary process whereby the 'saved' individual's status is symbolized not only by a new physical essence (new hands and new feet) but also by new behaviour, 'a new way of walkin and a new way of talkin'.

Next we turn to Celie, heroine of Alice Walker's Pulitzer Prize novel, *The Colour Purple* (1982: 183-4):

> Darlene trying to teach me how to talk.... Every time I say something the way I say it, she correct me until I say it some other way. Pretty soon it feel like I can't think. My mind run up on a thought, egit confuse, runback and sort of lay down.... She bring me a bunch of books. Whitefolks all over them, talking bout apples and dogs. What I care bout dogs?.... But I let Darlene worry on. Sometimes I think bout the apples and the dogs, sometimes I don't. Look like to

me only a fool would want you to talk in a way that feel peculiar to your mind.

At this point in her life Celie has at last been freed from the oppressive stranglehold, brutality and sexual exploitation of her father and husband. She has had to struggle against what Toni Morrison (1984) might refer to as the 'profound desolation of her reality.' In the process, she has been transformed into a new, empowered woman. Thus having finally found her voice - 'a new way of talkin' - she wisely admonishes us that only fools talk in ways peculiar to their minds.

My central thesis is this. Languages play a dominant role in the formation of ideology, consciousness, behaviour, and social relations; thus contemporary political and social theory must address the role of language in social change. I seek here to present a theory of languages within the framework of social and revolutionary transformation using the linguistic situation of US society where race, class and sex have historically (and often successfully) been manipulated in the consolidation of power. Borrowing from many sources and traditions, I am less concerned about theoretical neatness than about an explanatory framework that accounts for the observed phenomena. The theoretical formulations are grounded in an analysis of the historical formation of black English, non-standard English and white English and in empirical research in the African American speech community and among black and white auto workers in Detroit.

Let me clarify my use of 'language.' I refer, in a holistic sense, both to language as abstract structure and language in speech interaction, and to a symbolic system rooted in social formations. I view language and speech, i.e. individual and social expression structure and use, as a unified behavioural dialectic governing the cognitive and social life of men and women. I thus depart from prevailing tendencies in US mainstream linguistics which is dominated by two scholarly camps: sociolinguistics and Cartesian or Chomskyan linguistics. The former camp focuses on social and ethnic language, the latter on 'ideally competent' language, devoid of social influence. Neither is adequate to formulate a theory of language for social transformation since both schools, including black English studies, fail to locate language within the historical structuring of society and the class system. As Fowler and Kress (1979: 186) put it: '[Linguistics] has been neutralized... [there is need for a] critical linguistics... aware of the assumptions on which it is based... and prepared to reflect critically about the underlying causes of the phenomena it studies, and the nature of the society whose language it is.'

Language, Ideology and Consciousness

The issue of the relationship between language and thought continues to be an enduring one. (One is tempted to call it 'timeless.') What is the nature of reality? Is it only existent in what we name? For instance, given the differing types and numbers of colours in various languages, how many colours actually materially exist? Is language what I often call a 'marked deck of cards'? For example, given the historical oppression of people of colour in Western societies, is the white boss lady's reference to her 50 year-old black maid as 'my girl' a revelation of racist ideology? Do speakers of different grammatical systems have different conceptions of external and social reality? For instance, do 'standard average European' languages (Whorf 1941), with their structural reliance on the duality of 'agent-action' utterances, force their speakers to conceptualize their physical and social worlds into bipolar entities? Or is language neutral since it '"produces" nothing or "produces" words only' (Stalin 1951) and thus irrelevant in social and revolutionary change?

In the beginning was 'work and word.' As Marx (1968) said, 'speech is as old as consciousness'. In the evolution of human society, work provided the impetus for the word, and thus Marx was undoubtedly accurate in asserting that speech was the product of labour. However, once language started forming, work and word had mutually reinforcing effects on each other. Over historical time, the language-speech dialectic came to play a dominant role in the formation of ideology, consciousness and class relations. This dialectic acts as a filter through which material conditions and the struggle to change them is apprehended. Without the medium of language, real world experience is encoded as undifferentiated phenomena. As Vygotsky (1962: 122) says, 'reality is generalized and reflected in a word'.

Only in the most idealist sense can language be considered neutral because once it is employed in speech interaction, i.e. in social dialogue, it is 'filled with content and meaning drawn from behaviour or ideology' (Volosinov 1929: 70). Notwithstanding the existence of 'inner speech' and talking to oneself, language is social behaviour. The language-speech dialectic represents a society's theory of reality. As Fowler and Kress (1979: 196) put it, the 'society...impregnate[s] its language with social meanings.'

Can 'syntax code a world view' (Fowler and Kress 1979: 185)? Both von Humboldt in the nineteenth century and Whorf in this one argued the point convincingly. Von Humboldt (1810: 245) asserted that 'every language sets certain limits to the spirit of those who speak it; it assumes a certain direction and by doing so, excludes many others.' Further, he contended (ibid.) that 'thinking is not merely dependent on language in general, but up to a certain degree on each specific language.'

Whorf devoted most of his unfortunately short life to analyses of native American languages, contrasting their grammars and the cultural and social patterns they gave rise to with languages of the Western world. Whorf posited that 'meaning will be found to be intimately connected with the linguistic: its principle is symbolism, but language is the great symbolism from which other symbolisms take their cue.' Throughout all of his work, even during the time he was a fire investigator for an insurance company, he insisted (Whorf 1941: 26) on the power of language to shape and control thought and behaviour.

> The grammar of each language is not merely a reproducing instrument for voicing ideas, but rather is itself the shape of ideas, the programme and the guide for the individual's mental activity.... Formulation of ideas is not an independent process, strictly rational in the old sense, but it is part of a particular grammar and differs, from slightly to greatly between grammars.

For real-world evidence, we are given, for example, the morphology of Hopi verbs, which are marked not for time, but for the nature or source of validity. Hopi is thus a 'timeless' language. Because of Hopi grammar, Whorf argued, the culture conceives of time as fluid, in process, rather than static or fixed, and dialogic assertions about reality are to be weighed not by temporal standards but by truth criteria. Kress and Hodge (1979: 6) joked that we would want to buy a used car from a Hopi salesman, rather than from an Englishman.

While von Humboldt and Whorf may have overstated the case for language as *the* determiner of thought, consciousness, and behaviour, language *is*, as Volosinov (1929: 70) asserted, 'implicated in the current ideology', and thus it does 'constitute

the most important content and the most important instrument
of socialization' (Berger and Luckman 1966: 133). From this
vantage point, it is my contention that ideology and consciousness are largely the products of what I call the 'socio-linguistic
construction of reality.' Consider a few examples.

In US popular culture, the number 13 is considered symbolic
of bad luck. And so in high-rise hotels in the US, marketing
strategies require that there be no 13th floor. The elevator goes
from the 12th floor to the 14th floor, and hotel guests exit and
sleep soundly in $200.00 rooms located on the 14th floor, which
is, of course, floor 13, socio-linguistically constructed as non-
existent.

As another example, consider the language that marks power
relationships. Although English does not have formal and
informal forms of the second person pronoun which govern
forms of address (for example *du-Sie* in German, *tu-vous* in
French, *ty-vy* in Russian), US English speakers do have access to
other linguistic forms reflective of the class system. Peers and
subordinates are socio-linguistically differentiated through the
use of titles and first and last names. As a socio-linguistic class
marker, maids receive first names but must in return use the
boss lady or man's last name. Hence 'Rita Smith' becomes
simply 'Rita', but 'Phyllis Stein' is 'Mrs Stein', or occasionally,
'Stein'. As socio-linguistic markers of social subordination based
on race and sex, note the import of titles and their omission in
the following exchanges (Pouissant 1967: 53):

> (A scene on a public street, white policeman, black physician.)
> 'What's your name, boy?' the policeman asked.
> 'Dr Poussaint. I'm a physician'.
> 'What's your first name, boy?'
> 'Alvin'.

A similar example is provided in Smitherman-Donaldson et al.
1991:

> (A scene in a law office, two males, one female.) 'This is Dr Johnson;
> she's a new physician on our staff over at General', the chief surgeon
> said. 'How do you do, Ms Johnson', the senior partner in the law
> firm replied.

These socio-linguistic markers of address reflect historically
constituted patterns of classism, racism and sexism in the US.

From among the available linguistic options in English, each of the above speakers has chosen a form that socio-linguistically constructs and reproduces exploitation based on class, race and sex.

A sharp illustration is provided by various meanings assigned to the epithet 'nigger'. In the following dialogue, two workers at a Chrysler plant in Detroit are talking about the large number of Vietnamese (the 'boat people' as US citizens derisively called them) who attempted to enter the US in 1975/6 (Smitherman 1976):

> J.T.: The Viet Nam who didn't git off the boat, they was gon be the new nigguhs - for the whiteys and us.
> Sam: I wish they hadda come on out there to work, cause I'm tired of being the nigguh.

The racial epithet is taken beyond the historical oppression of African slaves and their descendants. On the automobile assembly line, the 'nigguh' is any exploited worker.

In a similar vein, during the social movements of the 1960s white counter-culture youth groups, mostly university students and emerging white feminists used 'nigger' to characterize their social oppression and exploitation. They viewed their status as akin to the historical enslavement of Africans and the oppression of their descendants, who typically work at the lowest and meanest jobs (in the auto plants as elsewhere). Hence phrases such as the 'student as nigger' and the 'woman (or wife) as nigger'. Students are constructed as 'niggers' because not only are they subservient and powerless, their intellectual labour is expropriated by professors in pursuit of their own self-interest (for example research grants, promotion, tenure). Women are 'niggers' by virtue of the domestic and sexual labour expropriated in their enslavement by men.

What we see illustrated here is the extension and socio-linguistic reinterpretation of the semantic range of a verbal symbol rooted in slave labour and subsequent racial exploitation. Contrary to *The Oxford English Dictionary*'s lexicographers, who attest that the term 'nigger' is 'incorrectly applied to members of other dark-skinned races', the language usage of black auto workers and progressive whites correctly reconstructs 'nigguhs' as both black and white, male and female, or any group whose labour is exploited.

Among power élites, the socio-linguistic construction of reality is linguistic trickeration writ large. Operating at the macrostructural level, with the powerful, pervasive force of the media to aid in the reproduction of thought control, US élites promote a national doublespeak which makes 'the bad seem good... the negative positive... [the] unpleasant... attractive, or at least tolerable' and 'which does not extend thought but limits it' (Lutz 1987: 10). When the US State Department decides, as it did in 1984, that 'killing' in US-supported countries would be replaced with 'unlawful or arbitrary deprivation of life'; when US nuclear strategists use 'countervalue attacks' to refer to destruction of entire cities (Elias 1986: 10); and when, in this age of nuclear weapons, President Reagan discoursed about Russia as an 'evil empire', Marxism as a 'virus', and communism as a 'cancer', thus inviting extermination of these 'micro-organisms and demons' (Bosmajian 1984: 5), such language was designed to 'distort reality and corrupt the mind' (Lutz 1987: 12).

Not only is the pernicious use of language evident in words, *qua* words, but also in syntactical contouring and discourse style, we can witness evidence of language to conceal, obfuscate and distort reality. Yes, syntax can code a world view (see for example, van Dijk 1988; Sykes 1988). Objects of action are nominalized rather than objectified resulting in a reversal of the realty of who does what to whom, as in the newspaper headline, RIOTING BLACKS SHOT DEAD. 'Thus someone who has something done to him by another can be made responsible for his own suffering' (Fowler and Kress 1979: 41). Actors and agents are buried in the passive voice so responsibility for action cannot be assigned. Thus, 'pain exists, but seldom blame' (Kozol 1975: 25). The passive voice is particularly problematic because of its rampant use in US academic discourse as well as in the national doublespeak, both of which have become discourse models for student writers and young learners. In a statement like, 'the invasion of Grenada was officially approved', a deletion transformation has been employed permitting the escape of the agent, 'President Reagan'. Further, the statement displaces the theme topic (in English utterances, generally found at the beginning of a statement), thus shifting the emphasis from Reagan to Grenada.

To recapitulate, language represents a society's theory of reality. It not only reflects that theory of reality, it explains interprets, constructs and reproduces that reality. In the global strug-

gle for social and revolutionary change, there must be concomitant linguistic change. The first to go should be the old adage,
'sticks and stones may break my bones, but words can never
hurt me.'

Black-White Non-Standard English in the US

The socio-linguistic construction of reality in the class system of
the US is made more complex by the contradiction of black and
white English which are the same and not the same. White
English (also known as standard English) is that language
spoken by power élites and those who aspire to upward social
mobility; non-standard English is that language spoken by
working class whites; black English is that language spoken by
African Americans. Significant and profound social and
economic distinctions accompany each of these three linguistic
phenomena.

White English is a class dialect derived from the speech of
power élites. Since this group is comprised of white upper-class
males, white English reflects and reproduces the classism,
racism and sexism of the US. Linguistic correctness is a function
of ruling class white male hegemony manifested in the historical
development of white English, concomitant with capitalist
formation in US history. Let us take a closer look at this socio-
linguistic development.

Early US linguists (for example Webster 1784; Murray 1795;
Brown 1851) were primarily school-oriented grammarians intent
upon the linguistic socialization of the new masses, particularly
impressionable youth, into the linguistic conventions and rules
of correctness of the emerging US bourgeoisie, rapidly consolidating itself into a capitalist formation on the basis of race and
sex. These linguists - like their counterparts in England (Lowth
1762) and France (the Port-Royal School of 1660; see for example
Arnauld and Lancelot 1975) - viewed their mission as that of
'purifying the dialect of the tribe' which had been unleashed by
the demise of feudalism and the rise of capitalism and expanding technology. Models of correct speech were developed, based
on *Pax Romana*, on the speech forms of the emerging capitalist
élite, and on the *ipse dixit* pronouncements and preferences of
the grammarians themselves. Although they were not above
biting the hand that was feeding them by criticizing the élites,
the primary purpose of these grammarians was to lay down the

linguistic law to the white masses and their children in the school. (Remember, black literacy and schooling were forbidden in this era.) In this way, the new social 'hordes' would be 'civilized' and brought into the language 'family' of the ruling class.

Twentieth century grammarians have abandoned all pretensions to Latinate norms and have flatly come out with the doctrine that 'standard English is that dialect used by those who carry on the affairs of the English-speaking people' (Fries 1940). Thus it behoves those wishing to partake of the American dream to master this class dialect (for example Golden 1960; Allen 1969). For both blacks and whites, such linguistic mastery is touted as a *sine qua non* of upward mobility. Blacks who lack this mastery are speakers of black English; whites who lack it are speakers of non-standard English. Since the norms of white English fluctuate according to the linguistic whims of those in power, an entire school of US linguists devotes significant amounts of time and State capital to chronicling the linguistic whereabouts of contemporary pace-setters. The products are voluminous guides to contemporary usage which become tools of linguistic (and hence ideological) indoctrination in our nationwide public and university educational systems.

Whereas white English and non-standard English are *class* dialects in US society, black English, by contrast, is a *racial* dialect within the class system. That is, black English is spoken across the class spectrum among African Americans; middle class blacks develop code-switching skills (i.e. from black to white English) which the black working and *unworking* classes generally do not possess.

Black English is a product of the free labour system of the African slave trade. It arose as a result of two sets of factors: the need for a *lingua franca* in the US slave community where it was the practice of slavers to intermingle linguistically diverse African ethnic groups so as to impede communication and hinder escape; and the need for a linguistic code intelligible to slaves but unintelligible to slave masters. In its formalistic dimensions, black English reflects a combination of British/US English with a West African deep structure. Its lexicon is largely English, its syntax, semantics and phonology a mixture of both linguistic traditions. For example, black English has elements of a surviving aspectual verb system which facilitates the expression of continuous versus static action, as in *the coffee be cold* (i.e.

habitually, frequently) versus *the coffee cold* (i.e. today, now). (See, for example, Dillard 1972; Alleyne 1981; Labov 1982). Although there are some few words of direct African origin that have survived in black English (for example Dalby 1969, 1970; Turner 1949), the African component is revealed more in the ethnographic realm. For example, the application of distinct meaning to white English words, often resulting in 'semantic inversion' (Holt 1972), thus generating an utterance like 'black English is so good it's bad.' Similarly, 'nigguh' can be used in affectionate, positive contexts, as in 'he my main nigguh,' i.e. *he is my best friend*, and 'she is a shonuff nigguh,' i.e., *she is culturally black and rooted in the experiences and aspirations of black people.* (Note that whites never use 'nigger' with these meanings.) Other significant examples can be found in norms of discourse and dialogic interaction. For instance, in the pattern of call-response, which obligates listeners verbally and actively to participate in speakers' messages and delivery (ritualized in the preacher's sermon style in the traditional black Church); in the speech acts of signifying, testifying, rapping, toast-telling and proverb use (see for example Smitherman 1976, 1986; Daniel 1974; Mitchell-Kernan 1969; Kochman 1972, 1981).

Black English is related to other African-European language mixtures - pidgins and Creoles - that developed in the slave trade. The development of black English reflects the modal experiences of African Americans and the continuing quest for freedom and literacy. For instance, black struggles for literacy have caused black English to de-Creolize considerably since the seventeenth century - i.e. blacks have de-Africanized black English linguistic structure and moved it in the direction of white English. Yet continuing US racism (i.e. as manifested in *de facto* racial segregation, economic and other forms of discrimination) creates the need for black solidarity and thus results in the maintenance of sufficient distinctiveness in black English deep structure to render aspects of it unintelligible to white English speakers, i.e. de-Creolization remains incomplete. Thus black English and white English are the same but not the same.

It is necessary to account for the linguistic contradiction of black-white English in order to grasp the socio-linguistic construction of reality in the US. This contradiction is a function of and helps to reproduce patterns of labour exploitation. During slavery, white workers had to relinquish wage demands in the face of competition from free (slave) labour. When slavery became non-profitable, culminating in the emancipation proclamation, US society was faced with the potential time bomb of its newly-emancipated African workers joining forces with white workers. Racism was the ruling class's tool to prevent this alliance. blacks were assigned the lowest-paying and meanest jobs in the society and relegated, in disproportionate numbers to the marginal working class and the unemployed. In language use, it was (and is) the practice to designate the race of a worker. And the term 'nigger' added to its semantic features the conceptual discourse 'at least I ain't no nigger' as ideological compensation for the exploitation of the working class. Further, although non-standard English is denigrated in the class system, black English remains at the very bottom of the US sociolinguistic hierarchy.

Black English - A Class Sociolect?

As is the nature of contradictions, the language at the bottom appears to be rising to the top. If we analyse languages-in-contact at the point of production, particularly in automobile manufacturing, there is evidence to suggest that black English is emerging as the *lingua franca* of the US industrial work place. Given that language usage reflects social network and solidarity, if US black English is indeed an emerging class sociolect, it points toward a linguistic index of shifting social relations and compels us to re-examine the traditional model of race relations in the US

Seeking empirical validation of the hypothesis that black English is the language of US workers, particularly those in automobile manufacturing, Botan and Smitherman devised the black English assessment, a language questionnaire (see Figure 5.1) to assess knowledge of black English semantics among production workers and non-production workers (i.e. professionals, plant supervisors, managers), both inside and outside the auto plants. The questionnaire consists of ten items drawn from the *Dictionary of American Regional English*. The items chosen have been designated by the *Dictionary of American Regional English* as 'black' or 'especially black' based on the frequency with which a certain meaning was given by blacks.

Figure 5.1: Questionnaire, 'Choose the Correct Definition' or 'Don't Know' (not shown)

Bid Whist
a. a bid made in an auction
b. a kind of dress
the habit of paying bills on time
d. a kind of card game

Call The Hogs
a. shout very loudly
b. snore
c. get angry and yell at someone
d. celebrate

Bo Dollar
a. a dollar owed a brother
b. silver dollar
c. last dollar you have to your name
d. a kind of hubcap

Chicken Eater
a. a Baptist preacher
b. a city dweller
c. a weasel or mink
d. one who raises chickens

Crack A Rib
a. eat spare ribs (or share them)
b. stomp someone in a fight
c. a kind of block in football
d. laugh very hard

Dead Cat
a. something suspicious
b. when a criminal is killed
c. to be badly beaten in a game of luck
d. a ringer in horseshoes

Jackleg
a. a good high jumper
b. a kind of spider
c. unprofessional or dishonest preacher
d. well tailored slacks

Nose Wide Open
a. injured in a fight
b. being openly and strongly in love
c. smelling nice flowers
d. just getting over a cold

Ig
a. a dance
b. to get a promotion
c. ignorant
d. ignore

Gall Shirt
a. undershirt
b. army uniform shirt
c. work shirt
d. spicy food

(See Table 5.1.) Informants were asked to select the correct definition of each item from a set of five definitions per item. The
usage given by the *Dictionary of American Regional English* informants was always one of the five options.

**Table 5.1: Black-White Responses in Black English
Assessment in Detroit Sample of Production Workers (%)**

Item	(1)	(2)	(3)
Bid Whist	82.7	94	45
Call the Hogs	61	67	17
Bo Dollar	79	73	12
Chicken Eater	100	64	37
Crack A Rib	60	73	37
Dead Cat	66.6	27	15
Jackleg	63	79	17
Nose Wide Open	100	97	51
IG	100	24	23
Gall Shirt	85.7	15	13

Key: (1) Black responses; (2) Correct Black responses; (3) Correct White
responses. (All shown in %)

Sources: *Dictionary of American Regional English*; See also Hirshberg
1982; Smitherman-Donaldson et al. 1991.

The *Dictionary of American Regional English* (Cassidy et. al. 1985)
presents the advantage of a national probability sample of US
citizens from every state, interviewed by trained fieldworkers,
who provided language data on a variety of topics of general
interest: foods, religion, attitudes towards others and social
activities. The number of informants in each state reflects that
state's proportion of the total US population; the number of
blacks in the sample is relative to the proportion of blacks in
each state. Altogether, the *Dictionary of American Regional English*
sample consists of 2,752 informants in 1,002 communities across
the US who were interviewed between 1965 and 1970. As many
as 2.5 million responses were obtained from informants and
computer analysed. So far dictionaries have been released in two
or three alphabetic sequences each year, beginning with 1985.

For the Detroit survey, informants were randomly selected

from the Detroit metropolitan area, using assembly line workers
to administer surveys in the auto plants, and university research
assistants for survey administration outside the plants. The
results reported here have been extrapolated from two surveys
conducted five years apart. While age and section of the US
where raised were analysed, it is the analysis of responses by
race and occupation that are of primary interest. In the 1982 data
(reported in Botan and Smitherman 1983), the comparison of
production workers with supervisors/professionals confirmed
our predictions. White auto workers scored higher than did
white professionals and managers, i.e. the production workers
exhibited greater familiarity with black English semantics.
However, black workers did not score significantly higher than
black professionals, as expected, given the linguistic homogene-
ity of the black community and the phenomenon of code
switching among black professionals. For the 1987/8 data
(reported in Smitherman-Donaldson et al. 1991), we have done a
preliminary item analysis of surveys from a subsample of
production workers. Results reflect a trend toward white
knowledge of 'especially black' terms - 'chicken eater', 'Bid
Whist' and 'nose wide open'. And although the percentages of
whites familiar with 'ig' (a 100 per cent black term) and 'gall
shirt' (85.7 per cent black) are lower, those percentages are
almost identical to the percentages of black workers who knew
these two terms. (See Table 5.1.)

Of course there are possible limitations to this kind of
language survey. The *Black English Assessment* is a written
survey of an *oral* language. White English can glean an index of
receptive competence only; the question remains to what degree,
if any, white workers use black English and in what contexts.
Related to this limitation is the effect of limited literacy skills on
both black and white workers' performance on the assessment.
And finally, there remains the question of the extent of white
workers' knowledge of black English beyond semantics. On the
other hand, we can pose several challenges to the question of
limitations. It is entirely possible that white workers exhibit
greater familiarity with black English in natural language envi-
ronments. When they returned their surveys, many of the workers, including whites, indicated recognition of some items when
they heard them pronounced; hence oral reading of the surveys
might have produced a greater number of correct responses
from whites. While it would be valuable to compare white

workers' knowledge of black English with their use of black English, and while the fully competent speaker possesses both receptive and productive competence in a given language, it remains an open question whether the ideological process requires competence in *both* linguistic dimensions. Conceptualizing language in a social change model raises the possibility that a person could be indoctrinated into a speech community's theory of reality solely on the basis of his or her *comprehension* of that community's language. Finally, while it might also be of some value to assess white workers' knowledge of black English beyond semantics into the realms of morpho-syntax and phonology, such an investigation is premised on the assumption - widely held among linguists in the Chomsky school - that the semantic component of language is subordinate to its syntactical and phonological dimensions. If we accept the principle that 'ideology is revealed in a word', a compelling case can be made for conceptualizing a model of language with semantics as the primary component.

Conclusions and Implications

Language should be assigned a central place in models of social change and in political and revolutionary theories. The language-speech dialectic represents habitual, systematic social behaviour. Its linguistic forms, embodying the world view of the society, are encoded in childhood in natural, developmental socialization processes. These forms construct and reproduce the society's theory of reality and become imbedded in the socio-cognitive structure of speakers, who in turn use their language in spontaneous, virtually reflexive ways largely inaccessible to consciousness. This language acquisition process is universal, transcending cultural space and societal time. In fact it is this process that gives validity to Cartesian assumptions about language as an inherent human trait. On these grounds, there is no quarrel with the Chomsky school. *Dico, ergo sum.* However, the 'I speak' and the 'I am' are functions of the class system. Through repetitive language use and social reinforcement in class relations, negative social meanings and class-biased socio-linguistic patterns come to sound common and innocuously 'natural'. Because speakers thus become oblivious to underlying deep structure, in the process of social transformation, we are all challenged to a new level of linguistic consciousness. We must learn to attend to habitual, socially encoded patterns of speech that construct and reproduce classism, racism and sexism.

Permit me to cite a personal example. Until a comrade in Chicano linguistics pulled my coat, I had never given thought to referring to the US as 'America'. Even as I criticized 'America' for its participation in the repression of the people of Nicaragua and elsewhere in the 'Americas,' I was unconsciously reinforcing US cultural chauvinism and its regressive ideology. The underlying social meaning conveyed by reference to the US as 'America' was that it was the only region among the 'Americas' worthy of the title 'America', the others being referred to as 'Central America', 'South America', 'Latin America'. I have thus consciously sought, throughout this paper, to use the term 'US' Such linguistic awareness has its practical problems. For example, the metaphorical construct 'American dream' is a linguistic register with immediate social familiarity whereas 'US dream' is not. However, the crucial point is that attention to language use re-raises social consciousness and ideological awareness each time speakers consciously select a linguistic option from their socio-linguistically constructed communication repertoire. Ultimately, 'natural' sounding negative language will come to sound as 'unnatural' and oppressive as race, class and sex exploitation.

An analysis of black-white-non-standard English calls into question the traditional model of race relations in the US. There is a need to redefine the semantics of race and class. Assumptions about who is black, who is white and about racial solidarity (i.e. all blacks versus all whites) must be re-examined. A critical lesson of the black movement of the 1960s and 1970s is that the verbal concept 'black' could not automatically be marked with the semantic features (+socially progressive), (+for the people), (-competitiveness), (-labour exploitation). As the National Organization for an American Revolution (1982: 37) asserts:

> The Black Power Movement degenerated into 'piece of the action' politics... blacks... resist engaging in the principled political struggles with other blacks that would force them to recognize how deeply blacks have been incorporated into the values of the capitalist system. So they cling to the illusion that changing the colour of those in city government will solve their problems, despite the mounting evidence that black mayors, black police chiefs and black school superintendents are only overseers on the corporate plantations and reservations that our big cities have become.

There is little evidence that the black middle class decries the machinations of capitalism. Many, if not most, seem to have bought into it as the pathway to the 'good life,' the only obstacle to which is white racism. While they have racial consciousness, there is little evidence of class consciousness. For example, though they use the concept 'nigguh' in the cultural ways in which working class blacks use it (see examples cited earlier), they do not use it to refer to exploited labour as do black workers and progressive whites.

The paramount role of black labour is underlined by black auto workers' verbalizations of class and in the emerging linguistic cross-over of black English in the work place. Though susceptible and often succumbing to the temptations of capitalist consumerism, the workers evidence a linguistic sense of class consciousness coexistent with their sense of racial consciousness. In analysing verbalizations of class in his 1960 study of black and white workers in Detroit, Leggett (1968) found strong evidence of class consciousness among the blacks in his study. In our interviews with black auto workers, there emerged distinctions between whites who are members of the power élite and those of the working class. Phrases such as 'whiteys with the shonuff money' and 'white boys with big paper' differentiate 'Po'ass whiteys' and 'Howard Beach suckers' who 'ain't in charge of nothin' (Smitherman-Donaldson et al. 1991). And there is evidence of an understanding of the manipulations of race by white élites (Smitherman 1976).

> Nigguhs know the real thang is bout money, so they sik them pecks [lower class whites] on the niggush to keep them from gittin too far.... They [whites] live out there in them lil funky shacks, driving the lil biddy funny riddes, stay on E [financially empty], and happy as a sissy in Jackson, long as the they got nigguhs to fuck wit.

The linguistic evidence from white workers indicating a trend toward the adoption of black English as the *lingua franca* in the work place suggests the emergence of black English as a class sociolect and raises the possibility of capitalizing on the resources of the language for social transformation. Not only is black English the workers' *lingua franca*, it is all US outsiders' language of choice. The ideological function and socio-linguistic status of black English is reminiscent of (though not identical to) an 'anti-language' (Halliday 1976). This is a linguistic system that reinforces group solidarity and excludes the 'other.' It is speech characteristic of a group which is in but not of a society. As an anti-language, black English emerges as a counter-ideology; it is the language of rebellion and the symbolic expression of solidarity among the oppressed. For whites and blacks outside the working class (i.e. in the US, not the Marxist sense), it is a language which permits progressives to commit 'class suicide' by socio-linguistically reconstructing themselves. One may well question whether this is not too great a claim for black English, and the answer may well be 'yes'. But one thing is certain: if we are to speak the truth to the people and usher in societal transformation, we must have 'a new way of walkin' and a new way of talkin'.'

6

Racist Discourse and the Language of Class

David Theo Goldberg

Race and Reduction

The prevailing tradition in social scientific analysis of 'race,' in both theoretical and empirical terms, has been reductionistic. In keeping with the scientific concern to explain complex phenomena in terms at once more simple, general, and real the complexities of racism are reduced to underlying motivational determinants. These include, most notably, social psychological attitudes, biological affinities, sexual identity, or economic class, and they are deemed more universal and substantial than the racist manifestations to which they are supposed to give rise. Racial discrimination is explained accordingly as so many rationalizations for questionable psychological attitudes or biological fitness, prohibition of unconscious drives, or most usually for class exploitation.[1] The primary theoretical concern underlying the appeal of reductionism here is the general consensus that 'race' has no ontological status: it is not a first cause.[2] Any division of humankind into 'races' has no rational or scientific basis. It is considered invalidated by the facts of nature.

Many difficulties face this standard view. First, racism is reduced accordingly to a single transhistorical phenomenon. It is treated as essentially the same social condition wherever and whenever it subsists. Yet there is considerable historical variance both in the conception of 'races' and in the kinds of social expression we characterize as racist. Racism transforms, continuously in some respects and discontinuously in others, from one period to another. Developments and changes in racist discourse may be demonstrated to be functions of dominant interests, aims, and purposes. But it can be shown also that forms of racism have developed in response to critical and practical resistances. Changes in the discursive representations of racism and the practices they inform are variously related to alterations in the conception and articulation of 'race,' and in the formation of races.[3]

Thus racism of all forms may be linked at the most abstract of theoretical levels in terms of their exclusionary or inclusionary undertakings. One major historical shift has been from past racist forms defining and fueling expansionist colonial aims and pursuits to contemporary expressions in nationalist terms.[4] Insistence upon racial inferiority in the past fed colonial appetites and imperialist self-definition. Now that neo-colonialist racism has become increasingly unfashionable, racist expressions have come more and more to inform the terms of isolationist national self-image; of cultural differentiation tied to custom, tradition, and heritage; and of exclusionary immigration policies, anti-immigrant practices, and criminality. These shifts may be found embedded in contemporary conceptions of state and legality, in constitution of class relations, and in family and gender formations.

A second difficulty facing reductionistic views is that it implies, if not presumes, that racism is inherently irrational. It is taken to be the set of rationalizations for, and so prompted by, some primitive irrational yet inevitable drives, whether psychological, physical, sexual, or economic. The drawback here, however, is that the presumed immorality of racism is thrown in question. For, where a drive or condition is inevitable, that is, caused by factors or conditions beyond the agent's control, no individual responsibility for its occurrence can be claimed. The misdirected actions of those suffering psychosis, physical or sexual maladjustment, economic deprivation, or disadvantage usually inspire varying degrees of sympathy for the agent rather than condemnation. If we are committed to insisting in any meaningful sense upon racism's unacceptability agent responsibility for racism's occurrence must be pressed, not mitigated. And this seems to entail abrogating the standard conception.

Third, the traditional view fails to account for the peculiarly *racial* component and effects of racist discrimination. This is not to concede the objectivity of race classifications; there is no objective scientific basis for such classifications.[5] Though lacking in scientific content, nevertheless, 'race' has wide *social* currency and effect. So it is important to distinguish between the biological and social concepts of 'race.' *Social race* is not a natural fact but is socially constructed; it is, in short, any group defined by others or defining itself as a race. As such, it has some analytic use value. Pressing in use the notion of 'social race' will enable a mapping of the different historical forms of racism and their range of discriminatory effects. Reducing racial discrimination exclusively to talk about class exploitation, say, fails to explain — if even to bring to our notice — the fact that it is *blacks* who benefit *less* from non-race-specific anti-poverty programmes than do whites. Race-neutral housing policies accordingly perpetuate existing deficiencies of given segregated urban housing arrangements.

My primary concern here is to argue for a non-reductionistic general account of racism. Reduction of race-talk to class-talk and class analysis is the most common and compelling form of reduction, if only because it tells part of the story.[6] The bulk of my critical concern will thus be directed at this form of reduction. It is my aim, in conclusion, to suggest ways in which analysis of race-talk and class-talk may be non-reductionistically integrated.

Race and Class Production

The claim that racism is analytically reducible to class formations and in particular to class exploitation is usually taken to mean that racism is *caused* by class interests, tensions, and struggles. Occurrence of racism is supposed to be *explained* as a function of the more primary social phenomena of class divisions and struggles. The implication of this reduction is that racism would disappear with eradication of classes and class struggles. By contrast, I aim to show that though racisms may (often) have a class component racism *qua* racism is in fundamental respects conceptually autonomous of, and to that extent irreducible to, class determinations.

Of course, if racism is not to be reduced to accounts simply in terms of class relations, it cannot be defined in terms of class exploitation. Racism will be characterized rather in terms of a model for picking out racists on the basis of the kinds of beliefs they hold. Racists are those who explicitly or implicitly ascribe racial characteristics of others which they take to differ from their own and those they consider like them. These characteristics may be biological or social. The ascriptions do not merely propose racial differences; they assign racial preferences, and they express desired, intended, or actual inclusions or exclusions, entitlements or restrictions. Racist acts based upon such beliefs fall under the general principle of discriminatory behaviour against others in virtue of their being deemed members of different racial groups. Nevertheless, in some instances behaviour may be racist on grounds only of its effects. The mark of racism in these cases will be whether the discriminatory behaviour reflects a persistent pattern or could reasonably have been avoided. Racist institutions are those the formative principles of which incorporate and whose social functions serve to institute and perpetuate the beliefs and acts in question.

My concern is to account for historical variations in the modes of racial formation, and for its articulations and exploitative forms, that differ from the modes of class formation with its articulations and exploitative forms. Methodologically, racial discrimination(s) and class formation(s) with the accompanying exploitation will be accounted for in terms of the more general notion of *social discourse*. Racism and class formation are to be considered fields of discourse. The discursive field in each case is sufficiently broad to incorporate the various entities constitutive of racism and class exploitation respectively. The constitutive entities, considered independently, fall under the category of expressions. Thus racist expressions and class expressions include the relevant beliefs and verbal outbursts (epithets, slurs, etc.); acts and their consequences under the relevant descriptions; and the principles upon which racist and class bound institutions are based. And expressions, whether racist or class determined, may assume widely divergent forms: economic, legal, bureaucratic, linguistic, scientific, philosophical, religious, pedagogic, and so forth.

A well-defined field of discourse arises out of a discursive formation. This consists of a totality of ordered relations and correlations — of subjects to each other and to objects; of

economic production and reproduction, cultural symbolism and
signification; of laws and moral rules; of economic, social, political, or legal inclusion and exclusion. The socio-discursive
formation consists of a range of rules that determine what can or
cannot be done, what falls within the range of the permissible or
what is excluded as impermissible. Conditions of existence,
production and reproduction, preservation, transformation, and
dissolution at a given historical conjuncture define an *object*
which can be spoken of and analysed. They determine also the
mode in terms of which the object can be approached, its
elements named and classified, its functions explained. Rules
constitutive of a discursive field are promoted in this elaboration
of object and mode.[7]

Racism and class constitution exist as the effects of — what
are given rise to by — established relations between subjects and
institutions, economic and social practices; by patterns and
principles of conduct and ethics, classificatory systems and
technologies of power. Neither racism nor class constitution are
simply present in these relations, nor are they reducible to them
or to any of their constitutive elements. Hence the failure of any
attempted explanation of racism — or for that matter of class
formation — *solely* on the basis of economic determinism, or
strictly in terms of psychological or biological reductionism.[8]

Specifying the genealogy and ontology of social formations
in this way highlights a point about racism often overlooked.
The ethnocentrisms of socio-epistemic conjunctures prior to the
seventeenth century, though forerunners of racism, were not
themselves forms of racist expression. 'Slavery' or 'barbarianism'
are discursive objects which are differently constituted and
structured than racism. They differ in making no legitimating
appeal to concepts like 'race' that originate in scientific
discourse. These differences are reflected in turn in the
discourses defining these respective forms of subjection,
exclusion, and subjugation. (Of course, this point is consistent
with class reductionistic accounts of racism, for class
reductionism need only claim that racism emerges with the
capitalist social formation.)

Elements of Racist Discourse

Three general elements constitute socio-discursive fields: socio-historical conjuncture; formal (grammatical) components and relations of the discourse; and subjective expression, that is, internalization, subjection in terms, and use of the discourse by subjects.

The socio-historical conjuncture of a discursive formation generally consists in the confluence of material *and* conceptual conditions over a given period of time that facilitates the definition of the discursive object and articulation of the field of discourse. Once the discursive field is constituted variations and transformations in these conditions may stimulate discursive modification, development, even dissolution.

The general socio-historical grounds of racism have been widely analysed, and I need simply summarize: The voyages of discovery from the sixteenth century on reported vast areas of 'unconquered' land with inestimable mineral wealth and natural resources, but cautioned that these lands were peopled by 'strange, often hostile beings.'[9] Nascent capitalism, fuelled by an ever-expanding appetite for profit, led very quickly to demands for cheap labour and raw materials, slavery, and the denuding of natural resources. The population increase in Europe in the early nineteenth century gave rise to colonial spread[10] while the unquenchable desire for profit stirred the accompanying drive for market expansion. The nineteenth century 'economic miracle' brought with it political solidification of the state, the forces of which were no longer directed just at the native barriers to colonial extension. They were soon employed to promote internal division and exclusion, domination and violence. Thus the terror conducted against Jews in Spain or Russia was extended by the mid-twentieth century into a well-oiled machine of annihilation in Germany; and the exclusion of Jews from British citizenship until the latter part of the eighteenth century, and again in 1890, has developed into state-sanctioned techniques of racial exclusion not only of blacks and Asians in Britain and some of its former colonies, particularly South Africa, but ironically of Palestinians in and from Israel. It has recently been argued also that the metropoles, utilizing scientific and technological developments, have internalized the dynamics of colonialism to maintain clear colour determined class lines 'at home.'[11] Clearly, these socio-historical grounds by virtue of which racism has unfolded is *consistent* with a class-reductionistic account of race-formation and discrimination. This consistency is magnified by reflecting upon the systems of underlying value and appropriation even at the level of socio-historical conjuncture and material interrelations. In the case of racism there is a remarkable confluence of the modes of economic and aesthetic valorization and appropriation, that is, of the general criteria according to which things are imbued with value and how such objects are made our own.

The rise of racist discourse rested upon the eighteenth century resurrection of classical values of beauty.[12] These values share a substantial similitude with the criteria of value in the classical economic tradition. Thus equilibrium and utility have functions in classical economic theory historically analogous to proportion, symmetry, and refinement for classical aesthetics. Both sets of criteria determine an order of balance and harmony, established on the basis of the geometric model. For classical aesthetics beauty is a property possession of which determines the ontological value of subjects, just as possession of economic goods creates the utility of classical economics. Possession of property is a sign of wealth, that which the agent is able to appropriate in the face of competition[13] To lack classical beauty is to be poor, which — as in *laissez faire* economic theory — is considered the subject's own fault. Where beauty is interpreted in terms of racial properties — fair skin, straight hair, head shape, well composed bodily proportions, and so on — to fail to possess them is considered a fault of inheritance, much as heirs are designated to maintain wealth within the confines of the family 'blood line.' So just as economic poverty (lack of ownership of property and the means of production) led agents inevitably to work for pittances in factories and coal mines, so 'racial poverty' was seen to justify property in humans. Locke's 'justifications' of property appropriation and ownership, on one hand, and human property in black slaves, on the other, provide perhaps the prototype of the confluence of values at work here.[14]

There lies at hand a further non-economic historical dimension that has moulded racist discourse. The criteria of value for classical aesthetics as for classical economics are thoroughly intellectualist. First, beauty is considered a property, present as an ideal essence to the intellect and characterized thus by its clarity and knowability.[15] Second, though 'utility' in the classical economic tradition appears to be defined in terms of 'satisfaction of desire,' the market mechanisms by virtue of which the classical model 'tends to equilibrium' are equally intellectualist.[16] This intellectualism is supported by a very strong naturalism. Objects are deemed beautiful in so far as they tend to or mirror the order of things, just as they are supposed to tend to their true or natural value (price) to the degree that they approach their natural equilibrium as demand and supply 'mirror' each other.[17] This common intellectualism and naturalism pervade the foundations of modern philosophic discourse. Both the rationalist and empiricist traditions rest ultimately upon common assumptions: truth as the correspondence of idea to reality, knowledge as mind mirroring nature.[18] This supports the conclusion that rationalism and empiricism in their own ways are equally prone to racist conjecture. Chomsky and Bracken have both argued that while empiricism enables the expression of racism rationalism offers a 'modest conceptual barrier' to the formulation of racist principles.[19] For empiricists, an unflawed perception of racial hierarchy or difference in nature will cause an idea of same to develop in the mind's eye. Nevertheless, rationalists are also bound to the view that mind mirrors nature. So if mind possesses a clear and distinct idea that one race is more intelligent or beautiful than another, it therefore must be true.

This pervasive intellectualism and naturalism led to the growth of the ideal that persons are to be considered beautiful on the basis of their 'natural' qualities. These qualities were supposed to be established on the a priori grounds of racial membership. In this way, aesthetic value solidified into natural law, becoming for the eighteenth century as compelling as the laws of nature, of economics, and of morality precisely because they were all deemed to derive from the same basis. It is for this reason that many natural historians, biologists, and anthropologists at the time classified humankind not only on grounds of physical criteria like 'measurement, climate, and environment' but according to the aesthetic values of 'beauty and ugliness.'[20] Thus the aesthetic values of bodily beauty referred to above were established as the mode for determining the individual's place in the racial (and therefore social) hierarchy. And perceived intellectual abilities (or their lack) were considered to reveal inherent racial differences in mental capacity.

Most commentators have assumed that racists inevitably combine these two strains into a spurious causal principle. It is assumed, in other words, that racial membership determines both one's degree of beauty and one's intellectual capacity, so that where an observer has access to one the other may be deduced. Unfortunately the entire racist tradition cannot be dismissed quite so hastily on grounds that it inevitably collapses 'aesthetic values' and 'natural qualities.' Based upon the inheritance of Cartesian dualism by the founding fathers of empiricism, some early racist thinkers had already begun to think of mind and nature as merely *correlated* in various ways.[21] It is this looser notion of causality as correlation (Humean constant conjunction) that enabled the extension of each strain into separate genealogical lines of racist discourse: On one hand, we find 'aesthetic racism' wedded to the physicality of bodily shape and colour, quality of bodily accoutrements like hair, and so forth.[22] On the other hand, 'intellectual racism' expanded into the technology of brain capacity measurements and IQ testing.[23] Immanuel Kant had already signalled a move in 1764 to merge these two trends in his own racist thinking. After he had more or less abandoned strict Cartesian dualism, Kant could turn Hume's correlation between race and intelligence back into a strictly causal relation. Kant did this by moving at the same time from the notion of 'beauty' as the basis of aesthetic classification to the concept of 'sublimity' as perfection. In typical Kantian synthesis, racial sublimity was taken to incorporate aesthetic and intellectual qualities and yielded a hierarchical classification of races, with white Germans and Englishmen at the top, Chinese and Negroes at the tail. This enabled Kant to conclude logically that 'the fellow was quite black from head to toe, *a clear proof* that what he said was stupid.'[24] Kant could consider himself in this way to have *derived* a 'Negro's stupidity' from his blackness.

My analysis has revealed a convergence of values, non-reducible and mutually determining, an interplay of factors — legal, political, economic, aesthetic, and philosophic — from which the field of racist discourse emerged. That these are the factors, which in many though not all instances also prompted class formations and exploitation, serves merely to underline the historical platitudes that racism has often reflected and served class interests, just as class formations have assumed racial form. Yet the foregoing line of analysis equally resists wholesale class reductionism of racial discrimination. Racist discourse has a specific, autonomous identity. Its causes and influences are a hybrid of social factors. But its identity, like the social marks and traces it leaves, are unique. The objectivity of causal factors and effects — social but never natural — is in sharp contrast with the *claimed* objectivity by racist discourse in legitimizing exclusivist social relations. Though the claim may sometimes succeed at the the level of (social) legitimation, it always fails as (moral) justification. This relatively autonomous identity of racist discourse can be conclusively established, then, only by outlining its distinctive 'grammar,' unique conceptual structure, rules of emergence, and social marks.

Racist Discourse and Class Formation

At given socio-historical conjunctures concepts, terms, and claims in scientific, legal, political, and moral discourse have fashioned ways of seeing, expressing, and acting that are distinctively racist. The particular histories, discursive structure, and exclusionary effects of racist discourse differ from the variations in class formations under capitalism, and at least in part from their exploitative effects.

The unity of racist discourse is established on the basis of a set of theoretically abstract but historically derived *primitive terms* and relations that 'ground' the discursive grammar of racism in its deep structure. The most general and so theoretically basic of these primitives are *racial exclusion/inclusion* and *exclusivity*. Yet these are *historically* derivative from the notions of *classification, order, value,* and *hierarchy, racial superiority* and *inferiority, identity* and *difference*. Changes in descriptions, hypotheses, rules, models, norms, and styles within racist discourse are a function of transformations in these preconceptual primitives. The structural unity of the discourse in contrast to, say, class discourse must be sought in a transformational schema of this set of primitives and 'in the interplay between their location, arrangement and displacement.'[25]

The classification of human groups on the basis of putatively natural (inherited or environmental) identities and differences gave rise by implication to a hierarchical ordering of human races. The *principle of gradation* considered inherent in rational classification of the universe was employed to ground the objectivity of racial classification. The subjectivity of aesthetic judgment and taste, of empathy and aversion, was applied to this objectification of human subjects. The full weight of eighteenth century science and rationality, philosophy, aesthetics, and religion merged in this way to circumscribe European representations of others. This chain of elements — classification, order, value, hierarchy — is supposed to delineate also the realm of possibilities at each putative level of existence, and thus to establish a range of moral commands and relations. Yet even if commitment to superiority and inferiority as a function of racial hierarchy is forgone in the face of critical attack, classificatory identities and differences in racial terms suffice to sustain the exclusions of racist practice. Domination of a particular race is established in respect of a series of differences from other individuals or groups, and by virtue of a series of identities between like beings.

Racial differentiation — the discrimination *between* races and their purported members — is not in and of itself racist. Racial identity even when externally ascribed implies unity. When this identity is internalized it prompts identification, a sense of belonging together. Only then does racial differentiation begin to define otherness, and discrimination *against* the other becomes at once *exclusion* of the different. Elaboration of racial differences and identities enables racists to applaud the debunking of social hierarchies while serving to establish unity for contemporary racist discourse.

Thus exclusion on the basis of difference furnishes common ground for the transformational schema generated by classification. *Differential exclusion* is *categorically* the most basic primitive term of the deep structure definitive of racist discourse. As the basic propositional content of racist desires, dispositions, beliefs, hypotheses and expressions (including acts, laws and institutions), racial exclusion conceptually motivates the entire superstructure of racist discourse. It establishes the racial mark of entitlement and restriction, endowment and appropriation. And racial exclusion functions in at least two general ways. It serves as *presumption* in the service of which rules or rationalizations may then be formulated or offered. Or it may be concluded as the *outcome* of practical deliberation in some domain, like economics, or legislation, or education.[26]

I am now at least tentatively in a position to differentiate racist discourse from that of class formation. First, the constitution of classes takes place primarily in terms of objective socioeconomic determinations and relations, while race formation, whether forced or self-ascribed, is a function largely of the 'grammatical' structure I have outlined above. Second, racist discriminations and exclusions may cut across class divisions as much as they coincides with and carries forward class differentiation and exploitation. Racist exclusion may in some contexts enable class exploitation, just as class exploitation may (often) take the form of racist exclusion. Nevertheless, there are forms of racist exclusion (separatism, for example, under some interpretations) that do not entail class exploitation, just as class exploitation need not require racist exclusivity. Race-formation has a history, even a history of class collusion; and class constitution is carried forward in part by ideological ascriptions (witness the most recent reference to ghettoized urban blacks as 'the new *under*class'). Yet the popular (non-academic) language of class differentiation, though equally unified as a discursive formation — at an abstract level it is also defined in terms of the primitives *classification, order, value, hierarchy* — perhaps plays only a supporting rather than a defining role in class constitution and exploitation. The difference here between racist and class discourse may be reflected in the difference between exclusion and exploitation: though both require social institutions for their respective effectiveness, the latter by definition requires actual class differentiations but not (necessarily) discursive rationalization while the former invokes questionable differentiations and succeeds only in so far as the terms it generates remain *subjectively* persuasive.

Racist and class discourse have together dominated the modern definition of otherness, the former furnishing the terms for the forceful exclusion of the different and the latter the relations of power for the exploitation of the powerless. It might be suggested that this makes the very point of class reductionistic accounts of racism. After all, the management of human subjects enabled by colour racism extended the space in which capital accumulation, the growth of productive forces, and the massive generation and redeployment of surplus value could take place. Yet this misses the deeper point I am insisting upon: namely, that it is *in virtue* of racist discourse and not merely rationalized by it that such forced manipulations of individual subjects and whole populations could have been affected. Instruments of exclusion — legal, cultural, political, or economic — are forged by subjects as they mould criteria for establishing racial otherness. Racism is promoted — perhaps entailed — by this discourse of the body, with its classificatory systems, order, and values, its ways of seeing particular bodies, and most fundamentally its modes of exclusion. Paradoxically, racist discourse has succeeded in drawing social subjects together, unifying them as subjects of authority. Subjects have been able to recognize identity in terms of this discourse, as they can be identified by it. The discourse of racism furnishes a cohesive foundation for the body politic, a continuity in time, across authorities. It is a discourse authors of the law might invoke as justification of entitlements or restrictions, endowments or lacks, incorporation or disenfranchisement.

Thus racist discourse enters the domains of morality and legality as a set of foundational claims. Its asserted title to establish differences is taken as an objective basis of inclusion and exclusion, whether natural or historical. This is offered in turn as a primary ground of entitlements, of rights of accessibility (to enfranchisement, opportunity, or treatment), and of endowments (goods and the means thereto); and conversely, of denial (disenfranchisement or restriction), of prohibition (to entry, participation, or services), and of alienation (of goods and the means to them). In general, the discourse of racism 'justifies' the exclusion of others by denying or ignoring their respective claims. It encourages active interference in establishing what the excluded, the disenfranchised and the restricted are entitled to and can properly expect.[27]

The unity of a discourse is promoted by transformational structures effected from a schema of preconceptual primitive terms. At specific socio-historical conjunctures the schema for racism generates the concepts peculiar to the enunciation of racism at that time and place, and thereby the categories, stereotypes, expressions, metaphors, styles and themes expressed in the field of racist discourse. To establish racism specifically as a discourse — independent from class discourse, say — the preconceptual schema must give rise also to racist hypotheses and presumptions, indeed, to racist argumentation, reasoning, and rationalization.

Race, Class and Social Subjectivity

If the widespread employment and influence of racist discourse is to be fully comprehended, non-reductively and *in its own terms*, it is the *persuasiveness* of racist argumentation that must be accounted for. In other words, to show how agents have so readily expressed racist discourse it must be illustrated how agents subject themselves to modes of expression, making these their own; towards whom subjects direct these expressions and reasoning, and why; and what subjects might hope to gain from this way of expressing themselves. To illustrate the autonomy of racist from class discourse I can only outline a response to these issues.

The full formation of subjectivity is necessarily social. I want to suggest that the social subject is constituted as the point of convergence, the bodily intersection, of multiple discourses. Social discourses are the intermediary between self and society, mediating the self as social subject. Discourses like racism are the product of economies of power, generated in the inter-relations of bodies, and characterized by relations of domination, subjugation, exclusion and exploitation. By converging with other discourses like that of class and interiorized by the individual, the discourse is able to define the identity both of subjectivity and of otherness. Actions are rendered meaningful in terms of the interests, values, and modes of rationality which the given discourse and its intersection with others represent and make available in moulding agents' relations.

The social subject consists in the intersection of social discourses in the body. The dimensions brought by the body to this formulation are the bounded capacities to desire, to think and to act. Discourses furnish the media for thought, for articulation of desires, and so for defining action types. Kant's famous dictum may be adapted to express the state of social subjectivity I am suggesting: Discourses without desires are empty, desires without discourses blind. Because human subjects fail to act save on impulsion of desires, discourses on their own would be unmotivated; they would be empty in the sense of producing no effect. Conversely, a desire not yet defined by a discourse could only be indiscriminate (or blind). The intentions, motives, dispositions, interests, and expressions of the racist are discourse specific. Their determination by discourse may be conscious and explicit or inadvertent, as with unconscious slips and misstatements that reveal repression and wish fulfillment.

At the conscious level discourses articulate and give definition to interests, intentions, dispositions, goals, and so reasons. I have argued that the general interest, intention, disposition, desire or goal of the racist is (relative) *racial exclusion*. For class they turn on *exploitation*.[28] The extension of each expression may include specific racist or class-bound reasons and goals respectively, whether cited as justification or rationalization. Racists may intend, desire, or be disposed to exclude, or have an interest in excluding racial others, just as a class or its representatives may be so defined in relation to exploiting class others (which as a matter of practical necessity is far less likely to require the sorts of exclusion fundamental to racism). The racist's explicit goal may be to dominate or subjugate; or to maximize profit by maintaining a cheap labour force, a reserve army of racial labour; or to reserve jobs for members of what they take to be their own race; or to maintain indigenous culture; and so forth. Notice that these goals need not coincide with that of exploitation or maximization of surplus value, or even of class domination, though in given circumstances they may. As reasons for the general principles they take to inform their acts racists may offer the goals themselves or various other categories of reason. These include — though they may not be limited to — scapegoating (for example a conspiracy theory), rationalizations (like inferiority), or rational stereotyping (for example a normative judgment appealing to factual evidence). These motivations a subject may have to act in a racist way are complemented by factors like fear and conformism, factors which may be independently motivated, or — more likely — a function of racist discourse (or some other) in the process of reproducing or reinforcing itself.

So the field of a given social discourse is a product of sociodiscursive *praxis* in determinate historical circumstances. The power of racist discourse conjoins with the power of other discourses — notably though not only those of class, gender and, lately, nation — to determine the subjectivity of agents at a given time and place. What emerges from this racial subjectivizing is a subjection to violence. The violence of racism is inherent in racist discourse, and afflicts both the objects of racist acts and the racist subject. Social subjects are generally defined in terms of the discourses of difference. Thus subjects recognize themselves for the most part only in contrast to others. Where identity is racially predicated or defined, self-assertion and promotion becomes a negation of the racial other, the other's exclusion. Tabulating racial differences so as to exclude racial others is at once to constitute the other as enemy, to engage her in relations of violence. Of course, class definition and differentiation may involve violence, but the *forms* assumed by class violence will often differ from those of racially predicated violence.[29]

Given this independence of racist discourse from class discourse as objects of analysis, questions both of conceptual and historical overlap, and of causal relations between race and class, may be addressed in detail. This is beyond my scope here. I conclude modestly that racist discrimination may occur *intra*-class, as it may *inter*-class. Indeed, it may at times have no identifiable class component. Thus there remains the distinct possibility that racism could be (largely) eliminated without eradicating class differentiations, and that racism could persist despite eradicating classes. There is nothing in my account, however, which commits me to denying that many forms assumed by racism may be class related or class based. Yet I emphasize that any merging of race- and class-defined concerns is a matter of historical contingency, not conceptual necessity, and it does not exhaust the scope of explanation.

Acknowledgement: This paper was completed with the assistance of a Drexel University Research Scholar Award. I am grateful to participants in The Washington Philosophy Club for their very helpful comments on an earlier draft.

Notes

1   Cf. respectively Pettigrew (1965) with Kovel (1970); van den Berghe (1981); Stember (1976); Gabriel and Ben-Tovim (1977); Cox (1948); and Gorz (1971).

2   Comaroff (1987: 302-3).

3   See Goldberg (1989a); and Omi and Winant (1986).

4   Cf. Gilroy (1989) and Balibar (1989).

5   See Appiah (1985: 21-37).

6   Recurring attempts to explain the occurrence of racism in biological terms, or to explain it away, inevitably fail. Socio-biological accounts are just the most recent of these attempts. Cf. van den Berghe (1981); and Kamin et al. (1984).

7   The analysis is given more fully in Goldberg (1989a). Cf. Foucault (1972: 38, 45, 179).

8   For a fuller argument supporting this claim, see Goldberg (1987: 58-71).

9   Consider, for example, the debate in Spain in 1550 between Las Casas, representative of the Church, and Sepulveda, Aristotelian spokesman for the imperial forces. See Hanke (1959).

10   For the best example see Hegel (1952: 241-7, originally published 1821).

11   Aronowitz (1981: 89-100).

12   Mosse (1979: 10-11, 21-22); Mosse is followed by West (1982: 53-4, 58-9).

13   Locke (1963: 327-44, first published 1690).

14   Locke (1963: 323, 325-7).

15   Plato (1972: 59b-69d); *Symposium* (1975: 2120a-212a).

16   This is a fact to which Adam Smith's 'invisible hand of reason' bears witness. See Smith (1978: 158, first published 1776). Of course, Smith does not use the concept of *equilibrium*, a later invention, but rather that of *natural price*.

17   Hauser (1951: 82); Marshall (1890: 323-50).

18   Rorty (1980: 129-312); cf. West (1982: 53).

19   Chomsky (1975: 132); Bracken (1978: 244, 250).

20   Mosse (1979: 11). For detailed documentation of this tendency
      amongst early racist thinkers like Buffon, Camper, and Lavater,
      and the influence upon their work of art historian J.J.
      Winckelmann, see Mosse (1979: 1-29); West (1982: 53-9); Gossett
      (1965: 32-9, 69-72); and Jordan (1969: 3-95).

21   'In Jamaica... they talk of one negroe as a man of parts and learn-
      ing; but 'tis *likely* he is admired for very slender accomplishments,
      like a parrot who speaks few words plainly.' Hume (1964: 250,
      emphasis added).

22   Witness, for example, the depiction of the 'Jewish nose' from Carl
      Gustav Carus in 19th century Germany, through Thomas
      Rawlandson (1921) to Nazi propaganda in the 1930s. Perhaps a
      less extreme, more sanitized version of this is Wilson's claim that
      bodily adornments, hair styles, and so forth, like the more readily
      accepted racial characteristics, are gene determined. Wilson (1975:
      22).

23   Consider, for example, the development in racist thinking from
      the likes of Gall and Spurzheim's phrenology, via Broca's brain
      capacity measurements, to the eugenics movement, and
      culminating with the contemporary intelligence testing of Shuey,
      Jensen, and Herrnstein. Cf. Gould (1981a).

24   Kant (1960: 113, emphasis added).

25   See Goldberg (1989a).

26   For the full argument, see ibid.

27   Ibid.

28   Cf. Thrift and Williams (1987: esp. 1-12); Wright (1985).

29   Again, for the full argument, see ibid.

7

The Reproduction of Labour-Market Discrimination in Competitive Capitalism

Mark Gould

In this chapter I formulate a theory that explains sustained labour-market discrimination within a competitive capitalist economy. I begin by explicating and criticizing orthodox, neo-classical, economic theory. The orthodox, Arrow-Debreu, general equilibrium model assumes perfect information and no transaction costs; it is unable to explain the persistence of labour-market discrimination within competitive markets. I then introduce an imperfect information version of neo-classical theory (the non-orthodox model). While it is able to explain the persistence of discrimination within competitive markets under certain restricted conditions, I argue that no neo-classical, utilitarian theory is capable of providing a convincing explanation of protracted discrimination under contemporary, competitive conditions in the USA. I contend that micro-economic theory must be sociologically reconstructed if an adequate explanation is to be provided.

I use very simple sociological principles to show how labour-market discrimination might persist even if inefficient, but I argue that while inefficient, discrimination may be cost effective and thus profitable. Further, I explain why this discrimination continues to affect blacks, rather than some other group, within the US.[1] The easiest entrée into this discussion is through an examination of the racist consequences that flow from utilitarian examinations of labour-market discrimination. Where racial discrimination has historically been an important factor in the distribution of persons into (and the evaluation of performances within) occupational roles, a theoretically consistent neo-classical theory will rationalize this discrimination as flowing from differences in the individual and/or aggregate attributes of blacks and whites.

Utilitarian Theory, Egalitarian and Universalistic Principles, and the Absence of Sustained Labour-Market Discrimination[2]

Utilitarian, Neo-classical Theory

Utilitarian, neo-classical economic theory[3] is characterized by the following attributes: atomism, a single positively defined normative orientation, taking each actor's ends as given and methodological empiricism.

Atomism involves the restriction of conceptualizations to individual unit acts and to systems of interaction between unit acts. The simplest system is the agent, understood as the aggregation of unit acts attributable to an individual or corporate actor. The relationships between unit acts may be enormously complex (as in general equilibrium theory in economics), but in an atomistic theory they are reducible to the attributes of the unit acts that constitute the system. A particular action is relevant to another only in so far as it affects the situation within which the second occurs.

In utilitarianism there is a single, positive conceptualization of the actor's normative orientation. This is usually seen as a form of instrumental rationality, where persons are viewed as selecting only from among ends attainable within the relevant situation and choosing those means most efficient to attain their ends. This is frequently analysed as 'maximization under constraints.' 'The assumption of rationality implies a consistency of response to general economic incentives and an adaptability to behaviour when those incentives change' (Ehrenberg and Smith 1982: 4).

When the theorist finds action to be inefficient, it is attributed to either error or ignorance (the absence of perfect information or uncertainty). Alternatively, it is possible to suggest that the analyst's attribution of the actor's end was erroneous; the agent may be seen to have been maximizing along a dimension different from the one the theorist previously suggested.

In addition, utilitarianism treats ends as given; tastes are 'unanalysable' (or at any rate unanalysed). They are independent of the actor's situation, but the theory says nothing about their selection (except that they must be consistent, transitive, and obtainable within the relevant situation). The only postulated relationships of one end to another are dependent on the consequences of one act, perhaps undertaken by a second actor, helping to constitute the environment of other actions. Thus one act may alter the situation within which another occurs, making a particular end attainable or not attainable within the new situation.

Finally, in this context empiricism may be briefly characterized as the methodological position that allows the introduction of concepts into the theory only when they are tied to directly observable 'phenomena'. Empiricists reject the introduction of 'constructs,' conceptualizations like the Freudian unconscious, Durkheim's collective conscience (1893) or, more generally, social structures not reducible to the actions of atomistically conceptualized actors.[4]

Orthodox Neo-Classical Theory and the Values of US Society

Orthodox neo-classical arguments contain all the attributes just enumerated. They are, however, more restrictive. While instrumental rationality is the sole normative orientation, there can be no deviations from it. In orthodox theories actors are endowed with perfect information and there are no transaction costs.[5] For example, in such theories each worker receives the value of his marginal product as his wage. There are no costs to monitoring the worker as information is perfect; both employer and employee know the value of the latter's marginal product. At the same time the employee has information concerning all other employment opportunities and is capable of shifting jobs instantaneously and at no cost. If the value of his marginal product increases, it is known to increase and he receives a higher wage. In a competitive equilibrium all economically homogeneous workers, all workers with a marginal product of the same value, must receive the same wage.

In the dominant orthodox explanation of labour-market discrimination employers are understood to sacrifice economic gain in order to maximize another goal, a taste for discrimination (Becker 1971). This discrimination is unstable in a competitive economy, as firms hiring relatively low-cost (let us say black, but otherwise economically equivalent) workers will make surplus profits and be able to expand production. In consequence their demand for black labour will increase, forcing higher the wages these employees receive. At the same time, firms paying white workers a premium wage will be driven out of business, increasing the supply of unemployed white workers and, in consequence, driving down their wages. These processes will result in a narrowing of the wage differential between black and white workers until, at equilibrium, economically homogeneous workers, whether black or white, receive equal wages.

If unequal wages persist for economically homogeneous blacks and whites at equilibrium, it must mean that there is a productivity difference associated with these racial attributes. In other words, this theory not only fails to explain the discrimination prevalent within a competitive economy, it rationalizes it as a residual productivity difference owing to individually aggregated racial characteristics of black and white workers, after controlling for pre-labour-market attributes.[6]

Neo-classical theorists have also postulated a statistical theory of discrimination. Here the goal is to explain why an individual black worker might be discriminated against, even in a competitive equilibrium. This theory assumes an aggregate, group, productivity differential between black and white workers and it assumes that there is a cost in differentiating between individual black workers who are as productive as the average white worker and those not so productive. Thus employers use race as a screening device and fail to hire blacks of comparable productivity to those whites who secure employment; alternatively they hire blacks at discounted wages.[7] This wage gap must, in equilibrium, be equivalent to the actual aggregate productivity differences between black and white employees, a gap attributed to the workers individually aggregated attributes (Aigner and Cain 1977; Bulow and Summers 1986: 398 n18; Blau 1984: 57).[8]

The empirical applications of this orthodox theory in both economics and sociology show that the process of inclusion for blacks in the US since the mid-1960s has lead to class differentiation within the black community and to a narrowing of the relative aggregative income gap between blacks and whites.

None the less, the absolute average income gap between blacks and whites has remained relatively constant. Both of these outcomes hold pre-labour-market characteristics constant.

In these empirical studies the residual income difference between blacks and whites, after controlling for all attributes deemed relevant to economic productivity, is usually attributed to the social variable, 'racism.' This attribution is, however, inconsistent with both the utilized theory and the empirical analyses. Utilitarian theory bars the use of hypothetical constructs and positively-stated, non-rational, normative orientations. In consequence, all other discussions in these empirical analyses focus on the individual attributes of actors and their aggregation by racial group as explanations for income differentials.

While 'racism' might be disaggregated into individual ends, we have seen that these tastes for discrimination are not sustainable in a competitive equilibrium. 'Racism' is not a theoretically consistent explanation for the residual gap in income between economically homogeneous blacks and whites within an orthodox neo-classical theory of economic competition. Thus these utilitarian analyses lead to unintended racist consequences; the individual and aggregate income gap between economically equivalent blacks and whites must be due to differential rates of productivity, differential marginal products associated with the worker's remaining individual attribute, race.

Even when the analysts draw the correct, if theoretically unwarranted conclusion, that the residual gap between the income of whites and blacks is due to 'racism,' this conclusion is belied by their own empirical analyses. These purport to show that even as US society has more closely adhered to values of equal opportunity, the average absolute income gap between otherwise equivalent blacks and whites has remained constant (Featherman and Hauser 1978).

US society is dominated by individualistic, universalistic, egalitarian values. Within the context of these values individuals are assessed in terms of their perceived performances. Most Americans view the US as a land of equal opportunity and see it as becoming progressively more egalitarian. In consequence they tend to view the degree of an individual's success within the society as a fair indication of his or her relative merit (Kluegel and Smith 1986).

An analysis of orthodox neo-classical theories of discrimination may be taken as a surrogate for a discussion of the nature of discrimination and its legitimation within contemporary US society. The utilitarian theoretical structure of neo-classical economics effectively mirrors the values of equal opportunity institutionalized in the US.[9] We have seen that the orthodox theory has the consequence of rationalizing equilibrium divergences in wage rates between black and white workers as a consequence of individually constituted productivity differentials associated with race. Likewise, in an individualist and egalitarian society where hierarchically ordered racial barriers are no longer visible, the failure of blacks to achieve the same level of success as their white counterparts is readily interpreted as a factual indication of the inferiority of those with black skins. The gap between blacks and whites is not seen as a measure of societal discrimination, as was often the case for fair-minded persons 40 years ago, but rather as an indication of the degree of black inferiority. If workers are paid fair, non-discriminatory wages (the value of their marginal product) and if otherwise comparable black workers receive lower wages than whites, an obvious conclusion is drawn that blacks are in some sense inferior to whites. In fact, approximately 45 per cent of the public believes that economic differences between blacks and whites are due to individual faults of blacks, to either a lack of motivation or to innately inferior ability (Kluegel and Smith 1986: 192). Many of these are the same persons who firmly accept the principles of equal opportunity that they see as in place (Schuman et al. 1985; Kluegel and Smith, 1986).

Thus it is clear how racist misperceptions may be generated within egalitarian values. It remains to be demonstrated how these misperceptions are reproduced within competitive capitalist relationships. To show this I will demonstrate two things. In the central sections of this chapter I will show how racist discrimination is sustainable within a competitive capitalist economy. This will involve a reconstruction of the economic models of discrimination. In the penultimate section I will briefly analyse the mechanisms whereby egalitarian values are able to legitimize racist inequality and I will draw a few simple, policy-oriented conclusions.

The Non-orthodox Model

In an orthodox neo-classical theory of a competitive economy all actors are constrained to act efficiently and such action is in the interest of each individual actor. Subject only to their starting position, their personal endowments and property, the self-interested actions of individual actors are in the interest of all.[10] It is plausible in this model to ignore imperfect information, as individual actors who fail to learn are subject to sanctions stemming from competitive constraints. While a worker might survive the consequences of his inefficiency, competition coerces employers to be(come) efficient.

In the orthodox model class or group membership is irrelevant. Assuming identical situations confronting their firm, members of one class will make the same economic decisions as the members of any other class.[11] In making decisions for their firms, both would be constrained by competition to act efficiently and would in consequence be incapable of pursuing group, instead of individual, interests. There can be no power in this model, for workers are protected by employers seeking profit. Given the fact that the worker can costlessly change jobs, no employer can pay an employee less than the value of his marginal product. Nor can an employer pay an employee more than the value of his marginal product without suffering the competitive consequences of inefficient production (Gould and Weinstein 1989). As Samuelson (1957: 894) correctly points out, 'in a perfectly competitive market it really doesn't matter who hires whom' (see also Roemer 1982 and 1986).

In this model economically homogeneous workers must receive the same wage; labour-market discrimination cannot be sustained in a model of a perfectly competitive economy. Discrimination is merely a form of inefficiency to be driven from the market. Unfortunately most of these conclusions — that there is no power in the economy, that group position does not matter, that it is irrelevant whether capital hires labour or labour capital, that discrimination is not sustainable — are not robust when we relax the assumptions of the model to represent more accurately the real world. This has become clear in recent developments of neo-classical micro-economic theory.[12] A demonstration of the lack of robustness of orthodox conclusions requires a brief exegesis of one strand of non-orthodox theory, the efficiency-wage model.

In recent years micro-economic theorists have developed numerous theories of imperfect information. When the assumption of perfect information is dropped, opportunistic action becomes a possibility and a distinction between consummate and perfunctory cooperation must be introduced.[13] Labour, work, must be motivated and in consequence crucial conclusions of the orthodox model are called into question. For example, the conclusion that markets must clear in equilibrium is no longer the case.

As is clear from the efficiency wage literature, 'imperfect monitoring necessitates unemployment in equilibrium' (Shapiro and Stiglitz 1986: 45).[14] Let us assume that all workers are economically homogeneous.

> Under the conventional competitive paradigm, in which all workers receive the market wage and there is no unemployment, the worst that can happen to a worker who shirks on the job is that he is fired. Since he can immediately be rehired, however, he pays no penalty for his misdemeanour. With imperfect monitoring and full employment, therefore, workers will choose to shirk. (ibid.)

In capitalism workers are paid for their capacity to work; their labour, work, is variable and must be motivated. While this makes profits possible for the employer, it assures that it is in the workers' interest to avoid working. The employer must be concerned with the workers' motivation, attitudes and work orientation (Littler and Salaman 1984: 54).

In the orthodox model, with perfect information, all this is irrelevant. The employee is simply paid for the work he undertakes. His marginal product is known and his wage equals the value of that product. In contrast, with imperfect information about the actual product of the work undertaken, the distinction between consummate and perfunctory cooperation (Williamson 1975: 69; 1985: 262-3) becomes crucial.

In the efficiency wage literature (Akerlof and Yellen 1986; Bulow and Summers 1986) it is recognized that employees must be motivated to work by proximate situational sanctions and that the threat of firing is the employer's most effective sanction. This threat is meaningfulness, however, if the fired employee can immediately and costlessly transfer to an alternative job. Thus a theory has emerged concerning the most cost effective wage and level of surveillance for getting employees not to shirk.[15] The employee's remuneration must be higher than the 'going wage,' thus providing an incentive to work. But since all employers face the same problem, this 'efficient wage' will be matched by other firms and it will become the equilibrium wage. As wages are raised, the demand for labour is reduced and unemployment results. Unemployed workers cannot undercut the 'efficiency wage,' as lower wages imply an incentive to shirk. Thus the title of Shapiro and Stiglitz's (1986) essay, 'Equilibrium Unemployment as a Worker Discipline Device'.

The actual efficiency wage depends on a number of factors, including the unemployment rate and thus the probable length of unemployment, the likely wage at re-employment, the level of unemployment compensation and other transfer payments (Shapiro and Stiglitz 1986; Gintis and Ishikawa n.d.: 2-3). It also depends on the ease and cost of monitoring a particular task. Bulow and Summers (1986) have formulated a theory of dual labour markets based on the level of autonomy and difficulty in monitoring certain types of jobs.

Each of these factors is an instance of the efficiency wage's crucial dependence upon the nature and degree of the power asymmetry between employers and employees. Any factor that contributes to this differential lowers the efficiency wage. For example, higher unemployment weakens employees and contributes to the power differential between them and employers; in consequence it lowers the efficiency wage.

According to this theory, in part because the employee is no longer able to assume that another comparably paying job will be immediately available, economically homogeneous workers need not garner the same wage package. Different wages for identical workers are a consequence of the characteristics of particular firms and jobs, most especially how easy it is to monitor workers' performances and how costly shirking is for particular firms (Shapiro and Stiglitz 1986: 47; Bulow and Summers 1986). Different jobs will have different efficiency wages.

Differential wages may also be a consequence of differences between workers that do not affect their productivity. In other words, economically homogeneous workers may differ along attributes irrelevant to their productive task and these differences may become the source of differences in their wage rates. It is this consequence that enables the conceptualization of sustained labour-market discrimination within a competitive economy.

The Possibility of Sustained Labour-Market Discrimination

The Failure of the Obvious Non-Orthodox Explanation

At first it appears as if non-orthodox theory makes it is easy to comprehend sustained labour-market discrimination within a competitive economy. In markets conceptualized within orthodox theory, if an employer chooses to hire white workers at wages higher than those garnered by economically homogeneous black workers, he will be subject to competitive pressures. In contrast, Stiglitz (1973: 290) argues, in the non-orthodox 'world, firms can exercise their prejudices in selecting among the applicants [for jobs] with impunity'.[16] There are various reasons that might be adduced for this contention, which appears to point the way towards an explanation of sustained discrimination within competitive markets. The simplest stems from the fact that employers have a choice among those workers available for employment. Thus even if employers are constrained to pay all economically homogeneous workers hired for the same job the same wage, they may choose to hire a lower proportion of one group of workers than another for higher paying jobs. In consequence the two groups will be maldistributed within the occupational structure and the average wage of one group may be lower than that of another (Stiglitz 1973: 290-1; cf. Bulow and Summers 1986: 397-9). It would appear that economically homogeneous blacks in low paying jobs cannot underbid whites in higher paying jobs, as the whites are being paid an efficiency wage. Even if the employer believes black employees to be as productive as their white counterparts (holding constant pre-labour-market variations), a black employee paid wages lower than the efficiency wage whites receive will not be expected to work.

It might be suggested that this form of occupational discrimination would persist in a competitive equilibrium. Even if this were the case, the principal-agent model says nothing about why this racial discrimination will occur, nor can it explain why one group will be favoured over another. In fact, however, this argument incorrectly presumes an equivalent efficiency wage for black and white workers. If black workers end up being more concentrated in secondary labour-market jobs and/or have higher rates of unemployment than their white counterparts, their efficiency wages will be lower than those of otherwise economically equivalent whites. Thus employers should be able to hire black workers at a wage lower than economically homogeneous white workers, with the expectation that they will perform in a comparably consummate fashion. Hiring black workers at a lower wage will instigate a process undermining the differences between their actual and their efficiency wages and will lead to an equilibrium outcome where equivalent wages are paid to economically homogeneous white and black employees.

In order to explain successfully the discrimination against blacks in the US two factors must be elaborated: the first stems from the explicit introduction of power into our model. An understanding of the role of power in a competitive labour market will help us to explain why what is profitable for employers may not be economically efficient and why discrimination, even though inefficient, may be profitable. Secondly, we must indicate how the racist attitudes discussed in the first sections of this chapter affect labour-market discrimination and enable us to explain why it is blacks who are discriminated against.

Power Asymmetries, the Disjunction between Efficiency and Profitability, and Racial Discrimination

In an earlier essay Weinstein and I explored the importance of class in a non-orthodox neo-classical competitive model (Gould and Weinstein 1989).[17] For class position to matter in such a model, power asymmetries must be manifest between persons in various class positions. We have just seen how the existence of unemployment generates power for employers over employees. In the first instance, assuming unemployed workers are available for employment, employers are likely to have more alternatives than workers. While it is true that they may suffer costs in terminating an employee and hiring a replacement, these costs are likely to be lower and less significant than those faced by workers in seeking new job opportunities. The smaller the cost that an agent confronts in walking away from an employment contract, the greater his power.

Employers often have non-labour sources of income. These capital assets provide a degree of freedom that the labourer does not possess. Employers need not hire particular, or any, workers to be confident that their families will be fed. Workers can have no such confidence. Finding alternative work may be costly, frightening or impossible. As Knight (1965: 351) writes:

> Freedom refers or should refer to the range of choices open to a person, and in its broad sense is nearly synonymous with 'power.' Freedom of contract, on the other hand, means simply an absence of formal restraint in disposal of 'one's own.' It may mean in fact the perfect antithesis of freedom in the sense of power to order one's life in accordance with one's desire and ideals. The actual content of freedom of contract depends entirely on what one owns.

In a non-orthodox situation where labour markets do not clear, where unemployment persists in equilibrium, employee bargaining power is eroded. Williamson (1985: 243, n5) argues that in a situation where neither employer nor employee has any interest in the continuity of their relationship, where there is no asset specificity, 'transition costs are asymmetrically concentrated on the employee side of the transaction. They mainly arise in conjunction with the disruptive effects on family and social life that job termination and reemployment sometimes produces. Protection against arbitrary dismissals is thus warranted even for nonspecific jobs.' As is demonstrated in numerous exchange models of power (for example, Blau 1964; Luhmann 1979: part II; Offe 1985: 181-2), the party in a relationship that is more willing or able to terminate it has power over the other party. Thus an employer may gain substantial power over an employee in so far as the latter's transaction costs when fired are greater than the employer's costs in replacing him.[18]

This is a far cry from orthodox markets where workers are capable of instantaneously finding new and equivalent employment. In non-orthodox markets, even though these remain competitive, if and when a fired worker finds a new job, the wages he receives may well be less than those afforded by his old job. In such markets competition constrains employers to act in ways to maximize their power advantage over workers. Certain economic institutions will prevail because they are profitable for individual employers and for capitalists as a class, not because they are efficient. Profitable organizational structures are as much determined by their capacity to increase profits as they are by the selection of efficient technology (see Marglin 1974). Class structure helps to determine what is profitable, since class structure conditions the nature of incentive problems that an economic system must solve and structures the relationships of power between employer and employee. If workers can offer different levels of labour intensity and creativity and if they will work harder in one institutional arrangement than another, one set of organizational structures will be favoured over another. Market structures that maximize profits under one class structure cannot be presumed to maximize profits under a different class structure.

In modern capitalist economies, economic efficiency is not a classless notion solely determined by technology. Capitalists hire workers; workers do not hire capital. And it matters. Economic decisions are driven by the employer's urge to maximize profits, including the urge to self-servingly redistribute income. In orthodox models, such self-serving ambitions do not rule because only economically efficient decisions are competitively viable; increases in profits represent increases in efficiency. But in unorthodox models, the intention to redistribute income can prevail because redistributive — profit-maximizing — decisions by individual employers can be competitively viable despite their inefficiency.

Consider a very simple example. Firm A uses 2X units of (homogeneous) labour and Y units of (homogeneous) equipment to produce a unit of output. Firm B, using more monitors, produces a unit of output with 3X units of labour (including monitors) and the same amount of equipment. If firm A's efficiency wage is more than 1.5 times firm B's efficiency wage, then firm B's technology will rule the market. Firm B drives firm A from the market even though it uses more of society's scarce (labour) resources.

Of course, were it profit-maximizing for firm A to lower wages, then its technology would rule. But paying lower wages, the efficiency wage literature teaches us, is not necessarily profit-maximizing. So, firm A does not *necessarily* find it profitable to offer the workers in firm B wages higher than firm B pays but lower than firm A's current rate. As firm B drives firm A from the market, capital's intention to redistribute income to itself prevails even though economic efficiency is sacrificed.

An analogous argument may be made about the effects of racial discrimination. Bowles (1985) argues that if employers offer racially distinct, but economically homogeneous workers different wage packages this will have the effect of weakening their capacity to organize. In other words, worker cooperation and power are assumed to be a function of worker unity and racially based wage distinctions are taken as inhibitions to worker unity. In these circumstances it may be rational for an employer to hire enough higher-priced white workers to inhibit unity among all workers and thus to debilitate worker solidarity and organization. This has the consequence of decreasing worker power *vis-à-vis* the employer and may allow for an increase in the average amount of labour actually extracted per unit wage. While economically inefficient, this strategy allows for the maximization of profit.

This capitalist strategy might well depress white wages below the level they would reach had black and white workers organized together. Thus it might result in an average wage per employee lower than the one that would have existed if the employer had hired only black workers. (The preceding two paragraphs follow Bowles's discussion, 1985: 29-31.)

While we can imagine divide and conquer arguments that do not involve the conscious manipulation of workers by capitalists, such arguments usually involve an assumption of white worker hierarchical prejudice towards blacks, and thus the inability of economically homogeneous workers to formulate a unified position across racial groups. In Bowles's argument, what precipitates this disunity is the employers paying employees in different or the same power positions unequal wages; implicit in his argument is the belief that it will be difficult for workers to organize to overcome employer discrimination.

While understanding the mechanisms of prejudice in contemporary US society helps in filling out his argument — the differential position of blacks is intelligible only if we understand the mechanisms which reproduce racist attitudes[19] - the question none the less arises whether it is conceivable that blacks might be paid lower wages than whites for work in the same job without the conscious manipulation of employers and the support of white workers who see themselves as relatively advantaged. Divide and conquer arguments are surely appropriate for certain historical periods, but they seem inappropriate for a time when most white employers and workers claim not to be prejudiced against blacks and when millions of white and blacks harmoniously work together every day. Thus Bowles's non-orthodox, utilitarian theory allows for an explanation of sustained discrimination within a competitive economy, but only under conditions that no longer appear to be manifest.

We must now attempt to provide an explanation for the persistence of labour-market discrimination that is applicable to current conditions in the US. Unlike Bowles (see note 19), we can base our argument on our sociological demonstration that egalitarian values in the US serve to generate racist attitudes as often as they undermine them.

Sustained Labour-Market Discrimination Against Blacks

The Devaluation of the Occupations Blacks Fulfil

We saw earlier that within egalitarian, individualistic, universalistic values a racial group that achieves less success within the economy, or elsewhere, may be seen to be deficient. This racist judgement need not be perceived by its adherent as prejudiced; instead it can be seen to be 'facing facts.' In contemporary US society, where achievement-oriented values are seen to be substantially in place by the majority of the population, discrimination appears to stem less from hierarchically structured prejudice than from the logical working out of the American 'creed.' While this outcome parallels the implicit conclusion of a utilitarian social science, in the everyday world persons do not bother to control for pre-labour-market attributes when evaluating the performance of blacks. Thus the conclusion is not subject to undermining by sophisticated statistical analyses.

Groups perceived as doing less well in situations of equal opportunity come to be treated as if they are inferior. Not surprisingly, these include the very groups that have previously suffered the most severe and longstanding hierarchical discrimination. In the US there are, broadly speaking, three such groups: blacks, Hispanics and women. One consequence of this prejudiced attitude is that blacks are likely to have fewer opportunities than otherwise comparable whites. Coupled with the fact that they have fewer resources than whites, this implies that their power position *vis-à-vis* employers is relatively weak.

This discrimination may have a series of consequences. One of the most indicative and important may be found in the devaluation of occupational positions when a substantial numbers of blacks take up these roles. Here we do not necessarily find blacks receiving lower wages than whites within the same job category; instead we find that the wages of the jobs incorporating a significant percentage of blacks decline relative to others remaining largely white. Paradoxically, the discrimination affects both black and white workers.[20]

This type of discrimination does not appear in most academic studies. It need not entail blacks receiving lower wages than whites for work in the same job, but does result in economically homogeneous blacks receiving lower wages than their white counterparts, as the jobs in which blacks cluster are devalued. The jobs that blacks fill become inferior jobs owing to their incumbency. Blacks are clustered in inferior jobs because societal attitudes towards them make their jobs inferior.

In situations where there is (legal) pressure to maintain approximately equal salaries for whites and blacks this prejudice 'rubs off' on the white workers employed alongside blacks. The consequence is similar to the one in Bowles's divide and conquer argument; in that case whites receive higher wages than blacks, none the less, as in the case of devaluation, the prejudice directed towards blacks lowers the wages of both groups.

The mechanism that operates in the case of devaluation is the power asymmetry between employers and employees, an asymmetry that is increased if prejudice is directed to one group of employees. If blacks are in a position where they have less power than otherwise comparable whites, their efficiency wage should be lower than that of whites. This is equivalent to the circumstance in which black unemployment rates are higher than white rates, where the reservation wage for blacks is lower than that of whites. Excluding the divide and conquer argument, in an analysis of a competitive market we would expect lower paid, yet economically homogeneous, workers to bid wages down in competing with their higher paid brethren. As blacks are allowed into jobs previously reserved for whites, this prejudice reduces the power of employees *vis-à-vis* employers. In consequence, wages fall.

According to neo-classical, competitive models, if black and white workers are economically homogeneous, the ignorance of seeing blacks as productively inferior should be driven from the market. 'As Aigner and Cain (1977) point out, discrimination based on employers' mistaken beliefs is as unlikely (or even more unlikely) to persist over time in the face of competitive forces as discrimination based on employer tastes' (Blau 1984:

57). This confidence in the transcendence of erroneous beliefs makes sense, however, only if racism is understood to be constituted as an individual attitude. It is possible that in its institutionalized form racism may result in different levels of productivity for different groupings of workers even when the differences between black and white workers are irrelevant to their economic attributes outside racist institutions.

It would seem that the most obvious case would be one in which the very presence of blacks within a particular occupation would cause white workers to disrupt production. Here, even assuming that the blacks and whites are economically homogeneous, levels of productivity in integrated firms would be lower than in segregated firms. While this disruption might, under certain conditions, result in the creation of segregated work sites, unless the white employees had the power to bar blacks from particular occupations (as they might in the context of Jim Crow laws or white union control over particular job categories), it is difficult to see how the competition of firms hiring black workers could be overcome (cf. Wright 1987). In other words, unless we abrogate the assumption of competitive markets or revert to a divide and conquer explanation, this argument will not work.

In the next section I will none the less show that one component of the prejudice blacks face in the US is institutionalized and organizationally structured. It results in placing blacks in situations constituted to enable whites to excel. This analysis will allow us to understand how it is possible to reproduce wage differentials for racially distinct and economically homogeneous workers within a competitive economy, differentials that are legitimized by the newly structured racist attitudes I have already discussed.

Institutional Racism and the Conflation of Capacities and Performances

It is essential that we understand how it is possible to reproduce discriminatory judgments within individualistic, universalistic and egalitarian values. One reason this happens is because we utilize a limited repertoire of performances as surrogates in the measurement of capacities. These performances are supposed to be indicative of the aptitudes required to master a particular set of activities.[21] In fact, while cognitive and other capacities are always mastered in actual performances, the activities within which these capacities are mastered may vary considerably by social group. Thus an 'objective test' measuring a determinant set of performances may well be biased in favour of one group as against another.

Even if we admit the bias inherent in many standardized tests, it is none the less true that success as measured by these tests may be correlated with success in the endeavours screened for by them. For example, Scholastic Aptitude Tests (SAT) are not intended to evaluate the specific skills required in college. They use particular performances in an attempt to measure aptitudes that, in gross terms, predict success in college, which in turn serves as a screening device for certain job-related skills, and thus as a reasonable credential for certain jobs. SAT tests, like IQ tests and many job-related 'ability' tests, were generated to predict performance within determinate social settings, so that it is not surprising that scores often correlate positively with such performance.[22]

If this relationship between an index of performance and success is real, it is unclear how using 'objective tests' as a basis of evaluation is discriminatory. We might assume either that an individual or a group (here an aggregation of individuals) measures up and succeeds or that it does not measure up and fails. This is the consistent utilitarian argument that leads to racist conclusions. The fallacy of this argument is revealed if we look at one link in this chain, the rational-legal procedures that underlie the standardized tests that are used as screening devices.

We may assume that intelligence (however we understand this concept) is randomly distributed in US society across all relevant social categories, including racial categories. We may further assume that all 'normal' persons pass through the stage-sequential progression of cognitive development outlined by Piaget. For example, as Piaget argues and as Labov (1972: ch. 5) seeks to demonstrate for black adolescents in Harlem, the ability to think hypothetically and deductively develops within egalitarian peer interaction. While different skills may be manifest within different racial and class groups, comparable intellectual capacities emerge for virtually all 'normal' adolescents. It is these capacities that form the basis of further learning. Yet, as is manifest in Labov's work, black working and 'under' class adolescents of comparable intelligence and cognitive development to middle class white students — as is demonstrated when the blacks are studied in their own social and cultural environment — do much worse than their white counterparts in school (and much worse on standardized tests). Labov attributes this difference to a cultural contradiction between the black adolescents and the schools they attend.[23] What is crucial about Labov's work is that he recognizes the importance of demonstrating that blacks and whites manifest equivalent cognitive capacities, while none the less pointing to the consequences of substantive differences between them. This can only be done within the context of a stage-sequential model where the stages are characterized as structured capacities allowing for the incorporation of various performances, and where blacks and whites manifest similar structural developments.

In contrast, rational-legal procedures treat all persons as if they were equal, as if they occupied the same social positions and developed through the mastery of the same performances, and in the process these procedures justify inequality. This happens because the standards of measurement assess determinate performances and not the capacities that underlie them, and because the tests themselves were developed to predict success in white and/or middle-class institutions.

If rational-legal (egalitarian, individualistic and universalistic) procedures measure the mastery of specific class or racially skewed performances and not the actual capacities required to perform successfully a particular type of job, these capacities might well be indicated by the mastery of a completely different set of performances not measured on the test.[24] In consequence, the procedure may be biased against one group *vis-à-vis* another. If the procedure, for example a standardized test, predicts job-related success, it may simply indicate that the institutional environment on the job is likewise biased.

While it is easy to label employment tests as biased, the fact that in gross terms these tests predict employment success indicates that the problem is not solely one of racist attitudes, but of racist institutions. Employers argue that they cannot hire workers who, they have reason to believe, will be relatively unproductive. Or if they hire these workers, it must be at a discounted wage.[25] They contend that we must change the individual worker to enable him to succeed in the employment system.[26] My argument leads to a different conclusion, that the structure of many US firms is biased in drawing on the performances of one group instead of another. The nature of the labour process on the job may be geared to the attributes of one group and ignore the equally relevant attributes of another group. The racism may be institutional.

This point might be clarified with a more concrete example. Bulow and Summers create a model explaining wage differentials between black and white workers in terms of the higher quit-rates blacks manifest.[27] The standard interpretation of this wage differential is in terms of human capital theory. Blacks are seen as less productive owing to lower levels of experience and, in consequence, they receive lower wages. However, Bulow and Summers's model does not presume a correlation between experience and productivity. Instead they assume that the utility of primary-sector employment is lower for blacks. 'Since women [and implicitly blacks] have a shorter horizon in primary-sector jobs, they must receive a greater inducement if they are not to shirk. With equal wages, this can occur only if secondary-sector women [blacks] have a smaller chance of moving to the primary sector than do secondary-sector men' (Bulow and Summers 1986: 400). Thus, for women and blacks to receive equal wages in the primary sector (which is, they suggest, mandated by competition) some occupational segregation (resulting in a higher proportion of women and blacks in the secondary sector) is required. This suggests to them that the discrimination that is manifest is not based on employer prejudice (ibid.: 401).

Yet if we look at Blau's data relating to the same issue, we find that 'all else equal (including job-related characteristics), white and black women were no more likely to quit their jobs than men of the same race... and also[,] that a high proportion of the observed sex differential in quitting was associated with job characteristics rather than personal characteristics' (Blau 1984: 69, where she cites Blau and Kahn 1981; Viscusi 1980). In addition, 'Both Blau and Kahn [1981: 571-2, 573] and Viscusi [1980: 393] found that, all else equal [including job characteristics], blacks were less likely to quit their jobs than white workers of the same sex' (Blau 1984: 69; see also Weiss 1984). Thus, in so far as there were differential quit rates for blacks and whites, and in so far as these are capable of explaining either differential wages for blacks and whites in common occupations (as in human capital theory), or occupational segregation and differential average wages for blacks and whites (as in Bulow and Summers), they are an artifact not of the measured attributes of the black and white workers, but rather of the job-related characteristics examined. 'The finding that women ([or] blacks) would be less likely than men (whites) to quit if given male (white) job characteristics may be, in part, a reflection of labour market discrimination' (Blau and Kahn 1981: 573; cf. Zax 1989).

One way of understanding what we might mean by job-related characteristics involves both the perception and the reality of black advancement. We know from studies of educational attainment that the expectation of a positive consequence deriving from hard work results in enhanced performance (Ogbu 1978). In occupational situations where blacks are not as likely to be positively rewarded as comparably performing whites, we would expect that their performance level would diminish.[28] This consequence is not created by any attribute they possess, but rather by an adaptation to the pressures of the institutionalized racism they confront.[29]

This may be seen in an illustrative case where a different outcome may be presumed. Some persons argue that 'underclass' blacks are incapable of adapting to the disciplined structure of the normal US labour process without considerable 'retraining.' But what if we imagine the talents that would be required in a small, group-centred, worker-controlled labour process in manufacturing. Here, in addition to generalized cognitive and motor capacities, the main skill required of entering workers is the capacity to bond in a group and loyally to perform group tasks. If incentives are structured so as to allow for group responsibility for individual performance, where individual rewards are grounded in group performance, then it is in the interest of each member of the group to secure the successful performance of all other members. In general, 'underclass' black workers will have had considerable experience in small peer groups and will understand the forms of loyalty necessary for successful performance in them. Since there is no reason to assume that they are incapable of learning the cognitive and motor skills necessary for successful functioning in entry-level tasks, there is every reason to expect that young black workers would succeed at rates at least equivalent to their white peers. In this situation the norms regulating worker interaction would have to accommodate individual and group based differences. Success would be forthcoming if the previously excluded blacks were economically homogeneous to the included whites.

In contrast, in most current situations, where blacks are at a disadvantage in actually functioning racist institutions, the predictions of the statistical theories of discrimination (Arrow 1985: chs 8, 9, 11; Phelps 1972) seem, but only seem, to be correct. In a competitive labour market, with imperfect information, blacks would be paid less than whites (Aigner and Cain 1977). Where the statistical theory is wrong is in inferring that the differences that generate this wage differential imply a deficiency on the part of the blacks; instead they reflect the institutional racism embedded in the US economy and society. This racism is sustainable because, in exacerbating the power differential between employer and employee, it increases profits.

Institutional racism is inefficient. When it is manifest, talent that should be available for productive work is underutilized, if it is utilized at all. None the less, institutional racism enhances the power of employers relative to employees; when it is present it restricts opportunities for black workers, lowers their reservation wage, and makes them available for work at lower efficiency wages. This, in turn, pulls down the wage of white workers. Thus while the devaluation of jobs occupied by large numbers of blacks entails that the average wage of blacks will be lower than the average wage of whites, white wages will be lower than they would have been in the absence of institutionalized racism. Costs are reduced and profits enhanced for capitalists operating within the current institutional structure.

In consequence, organizations manifesting this racism are competitive within the current institutional context, even though alternative organizational arrangements would enhance the efficiency of production. To eliminate the effects of racism from the US economy, firms will have to be restructured to take advantage of the capacities blacks possess. The integration of blacks into the work place will have to restructure firms, enabling them to take advantage of the culturally constituted talents of whites and blacks (and Hispanics and Asians, and men and women). A primary consequence of a successful reconstitution of the labour-process to accomplish this task will be an enhancement of economic efficiency. In fact, if such restructuring is to 'take-off,' the gains in efficiency will have to lower per unit costs to a point where they undercut the cost-cutting advantage generated by racist institutions.

Conclusion

Utilitarian theories are atomistic. They do not allow for the introduction of social structural concepts. In this they parallel US culture, which tends to view the outcome of an individual's achievement struggles as dependent upon that individual's personal attributes. Thus for both utilitarian social theory (if not for most utilitarian social scientists) and for our common-sense understanding, the differential success of blacks and whites translates into 'facts' apropos black inferiority.

In this chapter I have explored the possibility of conceptualizing various forms of labour-market discrimination within competitive markets. Unlike its orthodox predecessor, nonorthodox neo-classical economic theory appears to allow for the conceptualization of various forms of sustained discrimination in competitive markets. But, in fact, no neo-classical theory allows for the explanation of the specific forms of discrimination that derive from the institutionalized racism embedded in the contemporary fabric of US life. To explain this racism requires a paradigm shift within the social sciences (cf. Gould 1989). It requires that we overcome our natural empiricism in the recognition that what we have taken to be facts are merely a stylized interpretation of data controlled by a particular theoretical interpretation (cf. Lukács 1971: 5ff.).

In so far as the attributes of neo-classical theory are mirrored in the hegemonic culture embedded within US society, it is clear that a successful elimination of racism will require the generation of a counter-ideology capable of explaining the actual sources of labour-market — and other forms of — discrimination. It will also entail the construction of a political movement capable of bringing about the necessary structural changes.

The main ray of hope here is that, while profitable and thus sustainable, institutionalized racism is inefficient. It is not naturally driven out of the market as it sustains employer interests with the currently constituted economy, but its elimination none the less promises the prospect of not only a better, but a more prosperous world.

Acknowledgement: This chapter is based on work undertaken jointly with Michael M. Weinstein. While he is certainly not responsible for the views I have expressed, he is importantly responsible for my ability to express them.

Notes

1   Many varieties of labour market discrimination are sustainable in imperfectly competitive markets. In this chapter, however, I limit my attention to competitive settings.

2   The argument in this section is elaborated in Gould (1983).

3   Neo-classical economics is one variety of utilitarian social theory.

4   The discussion in this section is taken from Gould (1989), which in turn draws on Gould (1981). Both these discussions rely heavily on Parsons (1949).

5   In this essay I use the following terms interchangeably to refer to utilitarian theories that assume perfect information and no transaction costs: Arrow-Debreu, Walrasian, and orthodox. I refer to those utilitarian theories that introduce both transaction costs and imperfect information, including principal-agent theory and transaction cost economics, as non-orthodox.

6   Gavin Wright has informed me that an economist testifying in a court case adjudicating an employer discrimination suit adduced the attribute 'father's race' to explain the residual left after controlling for pre-labour-market factors.

7   One might argue that race serves as a surrogate for pre-labour-market attributes as well as for the residual difference in productivity between blacks and whites after correcting for these differences. In fact, these pre-labour-market attributes must be identified in securing whites suitable for any particular employment and there is no prima-facie reason why it would cost more to secure this information for blacks than for otherwise comparable whites. In the statistical discrimination theories the argument must be that otherwise equivalent blacks are on average less productive than their white counterparts (Cf. Aigner and Cain 1977; Thurow 1975: ch. 7).

8   Unlike orthodox general equilibrium theory, statistical theories of discrimination do not assume perfect information and they contain transaction costs. Both are, however, statistically controllable. Thus, in Knight's (1965) terms, the imperfect information represents 'risk' and not 'uncertainty' and, because no information is gathered on specific workers, transaction costs are not incurred in distinguishing between blacks and whites.

9   I am purposely overstating the case. I do not want to imply that hierarchically structured racism is dead in the US, only that it is on the decline and paradoxically that similar discriminatory consequences emerge from the implementation of egalitarian principles.

10   That is, the outcome is Pareto optimum. In so far as coercion is necessary it is only to guarantee contracts and to protect the starting endowments of the various actors (see Gould 1989).

11   Racist attitudes on the part of employers are, strictly speaking, impossible in the long run, for this taste for discrimination is unattainable. It violates the assumption of rationality.

12   In a later section we will see that even with these modifications — the introduction of imperfect, asymmetric information and transaction costs — a non-orthodox, neo-classical model remains incapable of explaining the persistence of labour-market discrimination within a competitive economy except in extraordinary circumstances. However, unlike the orthodox model, non-orthodox theory does create a space within which a sociological explanation of labour-market discrimination within a competitive economy becomes possible.

13   This distinction has the same importance as the one Marx draws between labour-power and labour, between the capacity to labour and actual work.

14   Strictly speaking this is misleading. What is crucial is that employers possess power over employees. The threat of unemployment is one particularly important source of this power.

15   In Shapiro and Stiglitz (1986) work is an on/off proposition. Either the worker works or he does not work. This simple assumption unnecessary for the operation of the model, but I adopt it for purposes of exposition.

16   This terminology is elliptic. The real world is always non-ortho-dox; only the assumptions of the economic model are orthodox. Even though one problem with orthodox theory is its tendency towards reification, treating the world as if it conformed to the model's assumptions, in this chapter I will generally refer to (non)orthodox markets to avoid the burdensome phrase, markets as analysed within (non)orthodox theory.

17   With few exceptions, the following several paragraphs closely follow the substance and wording of the Gould-Weinstein essay. In that essay we chose to formulate our analysis within the context of neo-classical, utilitarian, assumptions. Its findings can be generalized within a more sophisticated social structural model and in that model one can show how the proximate sanctions analysed by non-orthodox neo-classical economists are in fact socially structured (Gould 1987, 1989).

18   A more complete discussion of power asymmetries between employers and employees is found in Gould 1987, where the discussion cites both Durkheim and Weber as enunciating a viewpoint similar to the one Knight argues, and where my argument draws heavily on Offe 1985: ch 1.

19   Bowles comments that 'the above explains why identical workers may be paid differently. It does not explain why discrimination exists, or why... [advantaged] workers tend to be white, male, and neither very young nor very old' (Bowles 1985: 30. Cf. Roemer 1979).

20   This type of discrimination is very difficult to document. While there is some evidence, for example, that 'men tend to earn less when they work with women' (Blau 1984: 72), the adequate demonstration of gender or racial devaluation meets a number of problems. For example, the inclusion of blacks into middle-class occupations in the US economy since the mid-1960s has to a considerable extent been their incorporation into government jobs. This process has paralleled the unionization of many of these same jobs. In consequence, until the past decade, there was a considerable push to raise the salaries of governmental workers. My argument would suggest that if we construct a counterfactual excluding blacks from these jobs while allowing unionization to proceed at the same rate, wages for these occupational roles would have increased by an even more significant amount. No one to my knowledge has carried out sufficiently detailed comparative studies to determine the actual impact of devaluation — holding constant things like unionization and the supply and demand of workers.

21   In the orthodox neo-classical model, an equivalence between index and capacity must be manifest, since perfect information is assumed; there is no possibility of error or ignorance. Phelps (1972) discusses a number of cases that depend on the employer's view of the reliability of test scores for blacks and whites, but he does not discuss the case I emphasize.

22   In the text, I am drawing on an argument taken from work origi-
      nally undertaken on success in educational organizations. Conse-
      quently there is a tendency to conflate two different types of tests
      and two different outcomes. SAT tests do predict success in
      college in gross terms, though they do not do a good job of
      predicting success within a particular college once students have
      matriculated, and especially after their second year in school.
      While SAT type tests differentiate between blacks and whites at
      all levels of education, they are poor predictors of earnings
      differentials between blacks and whites. This may be because
      what schools try to teach relates poorly to subsequent earnings for
      either whites or blacks, or it may be that scores on these tests
      inadequately measure the things students sometimes learn that
      are relevant to economic success. It is none the less reasonable to
      expect that job-related 'objective tests' have some ability to predict
      occupational success.

23   Research similar in form to Labov's and focusing on women's
      language usage is beginning to appear. See Eliasoph (1987) and
      the research she cites.

24   The comparisons I am making assume economically homoge-
      neous blacks and whites, i.e. they control for skill differentials
      relevant to actual job performance. This is not a problem for entry-
      level manufacturing jobs in most primary labour markets, as these
      jobs do not generally require substantial experience. It is more of a
      problem for certain entry-level service jobs that may require
      specific job-related skills. I leave the latter complication for
      another time.

25   The importance of this argument is enhanced when the results of
      these tests are taken at face value by both blacks and whites.
      Blacks may accept lower wages owing to their belief that they are,
      in fact, less qualified than higher scoring whites. On the role of
      legitimation and justification in creating social order see Gould
      (1988), and on their role in the labour process Gould (1989).

26 Success is left intentionally ambiguous here. In entry level manufacturing jobs in internal labour markets, workers usually require minimal job-related skills. None the less, blacks may succeed less frequently because of culturally anomalous expectations unrelated to their job performance or because the ethos of a particular workplace entails more overt discrimination against blacks. This does not mean, needless to say, that no blacks overcome this discrimination and succeed. On the contrary, when given the opportunity many blacks have shown themselves capable of overcoming tremendous obstacles.

27 The model that Bulow and Summers construct is substantively based on the differential utility women and men are assumed to gain from secondary-sector, including home, employment. It is made empirical by noting the higher quit rates for married women than married men. None the less they begin this discussion by citing data indicating that there are large race (and age) differences in separation probabilities, as well as large differences in gender separation probabilities (1986: 399). Thus I feel justified in discussing their model as an explanation of racially grounded labour-market discrimination.

28 Viscusi (1980: 388) comments in a similar fashion about the quit-rates of women. 'To the extent that women have less precise notions of their prospects for advancement and their working conditions, such as the presence of co-worker discrimination, they will be more likely to use the initial period of employment as a period of experimentation and then quit if their experiences are sufficiently unfavourable' (see also Meitzen 1986). This is his explanation for the higher quit-rates women manifest in the first year of work. Blau and Kahn (1981: 569, table 2), who also find length of tenure negatively correlated with quit-rates, find more specifically that though all groups are responsive to their long-run earning opportunities, black men and women are a bit more sensitive to their perception of such opportunities than are their white counterparts.

8

Racial Formation Theory: The Contemporary Agenda[1]

Howard Winant

In a book called *Racial Formation in the United States*, Michael Omi and I (1986) systematically re-evaluated existing theories of race, both mainstream and radical. We argued that the tendency to *reduce* racial dynamics to manifestations of other, supposedly more deeply structured, dimensions of social relations was a major source of distortions and limitations in most contemporary racial theory. Three types of racial reductionism were identified, each generating a certain paradigm of racial theory — the ethnicity, class, and nation-based perspectives.

We suggested that these approaches, though certainly valuable in elaborating some dimensions of US race relations, also distorted and limited social scientific understanding of racial phenomena in very damaging ways. All three paradigms were incapable of grasping the ubiquity and comprehensiveness of racial dynamics in US society and all three were strikingly out of touch with the political complexity of racial phenomena.

Omi and I developed an alternative view: *racial formation theory*. This is an explicitly anti-reductionist approach. The racial formation perspective understands race as a phenomenon whose meaning is contested throughout social life. Race is seen as a constituent of the individual psyche and of relationships among individuals; it is also an irreducible component of collective identities and social structures.

This view seems far more capable of accounting for US racial dynamics. In US history, race has been a traditional source, not only of conflict and division, but also of renewal and cultural awareness. Race has been a key determinant of mass movements, state structure and, even, foreign policy.

In the twentieth century, racial meanings have been contested and racial ideologies mobilized in political relationships. The key factor in this contestation of meanings and mobilization of identities is *rearticulation*. This term denotes the process of rupturing and reconstructing the prevailing *commonsense* logic of race, the process of challenging individual and group identities.

Rearticulation is a complex concept, which I cannot present here in very great depth. But the basic idea is simple: in order to challenge an existing pattern of oppression, it is necessary to demystify that pattern, to demonstrate its vulnerability, its illogicality. But since commonsense (for example racial stereotyping) always has a certain logic, the elements of the old commonsense have to be taken apart, disarticulated, deconstructed. These elements may be political, religious, linguistic; they may be cultural norms and folkways. Successful social movements reinterpret, recombine, even reinvent these elements, constructing them (rearticulating them) in a new commonsense.[2]

Racial formation theory must consider the ways in which this process is carried out, how it succeeds and why it fails, and what its recent history has been. In respect to recent racial politics, a racial formation approach both integrates and goes beyond some increasingly dead-end debates. Two examples of such controversies whose reinterpretation the racial formation perspective facilitates are: (1) the individual versus group rights debate that has characterized neo-conservative attacks on affirmative action (see, for example, Glazer 1975; Pinkney 1984); and (2) the mainstream ethnicity theory debate with the radical class-based and nationalist positions (see Killian 1981).

Omi and I analyse recent racial politics — again I am being very schematic here — as follows:

Beginning in the 1950s and more intensively in the 1960s, racial movements initiated a *great transformation* of the American political universe, creating new organizations, new collective identities, and new social and political norms; challenging past racial practices and stereotypes; and ushering in a wave of democratizing social reform. The ability of racial movements to *rearticulate* traditional political and cultural themes — first among blacks and later among Latinos, Asian Americans and Indians — permitted the entry of millions of racial minority group members into the political process. Indeed, by making identity, the personal, and language itself political issues, the racial upsurge facilitated the appearance of the new social movements — such as the feminist, peace and gay movements — on the political stage.

The 1980s bore ironic witness to the impact of the racial minority upsurge on the overall political terrain in the US, for the racial movements of the 1950s and 1960s also provided the political space in which a *racial reaction* could incubate and develop its political agenda. By the latter 1960s, a substantial backlash had set in. The legacy of the great transformation, however, set limits on the reaction which succeeded it. The new politics of identity could not simply be reversed; it had to be rearticulated once again. This is why the current debate about opportunity is dominated by charges of reverse discrimination. Demands for community control have reappeared in opposition to school desegregation and high government officials claim that we are moving toward a colour-blind society.

Racial Formation Processes Today

All this represents a promising beginning, but much theory construction remains to be done. The racial formation approach does not yet provide an adequate account of US racial dynamics. Its theoretical logic needs further refining and extensive gaps and weaknesses remain.

Racial formation involves the interaction of subjective phenomena — racial identities and cultural processes — with social structural phenomena such as political movements and parties, state institutions and policies, or market processes. The rearticulation of racial meanings takes place unevenly, occurring where the old racial commonsense is at its weakest and where competing racial logics are at their strongest.[3] One aspect of racial formation theory thus involves the attempt to specify the *sites* at which racial meanings, identities and institutions can potentially change.

A second key dimension of racial formation theory involves the *levels* of racial dynamics: their specification, interrelationship and mobilization in political contestation. Sites and levels can be seen as two different dimensions of the racial formation process.

Sites

A site may be conceived, following the pioneering work of Bowles and Gintis (1981), as 'a region of social life with a coherent set of constitutive social relations.' (See also Bowles and Gintis 1983.) Each site has a set of rules which shape the social practices possible at that site. Thus we can understand political contestation as conflict over the rules in force at a given site. Conflict over voting rights, for example, takes place at the level of collectivity or macro-*level* racial dynamics, and within the *site* of the political system. Sites may be ideal-typically located within the economic, political, or cultural/ideological systems operating in a given society. Institutions can then be understood to belong — though always partially, never totally — to particular sites. The family, for example, by virtue of the centrality of social reproduction within it, can be understood as primarily a site within the cultural system, though it clearly has economic and political dimensions as well. By the same logic the workplace may be identified as a site within the economic system, and the state seen as a site within the political system.

Levels

We can picture racial dynamics as a series of social relationships occurring at two *levels* of society. The term level, then, would refer to micro- and macro-level racial relationships. In the US, no individual or collectivity can be wholly unaffected by racial dynamics.

At the micro level, racial identity, like any other form of subjectivity, must be discursively constructed. We must learn how to perceive ourselves and interact with others, how to manage our multiple identities — as workers, lovers, family members, as thinkers or philosophers in the Gramscian sense, and in a multitude of other social roles. All this is affected by racial meanings and awareness, yet in the US race is so deeply imbedded, so quintessentially ideological, that the racial commonsense underlying the formation of identities is nearly transparent. At the micro level, whether in the training of children within families or the operation of face-to-face relationships at other sites, identities are not fixed, but always subject to change and conflict. There is, then, a political dimension to the formation of racial identity at the micro level.

At the macro level, race is a matter of the dynamics of social structures. Racial conflict has emerged over recent decades in a host of institutional and organizational settings, from economic organizations (market processes, corporations, unions), to political parties and movement groups, to cultural systems (community or neighbourhood, audience for a certain style of music, for example, form of art, or type of cultural production through media). Macro-level racial conflict is about something broader than the traditional spoils of politics: wealth, power and prestige, to use Weberian terminology. These count of course, but in battles such as the one over racial equality the stakes are not just who gets the jobs or the admissions to medical school. What is at stake is the *meaning* of race for society. Is one's race a matter of individual or group identity? What loyalties does it imply? To what extent is it something that can be safely ignored? Sociologically, what we are discussing here is sometimes called the problem of foundations, but when sociologists talk about this, they usually mean the way individuality (i.e. the dynamics of identity and interest formation) structures collectivity.[4] There is certainly a connection between the micro and the macro level as far as racial formation is concerned, but in my view this linkage is a two-way street. Not only is identity the source of collective interests and movements, but collective processes also generate identity.

So, relationships of racial formation operate reciprocally at the micro and macro social level. *Racial meanings and identities, racial policies and practices, are shaped by interaction between the levels.* We live out our lives simultaneously as members of collectivities and as individuals. Our identities are neither purely subjective nor objective, but are constructed by the interaction among the various relationships in which we are imbedded. Although distinct phenomena, racially-based identity and racially-based social structure are inextricably linked.

An Experiential Synthesis

Every individual has to manage his or her identity in a social context which treats race as definitive of who one is. Conversely, every collectivity, every social institution, demands racially-oriented practices (in effect, a racial ID, an implicit 'passbook') of each individual with whom it comes into contact.

Let us consider two quick examples of these reciprocal interactions. Think back over the times in your life when you have met someone with whom you could not immediately identify racially: a sort of unease sets in as one struggles to 'place' the person within the prevailing racial commonsense.

Here racial formation is taking place at the micro level, in a cultural site: a personal, perhaps casual, social relationship. Yet this micro-level relationship is linked to larger, macro-level racial dynamics. The source of unease, after all, is not primarily within oneself, but in the system of racial categories by which large-scale society is organized.[5] Here collective racial practices challenge individual identities. What is going on here, then, is a micro-level 'crisis' of racial meaning.

A second example: black or Latino students who fail to act 'white' in the university setting, who do not adopt the institutional norms of, for example, language or dress, might precipitate an institutional crisis. Not their objective performance at the university, but their subjective style, can get them into trouble. They may be told to dress, speak, or socialize differently. Here racial identities challenge established collective racial practices. In this case racial formation is taking place at the macro-level, again in a cultural site, the university. Yet this macro-level 'crisis' is generated by micro-level racial dynamics.

Note that these are *contingent* outcomes. They are dependent upon social relationships whose results are uncertain, whose interactions may or may not be politically volatile at any given social site. In the example of an individual confronted with an 'other' of ambiguous racial identity, the person involved may choose to ignore the problem, to pretend he or she is colour blind. By the same token, the 'other' who is the source of the crisis (whose race is difficult to identify) may be oblivious to the problem or highly sensitive to it, or somewhere in between. In the case of the minority students who do not 'act white', this may be a choice that is not open to them (if, for example, they have not been sufficiently schooled in whiteness), or it may be a political decision. By the same token, university administrators may attempt to enforce their conception of what one neo-conservative commentator called 'the universal norms of European, Judeo-Christian culture,' or they may choose not to make an issue of the conflict. They may have students demonstrating for a more racially diverse university arrested, or they may send them baskets of fruit.

Theoretical Promises and Problems

These examples reveal both the promise and the problems of racial formation theory. Simply to argue that race is ubiquitous is insufficient. What is needed is a theoretical approach that spells out why at certain moments rearticulation of racial meanings and identities is possible, whereas at others it is not, why movements or the state (collective phenomena) at times succeed in rupturing the commonsense logic of race, while at other times they reinforce it. Conversely, we must understand what renders the effectivity of racial commonsense — which, after all, is a society-wide, macro-level phenomenon — vulnerable at some times and not at others. Why do the bonds of racial identity and racial meaning loosen? What makes racial logic vulnerable?

Two problems to emerge from the issues I have raised (and which point to future directions in research on racial formation) involve the *terrain* of racial conflict and the *actors* in the racial formation drama.

The Terrain of Racial Conflict

From the epoch of civil rights and desegregation to the present, the sites of racial contestation and rearticulation have shifted enormously. Omi and I suggest that during recent decades there have been *two* comprehensive, even epochal changes, in the key sites of racial contestation in the US.[6] The first was the great transformation — the movement upsurge of the 1950s and 1960s — which eliminated formal, legalized racial discrimination in the form of segregation, and which politicized racial identity, laying the foundations for all the new social movements (such as the feminist, peace and gay movements) which followed.

The second shift was the racial reaction of the 1970s and 1980s, which 'negated the negation.' That is, the new right and neo-conservatives, forced to play the game of rearticulation and confronted with the egalitarian legacy of the movement upsurge, adapted quite well. In fact they may have been the chief beneficiaries of the 1960s movements, since no united front of new social movements ever appeared that could match the political efficacy of the reaction led by Reagan. But already in the 1960s a loose coalition of new rightists and neo-conservatives was in the process of mobilizing the so-called silent majority around identity politics. They thereby threatened minority (and other) movement gains; the racial reaction was notably successful in confining the egalitarian themes of the movement upsurge within a conservative, individualistic commonsense. Equality was limited to opportunity and not results; discrimination was defined strictly in intentional as opposed to institutional terms and rights were not extended to groups, but only to individuals.

Without entering very far into the details of this argument, it is already possible to see that certain sites of contestation and rearticulation of racial meaning have proved particularly crucial in the postwar period. In general, cultural sites, having to do with the micro-level politics of race, have proved far more durable, far less susceptible to the roll backs, initiated by Reagan, that assaulted so many social policies (i.e. political sites). The deracialization of political identity has proved a far thornier problem for neo-conservatives than the deracialization of the welfare state.

Yet this is by no means the whole story. Electoral politics has been permanently transformed by the 1960s legacy, such that, for example, southern black votes placed the US Senate in Democratic hands in 1986, denied Robert Bork a seat on the US Supreme Court, and opposed the Reagan revolution in such areas as social spending, economic policy and interventionism in the third world. Electoral politics, by virtue of its ideological nature and pluralist, consensual imagery, remains a significant site for racial rearticulation.

Finally economic sites also retain an important racial dimension. William Julius Wilson (1987) argues in *The Truly Disadvantaged* that race-specific policies can no longer be relied upon to improve the economic conditions faced by significant numbers of minority poor. However, he suggests that redistributive economic policies (tight labour markets) can have the same effect, simply because there are disproportionately greater numbers of minority than of white poor.[7] Thus the economy appears to be reviving as a site of racial contestation for the first time since the late 1960s. This is an argument that will receive greater attention as the domestic crisis worsens.

A lot of work needs to be done in order to understand the role of race in these transformations. All the conventional wisdom, left as well as right, appears suspect. Certainly race is not declining in significance. Racial formation is becoming steadily more complex. Inter-minority conflicts (blacks versus Asians, for example) are on the rise. Class cleavages dramatically divide many minority communities. And patterns of racism vary significantly depending on who is being targeted.[8]

The Actors in the Racial Formation Drama?

We should understand that racial formation is a political outcome, a result of the demands and pressures placed on racial meanings and identities by particular social actors. There are three social actors potentially capable of articulating, or rearticulating, racial meanings.

The first of these are *individual actors* operating at the micro social level. Quotidian relationships, the relationships of everyday life, cut across all social sites (family, workplace, religion) and have key racial components. This may seem overly obvious, but such problems as racial socialization in the family, the interaction of race and class dynamics in the workplace, the role of religious themes in framing race as a political issue, are actually badly in need of reconceptualization. What is required is more attention to the micro level of racial formation: every individual must manage the complexities and contradictions of racial commonsense; one's ability to do this unquestioningly and with a minimum of conflict is undoubtedly a major factor in grounding that commonsense.

The second of these social actors is the *state*, which in the US today is itself a comprehensively racial institution. It is the fundamental political site of racial formation. The state *explicitly* defines and redefines racial meanings in many ways, for example by means of the census, in the formation and implementation of social policy, by organization and oversight of elections, through immigration control and as part of judicial activities (for example, adjudicating claims of discrimination). Beyond this, however, lies a vast realm of state action that is implicitly racial, in which even such matters as toxic waste disposal, the funding and organization of scientific investigation, monetary policy and foreign affairs have important racial dimensions.

The third social actor with the capacity to rearticulate racial meanings is the *social movement*.[9] Movements potentially bridge the levels of the racial formation process, challenging both the state and other macro-level institutions, on the one hand, and the individual's conception of his or her racial identity, on the other. Movements also potentially link racial sites: the demand for racial equality, the interrogation of previous racial common-sense, cannot be confined to one particular institution or group. In the movement upsurge of the 1960s, for example, the demand for political rights such as voting was intrinsically connected to the demand for an end to workplace discrimination, residential segregation, inequality in education, and even the absence of dark faces from the media. Similarly in the racial reaction of the 1970s and 1980s, the new right and neo-conservative movements successfully generalized their conception of equality (a largely individualistic, depoliticized vision) to these very same sites.[10] What is interesting about racial movements is that they only occasionally appear; only rarely is normal politics challenged by the emergence of an actor capable of rearticulating racial commonsense. When this happens, it occurs precisely because what the movement says and does resonates at both individual and collective levels, and spreads its contagious questioning to the many sites in which racial dynamics are present.

Here lies our hope, not only for social change, but also for theoretical progress. In a deep sense, our understanding of race can only advance as movements advance. The movements of the earlier postwar period have taken us this far and we are still working out their logic; this is certainly true of racial formation theory. In the future we shall no doubt see new racial dynamics, new struggles for identity, equality and social justice, and these will develop our understanding of race in ways that will surely be intriguing.

Notes

1   Earlier versions of this chapter were presented at the Conference
    on Comparative Perspectives on Race and Class, St Catherine's
    College, Oxford University, January 1988, and at the meetings of
    the Eastern Sociological Society, Philadelphia, March 1988. My
    thanks to the organizers of these events, and for the many useful
    criticisms I received.

2   Probably the most significant work to explore these processes, and
    the one which has most influenced our approach, is Mouffe and
    Laclau (1985).

3   The concept of commonsense derives, of course, from the work of
    Gramsci (1971).

4   While this is a vital endeavour, it often involves a reductionism of
    its own: social structures are seen as merely reflecting or
    mediating individual interests or even human nature — categories
    that are hardly self evident. A good example of this inadequacy is
    rational choice theory, which is currently in vogue; for a recent
    statement, see Hechter (1987).

5   Whole groups of people in the US — Arabs, Brazilians, and South
    Indians to name just three examples — have highly ambiguous
    racial identities.

6   As should be clear from reading our work, we do not argue that
    only one site is crucial, but in fact suggest that racial contestation
    is both ubiquitous and at the same time concentrated on key sites.
    See Omi and Winanat (1986, Chapter 4).

7   In our typology of sites Wilson's views straddle the political and
    the economic. His analysis of the class dimensions of racial
    dynamics focuses on the economic sites of racial formation; his
    policy recommendations concern political sites; how state activity
    can potentially change racial meanings and practices. On another
    point, it should be stressed that Wilson's recommendations
    include both 'class-specific' and 'race-specific policies,' though he
    places far greater importance on the former.

8   Whites' fears of blacks, for example, appear to be different from their fears of Latinos or Asians. Blacks are feared because they are seen as a threat to established white control of institutions such as neighbourhood schools, perhaps because of fears of crime, or because of fears about the stability of the family. But in my opinion there is an odour of superiority about whites' racism towards blacks: our schools are better, our families, our attitudes toward work are better. Asians, though, are feared because they may be *superior* to whites. They are seen as working too hard, as out-competing whites. At Berkeley recently (where the student body is now nearly 50 per cent Asian), white students told me that if there were too many Asians in a class they, the whites, would not take it, because they thought the Asians would drag the grade curve up. This is reminiscent of the kind of anti-Semitism that Jews used to face on campus.

9   Carl Boggs (1986) provides a good general treatment of social movement theory, which emphasizes the 'new social movements' but is nearly silent on race.

10   In my view one should be under no illusion that social movements are inherently progressive. The racial reaction of the 1970s and 1980s was powered by a genuine social movement. See Omi and Winant (1986, Chapter 7) for greater detail on this.

9

Race, Class and Political Economy: Reflections on an Unfinished Agenda

Thomas D. Boston

The most difficult aspects of race/class analysis are isolating racial class formations and identifying the forms of social consciousness that correspond to them. In *Race, Class and Conservatism* (Boston 1988) I attempt to accomplish this by first examining historically changes in the political economy of race relations and their effects on the external and internal character of African-American social classes. Second, I attempt there to specify the contemporary anatomy of classes using elements of the methodological approaches of Marx, Poulantzas, Weber and Giddens. This synthesis allows us both to define the external boundaries and internal structure of classes and to isolate the forms of social consciousness pertaining to each. Finally, I address arguments of authors who minimize the role of discrimination in the contemporary life chances of African-Americans. Such arguments take two forms; those that tend to over emphasize the role of class location *vis-à-vis* race (for example, Wilson 1978), and those that deny that contemporary discrimination continues to be a meaningful social force; typically neo-conservatives (Sowell 1984, 1981; Williams 1982a, 1982b; and Block and Walker 1982).

The critique of neo-conservative arguments emanates from a desire to reverse the current trend in public policy and the courts. Under the influence of this ideology social services to the poor have been drastically cut and the government has been disarmed of an aggressive role in preventing job discrimination and implementing affirmative action in employment and minority business development.

Early reviews of Boston (1988) focus solely on its critique of neo-conservatives' ideas (Banton 1989; Sampson 1989). But more recent reviews have come closer to capturing what I hope will be its enduring contribution. That is, the conceptualization of a racial class formation for contemporary black society and an elucidation of the historical interaction between race and class (Darity 1990).

In Boston (1988) the forms of social consciousness corresponding to class segments, i.e. strata, are identified largely by participatory observation and intuition and, as such, are still hypotheses. In a forthcoming study (Boston 1991) I hope to provide an empirical test of these relations. This is the *unfinished agenda* alluded to in the subtitle of this chapter. A second aspect of this agenda, although not touched on in this discussion, is the need to give greater articulation to the contemporary dynamics of the US and world economies and their effects on changes in the internal configuration of African-American social classes. In Boston (1988) I provide the abstract historical framework for this approach and argue that how changes in the political economy influence external boundaries and power relations is not the most important aspect to comprehend in class analysis. The real key to comprehending the race/class interaction as well as the nature of class relations in general is to consider what happens to the internal configuration of classes. That is where the race/class dynamic manifests itself most vividly. Finally, studies of race and class must give greater articulation to the role of gender relations.

Below I reiterate the main arguments pertaining to the internal structure of African-American social classes and corresponding forms of social consciousness. My objective is to set up the hypotheses more clearly for further verification or refutation. Despite their importance, I do not dwell in this chapter on the historical dynamics of race and class.

The Issues

Most studies of race and class have four fundamental shortcomings. First, the stratification of classes is incorrectly defined. Second, the internal structure of classes is usually ignored and, ironically, this is the very place where the historical and contemporary effects of racial antagonisms find their clearest expression. Third, many approaches are rigid, asserting that the status of African-American society is determined either by race or class and, too often, those arguing for a joint determination fail to elaborate sufficiently on the aspects of either. Finally, the historic role of racial domination in forming and regenerating the disarticulated class configuration of black society is usually neglected.

Historically, racial subjugation has created a unique class stratification among blacks; one whose internal composition differs both quantitatively and qualitatively from that of whites. This inferior status is constantly regenerated by economic dynamics and the legal, cultural, political and social apparatuses which support it. For example, the growing marginalization of the working class and the creation of a so-called 'black underclass' are the result of declining manufacturing employment and growing international competition, which hit blacks hardest because institutional and employment discrimination have concentrated them disproportionately in the most vulnerable occupations.

Investigations of race and class are difficult — particularly given the immense social and economic changes currently taking place. For example, the debasement or marginalization of the working class has occurred and is ever increasing the so-called 'underclass'. Consider the emergence of the new middle class or the growing divorce of ownership from control of the corporation. Leaving aside race, these developments alone turn the concept of class into an 'intellectual jellyfish' (Pryor 1981: 369). Yet, as Parkin (1979: 9) notes, 'now that racial, ethnic, and religious conflicts have moved towards the centre of the political stage in many industrial societies, any general model of class or stratification that does not fully incorporate this fact must forfeit all credibility'. Still, researchers have not adequately incorporated race into class analyses.

One reason for this omission is the mistaken belief that industrial societies dissolve ethnic differences; another is the use of methodological constructs that view ethnic factors as '"complicating features" that simply disturb the pure class model, rather than as integral elements of the system' (Parkin 1979: 32).

Three major issues are involved in race/class analyses. These are: (1) the need to define or identify the boundaries of the basic classes. More specifically we must determine what factors are responsible for constituting certain segments of the population into a social class. Included in this is the need to understand the problems presented by the intersection or overlap of certain class characteristics. Overlapping characteristics often give the impression that criteria used to define a class are not unique but are found also among members of another class; (2) the necessity to identify correlations between classes and forms of ideological consciousness; and (3) the need to analyse the interaction between racial subordination and class composition and to determine the impact of economic and social development on the existing class configuration. While each of these issues is difficult, little progress can be made until classes are sufficiently defined: a task which involves a good deal of abstraction.

The two most widely used concepts of class are those of Weber and Marx. In the latter approach classes are defined by the ownership relation to the means of production and forms of exploitation corresponding thereto. Furthermore, they are conceived of as dynamic agents of social transformation whose social consciousness is strongly correlated with their objective productive relations and economic situation. Within the Weberian conception, they are status groupings defined by a common set of socio-economic relations and life chances.

Most analyses of black classes employ the Weberian method, or a variation of it based on occupational criteria. Weber looks primarily to market relations as the basis of class divisions. He (Weber 1968: 927) states that: 'We may speak of a class when (1) a number of people have in common a specific causal component of their life chances, in so far as (2) this component is represented exclusively by economic interests in the possession of goods and opportunities for income, and (3) is represented under the conditions of the commodity or labour markets. This is "class situation."'

Several problems are common to most analyses of black stratification. The first and most serious involves merging the black capitalist class with the black middle class as if they constituted only one class. The small size of the former is usually the rationale. However, this practice leads to serious conceptual errors. Rather than overlooking this class, it is important to analyse the historical conditions responsible for maintaining its feeble existence because the black capitalist's weak state could well be a major aspect of modern racial inequality. The black capitalist is the victim of a long history of illegal property expro-

priation, financial discrimination and, for many decades, a
legalized system of racial segregation. And it is as incorrect to
subsume this class under the middle class in analysing US
race/class relations as it would be to subsume the dependent
capitalist class under the middle class in third world developing
countries. Why is the development of this class so distorted?
That is the question.

Many studies stratify classes by an arbitrary income boundary. Such approaches typically place all persons making
$25,000 or more in the middle or upper class. But the concept of
class in this instance is not a social phenomenon but rather a
sterile numerical statistic. There is also a conceptual problem in
dealing with the 'black underclass', an entity that is never defined precisely. Is it a class, a class segment, or is it a useful
concept at all? Furthermore, what are its internal differentiations? Surely an unwed mother living in poverty differs in
outlook, social consciousness and lifestyle from a drug dealer,
even if they both live in the same vicinity. Yet the typical approach is to lump all persons in the underclass if they live in
census tracts in which 40 per cent or more of the residents are
poor. Worse still, the economic dynamics that produce this
'underclass' are seldom discussed. Instead, the impression is
given that this stratum exists in isolation from the dynamics of
the economy and has cultural particularities that reproduce its
own impoverishment.

What is a Class?

To address this issue, we start at the abstract level and move to a
more concrete specification of social classes in African-American
society. Similarly, to understand the nature and interaction of
race and class, we must also start from the abstract historical
level by conceptualizing changes in the political economy of race
relations. Each significant change, or stage, produces specific
articulations of the class relations, both externally and internally.
The outlines for these two abstractions are provided in Boston
(1988: 9-31) and the interested reader is referred there.

Pryor (1981: 369-70) defines class as:

> the designation of a group into which persons are placed by either
> objective criteria, subjective criteria, self-identification, or mixed
> criteria. Depending upon the theory of social stratification that is
> proposed, 'class' can be defined in terms of 'objective' criteria (for

example, income, wealth, position), 'subjective' criteria (solidarity in terms of social or economic interests; or self-identification with some group) or mixed criteria (for example, evaluation by others in society in terms of esteem or some other scale of value). Depending upon the theory of social structure that is proposed, 'class' can be defined in terms of a group that is struggling together to change the structure; or statistically in terms of the position or power of the group concerning the operations of the society in equilibrium. Depending upon the theory of societal causation that is proposed, 'class' can embrace a difference defined in terms of a single criterion or of some combination of set of criteria.

The Marxian definition is based on objective criteria and views class positions as stations emanating from specific places in the economic hierarchy, as functional roles in the organization of production and as the relationship to the ownership of the means of production. The uniqueness of this approach is that classes are seen as instruments of social transformation.

Weber (1968: 927) introduces the idea of economic opportunity, or life chances, rather than economic station, as the element which binds classes together. In this regard, the behaviour of classes is determined as much by values and common circumstances as by position in the social hierarchy (Hacker 1979: 55). But if one of the principal objectives of class theory is to identify the main social cleavage or, as Parkin (1979: 3) says, 'the structural "fault" running through society to which the most serious disturbances on the political landscape are thought to be ultimately traceable,' then Weberian analysis is ambiguous. Its most obvious shortcoming is its inability to identify clear class boundaries: a problem traceable to its focus on the distribution system and status groups as opposed to production relations. In short, one may identify several sets of common values and circumstances. The theory's strength, however, is its recognition that individuals sharing common life chances and circumstances tend to share ideological outlooks.

The Marxian method (Lenin 1974: 421) defines classes as:

> large groups of people differing from each other by the place they occupy in a historically determined system of social production, by their relation (in most cases fixed and formulated by law) to the means of production, by their role in the social organization of labour, and, consequently, by the dimensions of the share of social wealth of which they dispose and the mode of acquiring it. Classes are groups of people one of which can appropriate the labour of another owing to the different places they occupy in a definite

system of social economy.

The definition embodies three elements: (1) the relations of individuals to the ownership of the means of production; (2) the division of labour and functions in the production process; and (3) the method of acquiring income and the pattern of its distribution. The first factor is considered to be most important in determining class formations.

Unlike the Weberian method, boundaries in the Marxian approach are more definitive. But the method experiences difficulty in attempting to correlate ideological and political attitudes with objective class locations. For example, a well known and frequently encountered problem is the incongruence of workers' class actions with their class station. Secondly, the derivation of objective class boundaries is problematic especially given the changing structures of advanced industrial economies. Is there a new ruling class now that 'family capitalism' has disappeared and ownership is divorced from control of production? Similarly, with the growing importance of information technology, service industries, financial services and the like, the classical industrial proletariat is disappearing. Does this mean there now exists a new working class or new middle class? These are complex issues which have not been fully resolved.

Neither the Marxian nor the Weberian methods have sufficiently resolved the boundary problem. The greater advantage displayed by the Weberian method in correlating consciousness with status groupings is offset by the limitless number of such groups that may be identified; the identification of boundaries is therefore problematic. On the other hand, the Marxian method has been plagued by the opposite problem, which is its inability to correlate boundaries with class consciousness. Finally, neither method accounts properly for complexities that arise when racial divisions are introduced (Parkin 1979: 4).

In Boston (1988) I argue that many definition and boundary problems in class analyses can be resolved if, instead of attempting to define impermeable boundaries, researchers recognize that overlapping class characteristics are perfectly normal. The object then is to build definitions incorporating this fact rather than skirting them with rigid and unrealistic assumptions. Sweezy (1953: 124) captures this notion of overlapping characteristics by asserting that:

It would be a mistake to think of a class as perfectly homogeneous internally and sharply marked off from other classes. Actually, there is variety within the class; and one class sometimes shades off very gradually and almost imperceptibly into another. We must, therefore, think of the class as being made up of a core surrounded by fringes which are in varying degrees attached to the core. A fringe may be more or less stable and have a well- defined function in relation to the class as a whole, or it may be temporary and accidental.

The 'new class' theory is another obstacle to the advance of class analysis. Specifically, is there a new working class or new middle class, or has the traditional capitalist class been superseded by a new managerial class? A major error in these theories is that authors describe them as separate and distinct classes, i.e. as classes in and of themselves. Contrary to this, we interpret 'new classes' as segments or internal divisions of existing classes. For example, the middle class has two segments, a new middle class and an old middle class. If instead we conceive of these new entities as separate and distinct classes, then 'new class' theories will encounter major boundary problems. But conceived as segments within classes, this problem is more easily addressed.

In Boston (1988) I propose a synthesis of class theory developed by Marx, Weber, Poulantzas, and Giddens. To delineate the boundary of each class I rely on an individual's relationship to the ownership of the means of production; a Marxian method. But several modifications are made to this. First, I attempt to demonstrate the interplay of race with economics, politics, and ideology in class composition. Second, the most important aspect of the analysis is its focus on the internal structure of classes, i.e. their segments and strata: an approach emphasized by Poulantzas. But where Poulantzas failed to define rigorously segments (or what he calls fractions) I do so by drawing upon Weber's notion of a class as constituted by similar life chances derived from the possession of goods and opportunities for income. Combining Weber's definition (which is rooted in the distribution process) with an individual's location within the division of labour (a more objective and functional criterion) we derive a definition of a class segment — which is closely related to Weber's notion of a status group. A segment is a sub-grouping within a class that is comprised of individuals sharing common life chances derived from their similarities in income and functional roles in the division of labour. Further, each class can be decomposed into strata. These consist of individuals within a class who share common ideological, political, and social orientations. In fact, strata are defined by the character of these ideological orientations. Most important of all, we expect there to exist a significant correlation between a segment and a given stratum of a class. Finally, Giddens's method is employed to explain the origin of the new middle class. But one difference we make is to interpret this development as a new segment of the existing middle class as opposed to a separate and distinct new class. Figure 9.1 presents a graphical representation of this abstract conceptualization.

Figure 9.1: The Internal Composition of a Class

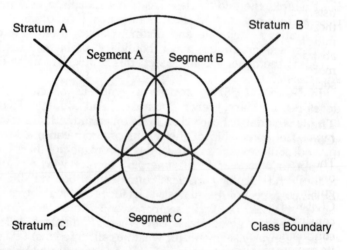

Class boundary: defined by one's ownership relation to the means of production.

Class segment; a sub-grouping within a class or a status grouping of individuals having similar 'life chances' derived from common locations within the division of labour and common patterns of income distribution.

Class stratum: defined by its political consciousness and social orientation. Significantly correlated with a particular segment.

Note: Our approach to class combines the methods of Marx, Weber, Poulantzas and Giddens.

In our approach there exist three classes in society: a capitalist class, a middle class, and a working class. The capitalist class consists of individuals having ownership, control, or possession of the means of production and the capacity to influence the means of livelihood of large numbers of workers. It has two segments, while the old segment of the capitalist class has ownership of the means of production, the new segment consists of individuals such as senior managers, executives and government officials having possession but not ownership of the instruments of production. The working class consists of individuals who do not own or control the means of production and must sell their labour to earn a living. The exception to this is provided by individuals whose labouring skills are so scarce that the possessor can command extraordinarily high wages and salaries in remuneration. Such individuals (for example scientists, engineers, technicians) sell their labour but are not a part of the working class. Instead we classify them as part of the new middle class, a segment of the middle class. This then is the abstract or general model of class to which I attempt to give more concrete specification by adapting it to African-American society. Figure 9.2 below specifies this more concrete model.

The Unfinished Agenda: Class Location and Class Consciousness

The black capitalist class is divided into two segments: an old one and a new one. The old segment has a number of distinguishing features. First, its enterprises mainly evolved before the Civil Rights era in an environment of racial segregation, which constrained its market to the black community. Second, this confinement to an exclusively black clientele not only restricted its growth, but also constrained the character of businesses that developed. These constraints, in turn, tie the fortunes of entrepreneurs of this segment to economic, political and social developments within the black community and force it to have a greater affiliation with the struggle for equality. In the lexicon of the community, these are 'responsible black businesses'. While segregation restricted the economic base and rate of accumulation of black capitalists, it provided them with greater political autonomy from whites in supporting movements for equality. For this reason most entrepreneurs within the old black bourgeoisie have ideological outlooks akin to the indigenous stratum of the black capitalist class.

Figure 9.2: The Class Structure of Black Society

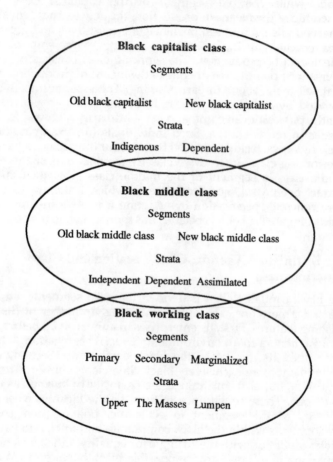

Black capitalist class

Segments

Old black capitalist   New black capitalist

Strata

Indigenous   Dependent

Black middle class

Segments

Old black middle class   New black middle class

Strata

Independent Dependent Assimilated

Black working class

Segments

Primary   Secondary   Marginalized

Strata

Upper   The Masses   Lumpen

There is a loose analogy between this stratum and the 'national bourgeoisie' in third world countries. Because the latter's economic operations are domestically financed and organized, it is perceived to have political interests that are linked more closely to indigenous development. This contrasts with the 'comprador bourgeoisie', or the segment of the capitalist class in a third world country whose economic operations are organized and financed by the multinational corporations of advanced industrial countries. Its foreign economic links are perceived to bind the local 'comprador' ideologically and politically to the foreign instead of the national interest (Poulantzas 1973: 39).

The new black capitalist enterprises contrast sharply with the old. Their development dates primarily to the transition period of the late 1960s and early 1970s. These new enterprises, which have transcended the boundaries segregation imposed upon the old black capitalists, depend to a greater extent on a non-black clientele for markets and resources, including debt and equity capital, and upon local, state and federal government procurement. As a result of their more diverse clientele, the economic fortunes of such enterprises are not tied as closely to the black community and so its ideological and political affiliation with the community is weaker.

Although more successful, the rapid growth of this new segment is still insufficient to alter the overall status of the entire black capitalist class. As such, whatever measure one chooses, whether number of employees or size of gross assets, the black capitalist class is minuscule. Its current state is the product of a history of racial subordination.

The black middle class may be subdivided into two segments which are analogous to those of the black capitalist class: an old black middle class and a new black middle class. While the origin of the former predates the Civil War, the latter is a consequence of new opportunities opened by the civil rights and black power movements. The old black middle class segment is distinguishable by the way it earns its means of livelihood: living mainly off its own effort through the ownership and operation of small businesses or services. In this category are self-employed persons such as doctors, lawyers, shopkeepers, barbers, beauticians, funeral directors, preachers (who engage in this occupation full time) and carpenters. Just as segregation forced most black businessmen of the old capitalist class to operate in a restricted market, it did likewise to small businesses of the old black middle class.

The new black middle class consists of individuals with scarce knowledge, skills or labouring abilities. These skills are usually acquired through advanced education, training or specialized apprenticeships. Individuals with these abilities include scientists, engineers, professors, technicians, professional athletes and entertainers. Whereas the old middle class is self-employed, these individual are not; they sell their labour to business and industry at high salaries. The relative scarcity of their skills permits this market power. These salaries distinguish this segment from ordinary workers, who also sell their labour.

There are three distinct ideological trends or strata within the middle class — the independent stratum, the dependent stratum and the assimilated stratum. The economic basis of the independent stratum is the old black middle class and its close economic and social ties to black society orients its consciousness towards grassroots ideas and movements, which means it is very liberal or even radical at times.

At the ideological centre of the middle class is the 'dependent' stratum. Its members are drawn simultaneously from segments of both the old and the new black middle class. In most cases they have close social, organizational, cultural and political connections with black society. But their economic means of livelihood are derived, in part or in total, from white society. A classic example of this dependent stratum is the traditional civil rights organization. This stratum's close social connection to black society, but economic dependence upon sources external to that society, most often places it in an intermediate or vacillating position *vis-à-vis* grassroots black political activity. While its members will always support non-violent social change and electoral politics, seldom will they support more radical movements. This stratum is torn between identifying with the demands of the black masses, with whom it has close social connections, and having to pacify the anxieties of white society, which provides its means of economic livelihood. Non-violence is usually a buzz word to identify this stratum. There has always been a tug-of-war for leadership over black society between the dependent and independent strata of this class.

I intend to argue that there is a significant correlation between class segments and class strata, but cannot attach a numerical value to the strength of the relation because it is derived from participatory observation rather than empirical investigation. I do not, however, mean to imply that everyone in the same economic position expresses a similar ideological outlook.

With the growing size of the new black middle class, a third ideological trend has developed and is represented by the assimilated stratum of the black middle class. The distinguishing feature of this stratum is an economic, social, cultural, political and organizational alienation from mainstream black society and black public opinion. Politically, this alienation forces it to the far right of the middle class and of black society in general and has given rise to the new black neo-conservatism. Today, many of the foremost ideologues of this stratum work for the government, for major universities or for private research foundations and are closely affiliated with the conservative political tide in mainstream politics in America.

The working class is distinguished by the way in which it earns its means of livelihood. Specifically, it must sell its labouring abilities to employers. This class consists of three segments: a primary segment, a secondary segment and a marginalized segment. These correspond respectively to three strata; the upper stratum, the masses, and the lumpen stratum. The segment scheme draws heavily upon the dual labour market literature developed over the last two decades (Piore 1969; Doeringer 1972; Harrison 1972; see also Boston 1991, 1988) where it is argued that there is a primary and secondary sector distinguished by the character of jobs, firms, earnings and the organization of work. Interested readers are referred to the literature above.

Marginalized workers constitute the third segment of the black working class. By marginalized we mean an involuntary situation where an individual does not have a full-time attachment to a job and may live under a variety of conditions — from homelessness or poverty to permanent part-time employment. Marginalized workers are surplus labourers, created by economic dynamics and by the displacement of primary and secondary workers.

The three strata of the black working class are the upper stratum, the masses and the lumpen stratum. The latter consists of totally disfranchised individuals who have turned to illegal ways of earning a means of livelihood. Its economic base is in the marginalized stratum of the working class. Members of the upper working stratum are mainly located in the primary sector and to a lesser extent the secondary sector. Their job stability, greater income and more prestigious occupations allow them a much better life style than the ordinary worker and this fact is reflected in their political consciousness. While they generally support popular political struggles, such support is usually channelled through established institutions such as churches, or civil rights, civic and community organizations. Individuals in this stratum believe very strongly in the 'American dream' and see racism as the only impediment to its achievement. As a result they are quite outspoken against discrimination. Generally they exhibit greater family stability, higher educational attainment and a much higher standard of living. Individuals in this stratum are typically secondary schoolteachers, low-level managers or supervisors, health technicians, people in sales related occupations, mechanics, construction workers and certain production workers. Some individuals within these same occupations have political outlooks that are characteristic of the 'masses'. But in most cases the consciousness expressed by the 'masses' is a reflection of its economic location in the secondary and marginalized segments.

The masses form the most left-wing stratum of the black working class and black society. This stratum has been the foundation of all significant struggles for social equality. Occupationally its members are usually secondary sector or marginalized workers — for example, labourers, cooks, housekeepers, nursing aids and orderlies, janitors, construction labourers, stock handlers, drivers, retail sales clerks and the unemployed. They are what Malcolm X calls the 'Field Negroes'. And while they are always very liberal and willing to engage in non-violent struggles, in the past many were quick to embrace the political slogan of change, 'by any means necessary'.

Conclusion

This discussion has attempted to outline the class structure of African-American society. An abstract definition of class was developed and the influence of racial antagonisms on class configurations illustrated. The most difficult yet an important aspect of classes to comprehend is their internal configuration. This is the level at which the effects of the interaction between race and class are seen most clearly. We have also established the framework for testing the validity of the class model by outlining the expected correlation between class station (or segments) and forms of political consciousness (i.e. strata). We refer to this test as the unfinished agenda. It is hoped that this framework will force class analysis beyond the persistent and often fruitless concentration on identifying boundaries. While a resolution of the boundary problem is certainly important, equally important are the continuous changes in the internal structure of social classes in response to changes in the political economy. It is here that the dynamics of race and class are most clearly manifested.

10

Race, Class and Civil Rights

Louis Kushnick

Introduction

The central thesis of this chapter is that, as far as the life conditions and chances of the mass of African-Americans were
concerned, the attainments of the Civil Rights Movement (CRM)
in the US were limited. For most blacks the removal of *de jure*
segregation was a necessary, but insufficient, condition for
fundamental changes.

In the US there is widespread structural inequality in the
distribution of wealth, income and power. Institutional racism
determines resource allocation: access to goods and services and
opportunities — including education, employment, health care
and housing — and assures that, compared with blacks, whites
get privileged access to scarce resources. This version of equality
in a *Herrenvolk* democracy maintains the class system by incul-
cating and reinforcing a race consciousness rather than a class
consciousness among the white working class (Kushnick 1981).
One has only to look at the history of 'race riots' — pogroms —
against people of colour in times of economic and political crisis,
for example, the race riots in Chicago and the current escalation
of racial violence among unemployed and alienated whites.

White working class racism represents an incorporation of
the dominant ideology, as reproduced through the schools, the
media and the political institutions of the society. This ideology
serves the interests of the ruling class and is encouraged and
reinforced both directly and indirectly (Murray 1986, 1986a;

Searle 1987). While it is true that white working class people are given psychic and, to a degree, material benefits from the racist system and, therefore, there is widespread acceptance of racism, it is important to note three points: (a) racism is not a genetically determined, or human nature determined, set of beliefs and practices; (b) the price white workers pay is very high indeed (as is the case for male workers and sexism); and (c) working class history contains many points at which the presence of an alternative ideology — an alternative way of explaining the world and alternative conceptions about the ability to change reality — lead to non- and anti-racist practice.

This threat fosters extensive political and ideological efforts on the part of the ruling classes (and their allies in the media and state institutions) to delegitimate these alternative ideologies. In the US, in the post-Second World War period, for example, massive state led anti-Communist hysteria and purges played a crucial role, not only in legitimating the cold war but also in isolating alternative visions about how US society itself should be organized. Central to this was a determined effort to prevent any linking of race and class in the black community and in black politics. Black people and their white allies have to overcome this ideological assault, which aims at separating race from class, intellectually and politically.

Civil Rights and the Cold War in the United States

In analysing the development of black politics in the period since the Second World War, we must look at the following: the interrelationship between political and economic spheres of life; the interrelationship between domestic and foreign policies; demographic, economic and political changes in the US; the class composition, ideology and hierarchies of the CRM; the incorporation of most industrial unions into the cold war, anti-Communist consensus; and the repression of those individuals and organizations that resisted.

This attempt to place the CRM in a framework of analysis is designed to enable us to understand its achievements as well as its limitations and to understand the position of black people in the US today. It is not intended in any way to deprecate the courage, determination and creativity of those who struggled, or the range of consequences which followed these struggles. It is clear, for example, that we cannot understand the politics of the

1960s and beyond — including the development of the New Left, the anti-war movement and, crucially, the Second Wave of Feminism — without understanding the impact of the CRM (see, for example, Cluster 1979; Evans 1979). But unless we situate the CRM in its appropriate framework, we are in danger of making a number of important and damaging mistakes. We would have to ignore (or fail to value) previous struggles of black people if we were unable to explain adequately why the CRM achieved what it did and why earlier struggles failed to achieve similar results. It is clear that African-Americans have struggled from the very beginning of their formation as a people — during slavery/resistance on the slave ships, through marronage and slave uprisings, and through their resistance to the re-establishment of the plantation economy, to Jim Crow and to institutional racism. The outcome of the struggles of any people is determined not merely by their will and determination but also by the range and balance of forces against which they are struggling and the range and balance of forces on which they can call. A second and related danger in failing to place the CRM in its context, is that we may fall prey to the neo-conservative ideological campaign which purports to explain the position of the mass of black people at the bottom of the society in terms of their culture of poverty, or of the broken, pathological Negro family, or of other similar victim blaming explanations.

Bearing these caveats in mind, let us look at some of the fundamental shifts which were occurring in the US and which consequently altered the context within which black people struggled and achieved changes. The fight against Jim Crow's *de jure* segregation united all sections of the black community and reshaped social and political structures in the South. It also changed the nature of black leadership and of class relations (discussed below). This legal form of racism denied fundamental rights to all blacks under its sway, irrespective of their class. It was a total system of racial humiliation designed not only to control blacks (then largely living in the former slave states), but also poor whites. By legislating in favour of racial supremacy the South's rulers gave poor whites a stake in a system which, in practice, kept them poor. Poor whites gave up their votes — when they had them — in return for this racial superiority and, consequently, their adherence to a highly unequal society was bought extremely cheaply. Whites in the South had lower wages, worse public services and fewer benefits than whites in the rest of the country. Any politician who dared to raise questions about this situation was defeated by demagogic appeals to racial superiority and unity.

It is important to see that, though *de jure* segregation was a powerful form of racial control, it was not the only one; Jim Crow did not embody all US racism and, therefore, its removal would not signal the end of racism. It was created to protect and reproduce the re-established plantation system of the South, in which 90 per cent of the nation's black people lived. The system depended on controlled (less than free) labour and terror and Jim Crow helped maintain the super-exploitation of a black rural proletariat for the benefit of Southern and northern capitalists. The system served the interests of all dominant financial and industrial capitalists — not merely the Southern white ones (see Alkalimat et al. 1986).

The origins of the dismantling of Jim Crow can be traced back to the recruiting of black labour by Northern industry during the First World War. Despite the opposition of Southern political and economic élites, the imperatives of Northern capital proved too powerful to be resisted. This led to increased mechanization of Southern agriculture, which was further encouraged by the New Deal, AAA and other programmes which began the process of creating a capital- rather than a labour-intensive system of agriculture. This had the consequence of lessening the region's dependence on black labour and, therefore, its need to keep black people out of the national labour market and, thus, ultimately its need of Jim Crow itself. This is not to say, however, that there was not a strong determination on the part of large numbers of whites (or even of a majority of them) to maintain the system of petty apartheid. It is, however, to say that for the dominant section of large-scale Southern agriculture, Jim Crow was no longer necessary for its hegemony.

The South was also changing in terms of the mix of industry and agriculture. The Federal government played a crucial role during and after the Second World War in encouraging the industrialization of the South and Southwest. This process increased the political and economic importance of industrialists (including Northern based ones) in determining the future direction of the region. This dependence on outside capital provided a very important counter-pressure against Southern opponents of civil rights.

The experience of Northern industrialists throughout the

20th century — but particularly since the First World War — proved to them that *de jure* segregation was unnecessary. When black labour was recruited for jobs in Chicago, Detroit, Pittsburgh and other industrial centres, it entered communities in which *de jure* segregation was not the norm and in which it was not created. Instead, institutional racism was created to contain and control black people, to facilitate their super-exploitation, to ration scarce resources so that the unequal system which had produced that scarcity in the first place could be maintained, and to separate white and black workers. It was, therefore, clear to industrialists that, however desirable, Jim Crow was unnecessary. Therefore, in a highly charged political atmosphere in which Jim Crow acted as the target, or lightening rod, of all black anger and political mobilization, it was no longer clear that agribusiness and industrial leaders could, in the face of escalating disorder and instability, be counted on as steadfast allies of those determined to maintain Jim Crow.

As indicated earlier, black people were struggling in the years prior to the emergence of the CRM. In the post-First World War period Marcus Garvey's UNIA (Universal Negro Improvement Association) became the largest mass movement of blacks in US history. The UNIA represented the nationalist strand of black struggle and its appeal is indicative of the massive anger against white racism felt by African-Americans (Hill and Bair 1987; Vincent 1971). During the late 1920s and 1930s the Communist Party gave high priority to working with blacks and, though it never obtained great numbers of black members, it did put the concept of the links between race and class on the political agenda. It also was the most important white-led organization to challenge white racism — particularly in an era of unchallenged white supremacy. In 1945, Representative Adam Clayton Powell Jr said, 'There is no group in America, including the Christian Church, that practices racial brotherhood one-tenth as much as the Communist Party' (Marable 1986: 171; see also Naison 1983). The relationship between the CPUSA (Communist Party of the United States of America) and blacks, between race and class, was to be of growing importance and was a central target of the efforts of the US government and of white liberals and middle class black leaders.

Questions of who the leaders are and of who determines priorities are crucial to any discussion of black politics, as they are to the politics of any group. In his overview of black American politics, Manning Marable (1985: 172-3) argues that:

> The central fact about black political culture from 1865 to 1985 is that only a small segment of the Afro-American social fraction, the petty bourgeoisie, has dominated the electoral machinery and patronage positions that regulate black life and perpetuate the exploitation of black labour. The buffer stratum has historically focused its energies on non-economic issues, such as the abolition of legal segregation; and when it has developed explicitly economic agendas, more frequently than not it presumes the hegemony of capital over labour. Even during periods of black working-class insurgency within electoral politics, the Negro petty bourgeoisie tend to surface on the crest of such movements.

The system of white supremacy that had been created with the defeat of the First Reconstruction involved the shaping of the black community's leadership structures. As Bloom (1987: 120) has written:

> White power was able to reach into the black community itself and to shape it, to help determine the goals the black community sought, the means desired to seek these goals, the leadership the black community had, the kinds of personal options blacks often felt they had, and even the view that blacks had of themselves. As a result of the victory of white supremacy, blacks had few options. They were not in a position to confront the white-created social, political, and economic world in order to change its terms; rather, they had to find a way to survive in it, to adjust to it. Accomodation meant looking to powerful whites as benefactors, requesting 'favours,' accepting paternalism and subordination. It meant that whites determined the black community's leaders by deciding with whom they would communicate and to whom they would grant their 'largesse.'

Bloom (1987: 218) goes on to argue that, as a consequence,

> the dynamics of the old system had divided blacks along class lines. The divisions in the old system had a weak objective basis. Those considered of higher social rank often had a tenuous hold on their status. That was all the more reason for their subjective insistence upon an exaggerated social distance separating them from poorer and (in their view) less cultured blacks.

Emphasis on economic issues, especially for a socialist position, represented a threat to the interests of this petit bourgeois stratum. It challenged its class interests and the acceptability of its leaders — acceptable, that is, to the white power structure. It is interesting and important to note that W.E.B. DuBois represented just such a threat and thus was removed twice from leadership in the National Association for the Advancement of Colored People (NAACP). His writings were apt and very prescient. During the Depression he 'urged the NAACP to develop a meaningful economic programme to assist African-Americans. In May 1932, the Crisis reported that the "first job" of the Association was "to fight color discrimination" but it also stated that "our fight for economic equality" must include economic cooperation and "socialization of wealth".' (Marable 1986: 193.) He went on to declare (ibid.: 140) that the NAACP had to devise 'a positive program rather than mere negative attempts to avoid segregation and discrimination.... The interests of the masses are the interests of this Association, and the masses have got to voice themselves through it.'

This emphasis on economic issues and on the masses having power continued to be stressed by Dr Dubois and continued to be denied by the established leadership. Yet the Second World War brought to the forefront the reality of the mass of black people's anger and sense of alienation from US institutions. The Office of War Information carried out a survey in Harlem in the Spring of 1942 to determine black attitudes towards the war. It concluded (Finkle 1973/4: 701) that, 'resentment at Negro discrimination [was] fairly widespread throughout the Negro population.' Only 11 per cent said they expected conditions to improve if America won the war. Lee Finkle quotes Ollie Stewart, a reporter who had visited many army camps, reporting that 'black soldiers were ready to start the fight at home before the European war ended. He said that with some encouragement and ammunition they would head for Washington to end discrimination.' He also quotes Joel A. Rogers (ibid.: 707-8) reporting a letter from a hostile reader complaining about 'so-called intelligent race leaders... yapping all out for victory. I ask what victory? The white man feeds his jive to the race leaders and they take up the yapping and feed it to the ignorant masses.... Each week when I read how the whites do the race it cements me against them and their war.' George Schuyler reported, 'the masses of Negroes are far more ready to fight and die than their leaders and spokesmen' (i.e. for their rights at home rather than for the US abroad). E. Washington Rhodes of the *Philadelphia Tribune* reported (ibid.: 696), 'the mass of Negroes is more radical than... those of us who publish Negro newspapers. The less vocal Negro... is thinking more radical thoughts than we are thinking.'

These concerns were central to Gunnar Myrdal's *An American Dilemma* (1962), a classic liberal statement on race relations, in which he lays out the liberal agenda for the post-war period, including a clear statement on the underlying assumptions of that agenda. Themes running through this statement include the need for white Americans to re-evaluate race relations; the need to contain black militancy; and the international implications of American race relations. He makes clear that reforms are a necessary consequence of the growing black militancy. As he put it (Myrdal 1962: 1004), 'America can never more regard its Negroes as a patient, submissive minority.' He was also at pains to stress that Negroes in America could count on the 'glorious American ideals of democracy, liberty, and equality' and the adherence to these ideals by white Americans. Therefore, 'the Negroes do not need any other allies' (ibid.). Presumably included among those allies they did not need was the Communist Party. Given that it was *An American Dilemma* and would be solved by white Americans being true to the *American Creed*, blacks would not need Pan-Africanism either.

Myrdal (1962: 1006-7) then elaborates on the new mood among the Negroes:

> Reading the Negro press and hearing all the reports from observers who have been out among common Negroes in the South and the North convinces me that there is much sullen scepticism, and even cynicism, and vague, tired, angry dissatisfaction among American Negroes today. The general bitterness is reflected in the stories that are circulating in the Negro communities: A young Negro, about to [be] inducted into the Army, said 'Just carve on my tombstone, Here lies a black man killed fighting a yellow man for the protection of a white man'. Another Negro boy expressed the same feeling when he said he was going to get his eyes slanted to that the next time a white man shoved him around he could fight back.... There is more money in circulation and some trickles down to the Negroes. With a little money in his pocket even the poor Negro day labourer or domestic worker feels that he can afford to stiffen himself. Many white housewives notice strange thoughts and behaviour on the part of their Negro servants these days.

He quotes the 'troubled view' of a Negro clergyman, Dr J.S. Nathaniel Tross: 'I am afraid for my people. They have grown restless. They are not happy. They no longer laugh. There is a new policy among them — something strange, perhaps terrible (ibid.: 1013). The international implications are clearly stated by Myrdal, who is worth quoting at length again:

> What has actually happened within the last few years is not only that the Negro problem has become national in scope after having been mainly a Southern worry. [The language is interesting: who has the problem and whose worry? It is also misleading in that it was always national in the obvious sense that blacks were American citizens denied their constitutional rights — with the acquiescence of the national government — and in the interests of the national economic system.] It has also acquired tremendous international implications, and this is another and decisive reason why the white North is prevented from compromising with the white South regarding the Negro. The situation is actually such that any and all concessions to Negro rights in this phase of the history of the world will repay the nation many times, while any and all injustices inflicted upon him will be extremely costly. (ibid.: 1015)

> The main international implication is... that America, for its international prestige, power, and future security, needs to demonstrate to the world that American Negroes can be satisfactorily integrated into democracy.... The treatment of the Negro in America has not made good propaganda for America abroad and particularly not among coloured nations. (ibid.: 1016)

And crucially in Myrdal's felicitous phrase:

> Particularly as Russia cannot be reckoned on to adhere to white supremacy, it is evident from the facts... that within a short period the shrinking minority of white people in our Western lands will either have to succumb or to find ways of living on peaceful terms with coloured people. (ibid.: 1018)

Thus, the stage was set. Fundamental economic and demographic forces had lessened the centrality of *de jure* segregation for the leaders of the New South. Blacks had become more urban and more Northern and, consequently, more important in terms of electoral politics and were, at the same time, being seen as potentially dangerous or possibly disloyal in future wars — particularly against coloured nations. The threat of renewed links between blacks and the CP red was worrying. Centrally for the politics of post-war America, Pax Americana was replacing Pax Britannica and this was to have race implications within the US. And crucially Southern blacks were increasingly prepared to resist racist intimidation and the domination of the white power structure and their own accommodationist leaders. The dynamics of growing willingness to fight, the delegitimation of *de jure* segregation by the Supreme Court and other institutions, the rejection of leaders who refused to oppose segregation *per se* as opposed to negotiating marginal variations or concessions in its operation, the white Southern resistance to the Brown decision, and the determination to obtain freedom and equality led to what Jack Bloom has called, after the example of blacks in Harlem in the 1920s, the New Negro. This all took place in a world being reshaped by the development of television, ensuring regional, national, and worldwide coverage of the resistance, which in turn ensured that the uprisings of the post-Montgomery period — unlike those of the earlier period — became part of the public consciousness of blacks, North and South, of whites throughout the US and of people throughout the world.

The black led coalition which reshaped Southern society included, in Bloom's analysis (1987: 5), 'Southern business and middle classes, the Northern middle class, the national Democratic Party, and the federal government.' This coalition 'was the key to the victory of the civil rights movement.' The nature of this coalition was also the key to the limits of what the CRM could achieve. The essence of black politics was the understanding of the different goals of the various components of the coalition and of how to play one sector of the Southern élites off against the other and of how to put pressure on the various Northern components to act. The strategy was effective as long as the CRM's demands for freedom and equality were contained within the parameters of the dominant ideology, i.e. freedom from segregation and overt discrimination and equality of opportunity. These were the limits of the dominant ideology and the limits imposed by the structural interests of the white middle and business classes, North and South, of the national Democratic Party and of the federal government. These demands were also congruent with the class interests of the black middle class. When, as a result of the greater involvement of the black masses — in the South in the mass actions of the CRM and in the North in the ghetto uprisings — the meaning of freedom and equality was expanded to include an economic dimension, a demand for structural change, the coalition broke apart.

The range of political forces supporting the status quo are very great. In the case of the status quo of *de jure* segregation these included: the dominant ideology and popular culture of the US which were racist; the effects on the legislative process of the combination of the Seniority system in Congress and the Solid South (the one-party system dominating post-reconstruction Southern politics; racist attitudes among decision makers themselves; and, generally, the weakness of those wanting change in terms of political and economic resources.

Therefore, for the CRM to succeed in overturning a system of legalized segregation a range of pressures had to be brought to bear on decision makers so that these forces could be overcome. Among these forces were, political pressure from Democratic politicians in the urban centres of the North and Mid West (who were becoming increasingly dependent upon the black vote); the moral delegitimation of overt racism as a result of the horrors of Nazism and the moral imperatives of the Second World War (which placed the defenders of Jim Crow and their allies on the defensive); threats to the order and stability of the wider society (particularly after the widening of support for the CRM in the non-South) through sympathetic boycotts and picketing; threats to order in the South, which increasingly came to be seen as putting at risk new investment; and threats to the US position in the world from Soviet use of Jim Crow and later of Bull Connor, Jim Clark and George Wallace.

The removal of Jim Crow, therefore, had to be forced onto the agenda of an unwilling political system. There were forces which operated to limit the changes being made (under duress) to the removal of *de jure* segregation and overt discrimination. Equality of opportunity would require the removal of the latter so that blacks could compete like everyone else. It might represent a threat to particular whites or to particular institutions in terms of their current practices, but the wider imperatives of the system would work through these problems — as in the range of measures which had been taken and which involved limitations in the absolute rights of property for the greater good. Factory safety, social security and child labour laws had all been opposed as interferences with freedom, but, in the face of greater threats, threats of more fundamental demands and radicalization, concessions had been made. It is important to note that these concessions, as the ones made in response to the demands of black people and their allies, were limited, did not involve fundamental shifts in the distribution of wealth or power and would be secure only to the extent that the forces which extracted the concessions remained strong.

If we now look in detail at how these forces and processes were played out we can see the salience of Myrdal's international agenda in forming the liberal agenda within which the CRM developed and was shaped. The final report of President Truman's Committee on Civil Rights defined 'moral' and 'economic' reasons for ending discrimination and then defined the 'international' reasons (quoted in Zinn 1980: 440):

> Our position in the post-war world is so vital to the future that our smallest actions have far-reaching effects.... We cannot escape the fact that our civil rights record has been an issue in world politics. The world's press and radios are full of it.... Those with competing philosophies have stressed — and are shamelessly distorting — our shortcomings.... They have tried to prove our democracy an empty fraud, and our nation a consistent oppressor of under-privileged people. This may seem ludicrous to Americans [which Americans? Presumably Afro-Americans, Native Americans, Asian-Americans, Latino-Americans do now count] but it is sufficiently important to worry our friends. The United States is not so strong, the final triumph of the democratic ideal is not so inevitable that we can ignore what the world thinks of us or our record.

The centrality of the cold war and of anti-communism is crucial to our understanding of post-war US society and institutions. The cold war provided the framework for the creation of a 'permanent wartime economy' — as had been called for by Charles E. Wilson, President of General Electric in 1944 — and for the opening up of the markets and economies of the 'free world' for US exports and investment — as Dean Acheson had declared was necessary if the US were not to return to depression after the war (see Gardner 1976; Kolko 1968; Williams 1972). The use by the Soviets and by nationalists in Third World countries of US apartheid to challenge US claims to leadership of the democratic, free world had to be limited. The records of the Truman, Eisenhower and Kennedy administrations, for example, are full of indications of how sensitive was the US government. These concerns worked their way through into the decisions of the executive branch of the federal government and were instrumental in the Supreme Court's landmark decision in the Brown case, as in many others.

The international benefits to the US of removing petty apartheid would be reinforced by anti-Communist benefits at home for the federal government. Since the Communists were supposedly concerned to exploit Jim Crow for their own purposes of destabilizing US society, the removal of Jim Crow would presumably end that threat. Despite the limited membership of blacks in the CPUSA, it is clear that decision makers were conscious of the danger, in their terms, of black-white unity around class issues which a black-red alliance represented and, therefore, were determined to combine repression of the left with their anti-Jim Crow policies.

The anti-Communist hegemony, which was established, shaped the debate on black rights — as it did all other debates. The determination to prevent the linking of black and red was central — so central that the FBI and other agencies used as prima facie evidence of probable disloyalty the fact that a white person had black friends or invited black people for a meal. The purges of the Communists, fellow travellers, 'comsymps' and others unable to prove their loyalty became the dominant feature of life in the US. Most individuals and organizations succumbed and often tried to use the terms of the anti-Communist hysteria for their own purposes. In his book on W.E.B. DuBois, Gerald Horne (1986), reports that, after the firing of Dr DuBois, the NAACP 'strongly implied that those Euro-Americans most opposed to Jim Crow and racism were Communists and should be carefully watched in the branches.'

Naturally this heavy-handed approach caused a wail of protest and was 'corrected' in a subsequent editorial. But this episode was indicative of how far anti-Communism had gone, for apparently there was sentiment for routing out white members of the Association (who often were influential and sizable financial contributors) in a spurious anti-Communist crusade (Horne 1986: 64).

So central was anti-Communism that people in every walk of life identified as Communists were purged from public life. In this context Paul Robeson's prominence as a fighter for black rights in the US and for the freedom of the colonized peoples, his openly leftist position on questions about the political economy and his opposition to the cold war, marked him out as a prime target. The US government took away his passport so that he could not travel abroad. This was accompanied by a massive propaganda campaign to label him a subversive, a false prophet who was misleading his people. The House Un-American Activities Committee (HUAC) and other committees not only regularly called him to testify but also had a succession of prominent Negroes appear before them to attack him. It was said at the time that a condition for employment for black actors (for what little work was available for blacks in Hollywood) was that they had to attack Paul Robeson publicly. This campaign succeeded in denying Paul Robeson work in the US — threats of economic and/or physical retaliation were sufficient to prevent venues being made available to him.

The intimidation increased and there was violence against him and those who came to hear him sing. Listening to and applauding his songs were considered proof of being a Communist, at least by Adolph Menjou's testimony before the HUAC. The pressure to turn Robeson into a non-person continued unabated. Gerald Horne recounts (1986: 208) what happened when Dr DuBois received a copy of Langston Hughes's book, *Famous Negro Music Makers*, and discovered that Paul Robeson had been totally excluded. DuBois wrote to the publisher and received a 'remarkably candid' reply from Edward H. Dodd Jr, president of Dodd, Mead & Company: '[Hughes] was told by experts of his acquaintance and probably also told by our library advisers that the inclusion of Robeson would probably eliminate the book from acceptance by a good many school libraries, state adoption lists, etc.' (See Robeson Jr 1971: 24-5 for a discussion of the processes involved in books about the theatre.)

Other examples of the creation of a non-person in a democracy are provided by his son, Paul Robeson Jr, who quotes contemporary experts rating his father as one of the greatest football players of all time. He goes on (Robeson Jr 1971: 23) to declare that:

> In spite of these credentials, my father is the only two-time Walter Camp All-American who is not in the College Football Hall of Fame. Not only that, the Hall of Fame is located at Rutgers, and Paul Robeson was the first Rutgers player to win All-American honours. It is also a fact that the book *College Football*, published in 1950 by Murray & Co. and labelled 'the most complete record compiled on college football,' listed a ten-man All-America team for 1918, the only ten-man team in All-America history. The missing man was an end named Paul Robeson.

The NAACP supported US foreign policy and tried to use that support as a way of obtaining federal government backing for its anti-discrimination agenda. The following statement to rank and file members by Alfred Baker, an NAACP board

member, is an example of this approach: 'If there is... a group
interested in the discussion of foreign policy, they might take a
speaker on the bad effect of racial discrimination on our foreign
relations... [they] should be able to answer questions about... our
exclusion of Communists and our support of anti-Communist
foreign policy measures' (Horne 1986: 280). Horne's conclusion
is that 'the NAACP was trying to run with the hares and hunt
with the hounds; attempting to tweak Uncle Sam, they
hammered on the hypocrisy of foreign policy when it came to
race while eagerly supporting the glue that held the policy
together — anti-Communism' (ibid.).

This anti-Communist campaign involved political élites on
the national and local scene (governmental and non-govern-
mental officials alike) and had an anti-union, anti-welfare state,
pro-cold war, pro-military-industrial complex agenda. Racism
was always part of this campaign — either up front or *sub rosa*.
The consequences included the retarding and weakening of
black struggles for structural change, as well as channelling
struggles into an anti-Jim Crow, anti-*de jure* segregation mode —
and thus retarding the wider struggle for black rights and, even,
as we shall see, distorting and retarding the limited, legitimate
campaign. Victor Bernstein, writing prophetically in 1943 (337-
8), argued that:

> Since the Wagner Act made open union-busting illegal, race-baiting
> has become almost the chief weapon of the anti-labour storm
> troops. Certainly this is true in the South where the union man,
> himself torn by prejudice, is inclined to fall easy prey to the anti-
> Negro mouthings of demagogues like [Eugene] Talmadge and
> ['Pappy'] O'Daniel... and professional hate promoters like Vance
> Muste, who once described the non-existent Eleanor Clubs as a 'Red
> Radical scheme to organize Negro maids, cooks, and nurses in order
> to have a Communist informer in every Southern home.

This link between black rights and Bolshevism has a long
history in the US. President Truman's secretary of state, James F.
Byrnes had an equally long history of mouthing such hysteria
and hate. In a speech on the floor of the House of Representatives in 1919 (Congressional Record, 66th Congress, 1st Session,
Volume 58, Part V, 25 August-September 1919, 4303-5. Quoted
in Clark 1976: 9), he attacked the *Messenger*, the socialist newspaper published by A. Philip Randolph and Chandler Owen, in
the following terms:

The material in the magazine would indicate that the source from which the support comes is antagonistic to the Government of the United States. It appeals for the establishment in this country of a Soviet Government.... It urges the negro to join the IWW's [*sic*], pays tribute to Eugene Debs and every other convicted enemy of the Government, and prays for the establishment of a Bolshevik Government in this land. It is evident that the IWEW's [*sic*] are financing it in an effort to have the negro of America join them in their revolutionary plans.

This anti-red, anti-black rhetoric was used by capitalists in their attempts to divide black and white workers and to destroy industrial unionism. Victor Bernstein gives a number of examples of this in the campaign by Humble Oil, a Standard Oil subsidiary in Beaumont, Texas in 1943 against the Oil Workers International (CIO) organizing drive. He (Bernstein 1943: 330) quotes from two issues of the company union's publication (*Baytown Employees Federation Bulletin*, nos. 72 and 9 respectively):

The CIO is openly committed to a policy of complete elevation of the Negro to absolute social and economic equality with the white.... They want political power, and to have this power, they must have votes... and a coloured vote unrestricted and unrestrained represents the greatest single block of solid voting power in America.... That is why they promise [the Negroes] white men's jobs, white men's houses and complete social equality with the white race on and off the job.

The CIO has come into our Southern State of Texas brandishing the torch of racial hatred, seeking to tear down the hundreds of years of good feeling and understanding which has always existed here between white and coloured races. The place to check them is here and now. Tomorrow may be too late.

There is widespread agreement among those who have looked at these developments that, in the words of Wayne Clark (1976: 87), 'race relations in the 1950s and early 1960s were shaped to a great extent by the pronouncements of those individual members of the political élite who assumed responsibility not only for preserving white supremacy but also for awakening the nation to what they considered the inherent dangers of international communism.'

Don Carleton (1985: 72), writing about Houston, found a similar pattern:

After World War II, Houston's establishment began to perceive a threat to its wealth and power from the growing labour movement in Texas and an ever-expanding Federal government. Houston's leaders faced a federal government they believed to be controlled by Socialists and left-wingers. They saw Washington attempting to make further incursions into sacred areas such as the oil-depletion allowance, labour relations, corporate tax reform, medicine, education and race relations.

They used the red scare to achieve ideological, political and economic hegemony. On the national scale this process was being encouraged and orchestrated by the Chamber of Commerce. Leslie Adler (1970: 94-5) writes that:

> Recovering from a serious decline in status, wealth and power suffered during the depression decade, business leaders were clearly making an all-out effort at the war's end to regain control over the domestic sector of the economy and to reorient national priorities away from social reform and toward the business foundation they believed to be central to the American way of life. Efforts to curb newly-established labour union power were high on their own list of priorities, and given the longstanding link in business thinking between unionism and communism, it would seem natural that the communists-in-unions theme would appeal to businessmen.

Adler (1970: 97) then discusses how they accomplished their goals:

> Seeing themselves in the position to bring a great deal of influence and pressure to bear on American thinking, members of the Committee on Socialism and Communism did not take their self-appointed task lightly, and set about to research those who could best shape public opinion. 'Authorities who have studied this type of problem carefully,' [Emerson P.] Schmidt wrote to Committee members in early 1946, 'are convinced that approximately 8,000 American people are the genuine creators of public opinion — the rest merely follow. If we can reach a goodly portion of these 8,000 with such a brochure, its influence will automatically tend to spread into the lives and homes of most of the people.' Careful planning such as this and a thorough knowledge of how to appeal to the American public marked the entire Chamber of Commerce crusade.

Along with the related activities of HUAC (see Caute 1978; Goodman 1969; Pomerantz 1963), this campaign led the Senate Internal Affairs Committee; President Truman's Loyalty Security Programme, the attorney general's List of Subversive Organizations and the activities of the FBI and state and local 'red squads' succeeded in purging those who disagreed with the dominant ideology (see, for example, Freeland 1971; Griffith and Theoharis 1974). Clark (1976: 197-8) concludes that:

There is little doubt that resistance activities hindered the organizing efforts of the labour movement and protracted the civil rights struggle in the Deep South. The white leadership understood that picket lines, boycotts, marches, and other forms of organized protest could be used to fight segregation before these methods were actively used by civil rights activists. They instinctively associated those tactics with communists, labour militants, and agitators for integration. As a result, public opinion was strongly united against protest methods, particularly those involving direct action. The cold war consensus contributed to this climate of hostility towards groups and individuals who exerted pressure for social change. It facilitated the development by anti-union and segregationist forces of a resistance to racial integration that was based, in part, on the knowledge that segregation was as effective in maintaining class barriers as it was in sustaining the colour line between whites and blacks.

In the South this campaign had the effect of thwarting unionization and struggles for the tenant farmers. In his study of Southern radicalism in the 1929-59 period, Anthony Dunbar (1981: 256) wrote that:

Though Southern plantations were still inhabited by poorly paid, educated, and housed workers, there were few fresh attempts to rekindle the union spirit of the 1930s. One of the reasons, of course, was the history of failure. But another was that there was no longer a Socialist party or a coherent progressive community willing to underwrite the cost of pressing the one demand that had traditionally rallied Southern farm workers: 'land for the landless.'

The purge of leftists from CIO unions and of leftist unions from the CIO had particularly deleterious consequences for blacks. Sumner Rosen (1969: 199-200) argues that, 'to the extent that the unions expelled had been the more militant and devoted advocates of racial justice, the cause itself lost much of its meaning and appeal.' Boyer and Morais (1965: 361) write that:

The expelled unions were the soul of the CIO.... It was those unions that had fought the hardest for Negro representation in trade union office. It was they that had led the fight for equal pay for equal work for women and it was they that had fought for the rights of such minorities as Puerto Ricans and Mexican miners. And what organization had been accomplished in the South had been done mostly by them.

The consequences were starkly summarised by Charles W. Cheng (1973: 195):

> the drive to organize the unorganized in the South never fully materialized. Certainly a concerted effort by either the CIO or AFL would have increased the number of blacks in the labour movement. Instead, black workers in particular and large numbers of white workers, in general, continued to be economically exploited. The wall of white supremacy gained a new lease on life, and this wall would not be massively confronted until the 1960s. In any case, it seems probable that the expulsions, and thus the fragmentation of labour, were in part responsible for the failure of labour to organize in the South.

These purges, including those in Hollywood and in academic institutions at every level and in every area of the United States, reinforced the ideological hegemony of corporate America. In an interesting discussion of the issues dealt with (or avoided) by Hollywood in this period, Leslie Adler (1970: 427-8) has written:

> Though the changing composition of Hollywood films after 1947 cannot be attributed entirely to the impact of HUAC, a basic change did occur which oriented the industry further away from dealing with serious social themes and which seems clearly related to the investigations. The 1945-1947 period had seen an increase in the film treatment of such themes, and as calculated by Dorothy B. Jones, approximately 28 per cent of the films in 1947 were of a serious social bent. From 1947-1949, however, the trend was reversed, with only approximately 18 per cent of the films in 1949 qualifying. An even sharper break occurred from 1950-1952 with an upswing in war films, pure entertainment films, escapist films, and a larger number of anti-Communist films. In 1950 only 11 per cent dealt with social questions and by 1953 that figure was further reduced to 9 per cent.

J. Fred MacDonald (1985: 11, 12), discussing similar developments in the newly emerging medium of television, reports:

> The broadcast industry readily fell in with the government purgists. Entertainers adversely touched by the [HUAC] hearings found themselves blacklisted from radio and, more important, the burgeoning new medium, television. It made little difference to broadcasters if, in the jargon of the day, these political deviates were 'card-carrying members' (actual dues-paying members of the CPUSA), 'dupes' (those fooled into supporting Red goals without

realizing the error of their ways), 'Pinkos' (those who were leftists, but not Red enough), or 'comsymps' or 'fellow travellers' (those who sympathized with Communist ends without joining the party). The CPUSA was considered to be an arm of the Soviet Union, not a legitimate political party springing from the fabric of American society. Those said to be associated with Communism, then, were considered anti-American conspirators. They were unwelcome in broadcasting. In this way the entertainment business became a political arena in which cold war fears and ignorance became the basis for exclusionary professional policy. This was to be expected in a business that had been heavily politicized during the war.... In news and entertainment programmes television presented Americans a picture of world affairs in which the honest, selfless United States was forced to defend the Free World against the barbarous onslaught of Communism — with its godless ideologues and automaton commissars intent upon conquering the planet. Those not wholeheartedly in favour of the national crusade were often suspected of being at least tolerant of the evil empire. It was an over-simplified picture. But in the context of the United States at mid-century, it was widely perceived as genuine.

The Truman administration fully supported the development of this ideological strait-jacket and gave its highest priority to the pursuance of the cold war and the creation of the national security state. Its tactical support for civil rights was always a lower priority, despite the periodic rhetorical emphasis on equal rights. Symbolic appointments and policy statements, combined with a limited number of executive actions (forced by pressure from blacks and from the foreign policy pressures of the cold war) were the major aspects of the administration's practices. The red-baiting and purges, as has been discussed, actually adversely affected the struggle for black rights.

That struggle escalated in the 1950s, particularly after the Brown decision. What should have been the crowning glory of the NAACP's élite dominated strategy of litigation and lobbying, in practice turned out to be the beginning of a new phase of black struggle. The reason for this apparent contradiction is that the Court in Brown II — its implementation decision — developed the unique concept of black children being granted their constitutional rights 'with all deliberate speed' and with the onus on black parents throughout the South having to go to court to obtain desegregation. Not surprisingly, this provided valuable breathing space for Southern racists determined to resist integration — especially as the president, Dwight D.

Eisenhower, never supported the moral imperative of the decision and did not throw the weight of his tremendous popularity into the fray on behalf of the constitutional rights of black people.

Following the massive resistance to the Brown decision there was a growing disillusionment among blacks with the NAACP strategy and a receptivity to new forms of struggle. This disillusionment must be seen as being directed primarily at the NAACP on the national level. Local chapters and leaders were often in the vanguard of struggle, were subjected to local government and State repression, and often cooperated with other more activist groups. The most famous example of this new strategy developed in Montgomery, Alabama in 1955 when the black community carried out a year-long boycott of the bus company. This strategy of non-violent direct action became associated with the teachings of Dr Martin Luther King Jr and the Southern Christian Leadership Conference (SCLC), which emerged out of the Montgomery struggle and related struggles throughout the South. Dr King and non-violent direct action held centre stage for more than a decade. Following student sit-ins in 1960 and the formation of the Student Non-Violent Co-ordinating Committee (SNCC), there was mass mobilization of Southern blacks and mobilization of Northern support, among blacks and whites (Carson 1981).

These struggles received the attention of the print and visual media of the world, as they were intended to do. The strategy required the intervention of the federal government in all its forms, but to overcome the power of the Southern Committee Chairs in Congress, the lack of interest on the part of the FBI and other governmental agencies, and the electoral interests of Kennedy, countervailing pressures had to be brought. For example, the pressures on President Kennedy as a result of the Birmingham, Alabama campaign were dramatic. Carl Brauer (quoted in Horne 1986: 278-9) writes that:

> The Birmingham crisis touched another sensitive Kennedy nerve when it attracted a great deal of publicity abroad.... In several countries, particularly in Ghana and Nigeria, the media poured out caustic denunciation of the racial outrage. Radio Moscow, after a hesitant beginning, was currently diverting a quarter of its output to Birmingham, much of it beamed to African audiences. Given Kennedy's expansionist view of his country's role in the world, the damage Birmingham had done to America's image undoubtedly

concerned him.

This strategy clearly worked in terms of forcing President Kennedy to introduce civil rights legislation. He told civil rights leaders that, 'the demonstrations in the streets had brought results, they had made the executive branch act faster and were now forcing Congress to entertain legislation which a few weeks before would have had no chance' (Marable 1985: 90). The problem black people and others would face in the years following these victories, was what would happen when the protestors' demands touched on structural racism and the bases of inequality in the US political economy?

There were, however, important differences within the black community about both strategies and goals. The major (moderate) establishment groups defined the problem as that of blacks being excluded from an otherwise fair, just and democratic system — much like the later bourgeois, mainstream feminists. The solution was to allow blacks (or women) into that system on the same bases of competition and individualism as was presumed to be the norm in the US meritocratic system. These groups either supported US foreign policy or did not comment on it — an implicit recognition that the limits of assimilation, integration for blacks, meant that blacks could speak on race questions but not on foreign policy or other fundamental questions of the political economy. The radical black groups challenged these positions across the board. They did not accept the view that, apart from the exclusion of black people (or women in the case of the socialist feminists), the US was a fair, just and democratic society. Instead, they argued that the political economy was a highly unequal, unjust system, not just for blacks but for all. The solution, therefore, involved not the integration of individual blacks into that competitive system, but more collective responses designed to change the system as a whole. Increasingly these tendencies came to oppose US foreign policy, particularly in Africa and Vietnam. The established groups bitterly attacked these interventions on the grounds that they would put at risk the gains that had been made.

The political repression of Paul Robeson and W.E.B. DuBois — and the collaboration of the NAACP and other moderate groups in the repression — focused very directly on their opposition to US foreign policy. As indicated above, Paul Robeson's passport had been taken away by the State Department. The

government's reasoning is apparent in the following extract of
the US State Department's deposition (Robeson Jr 1971: 28):

> Furthermore even if the complaint had alleged... that the passport
> was cancelled solely because of applicant's recognized status as
> spokesman for large sections of Negro Americans, we submit that
> this would not amount to an abuse of discretion in view of the
> applicant's frank admission that he has been for years extremely
> active politically on behalf of the colonial people of Africa.

If it appears surprising that the government of the US, which
prides itself on being the leader of the free world and an anti-
colonial nation, used as the basis of denying a passport to an
American citizen the fact that he had frankly admitted to having
worked on behalf of the colonial people of Africa, it is because of
the widespread acceptance of US bona fides. It is important,
therefore, to look behind the façade of US beneficence and anti-
colonialism. The *New York Times*, as much an establishment
newspaper as one could wish for, wrote in its editorial on 22
November 1949 that, 'Africa is the continent of the future. We
learned its strategic value in the Second World War. Its
economic potentialities are the hope of Western Europe... as well
as the rest of the world.... The United States need not be afraid of
the label of reactionary if [we] oppose too hasty independence'
(quoted in Horne 1986: 184).

Given the economic importance of Africa and the US
government's acceptance of the advice of *New York Times* leader
writers, it is not surprising to find the US expanding its
economic and political role in Africa and acting as a leading
anti-revolutionary power in conjunction with South Africa and
Israel — propping up an array of corrupt and brutal client
regimes and destabalizing nationalist and socialist governments.
It is also not surprising to find W.E.B. DuBois a target of the US
government alongside Paul Robeson. Dr DuBois had a long
history of support for the 'colonial people of Africa' and for Pan-
Africanism. Manning Marable and Gerald Horne have written
about this aspect of DuBois's politics, which linked Pan-
Africanism, the struggle for black rights and freedom inside the
US to a critique of the reactionary role played by the petit bourgeois leaders of establishment oriented moderate groups. Horne
(1986: 184, 188) writes:

> DuBois and the Council [on African Affairs] were rooting on a hasty
> independence for the continent and the fact that he was both black

and influential was guaranteed to cause tensions. It was important that those of African ancestry in the United States be brought into line in support of US foreign policy, but DuBois and the Council were not cooperative.... The Council was not only sharply critical of the State Department and the United States-based transnational corporations but they also turned their microscope on potential friends and allies. They commended the NAACP for their resolution on colonialism in 1953 but criticized the use of the term 'natives' and the equating of the 'persecution' of Britons in South Africa with blacks; they questioned their lack of forthright support for specific organizations — like the ANC — and United States votes in the United Nations on Africa. A specific reference to East Africa by the Association — 'We view with alarm the terrorist methods of the Mau Mau in Kenya' — was strenuously attacked.

Marable (1986: 198) quotes DuBois saying that 'American Negroes freed of their baseless fear of Communism will again begin to turn their attention and aim their activity toward Africa.' They would soon recognize the role of American capitalism in the exploitation of African people. 'When once the blacks of the United States, the West Indies, and Africa work and think together,' DuBois concluded hopefully (ibid.), 'the future of the black man in the modern world is safe.' DuBois's foreign policy activities were sufficiently threatening to US government and business interests that not only was his passport taken away but he was 'indicted for allegedly serving as an "agent of a foreign principal" in his work with the Peace Information Center in New York.'

The 82-year-old black man was handcuffed, fingerprinted and portrayed in the national media as a common criminal. Before his trial, the *New York Herald Tribune* convicted him in a prominent editorial: 'The DuBois outfit was set up to promote a tricky appeal of Soviet origin, poisonous in its surface innocence which made it appear that a signature against the use of atomic weapons would forthwith insure world peace. It was, in short, an attempt to disarm America and yet ignore every form of Communist aggression' (Marable 1983: 28-9). The charges were dismissed but the government's determination to silence Dr DuBois was clear for all to see.

When Dr King came out in opposition to the war in Vietnam he was subjected to the same vitriol. Henry Darby and Margaret Rowley (1986: 49) studied these responses and have written:

Well-known civil rights leaders and other prominent blacks such as

James Farmer, director of the Congress of Racial Equality; Roy Wilkins of the National Association for the Advancement of Colored People; Ralph Bunche, former United Nations under-secretary; Edward Brooke, senator from Massachusetts; Carl T. Rowan, newspaper columnist; Jackie Robinson, then special assis-tant on Community Affairs to Governor Rockefeller of New York; and some members of SCLC were fearful that King's opposition would result in a loss of support for the civil rights movement.

Charles Cheng (1973: 288) argues that, 'the NAACP's Roy Wilkins adopted the stance that the Vietnam War was not "a proper sphere for public analysis or criticism" at least not by a civil rights organization.'

One of the most fundamental conflicts between the moderate and the radical black organizations was over anti-Communism. As the former had accepted the cold war so had they accepted anti-Communism — both were the price of admission into liberal America. The SNCC from the beginning had refused to accept the hegemony of cold war liberalism, had refused to use the standard anti-Communist disclaimer as a condition for membership and had refused to follow the anti-Communist dictates about which organizations they could work with. This was particularly contentious in the run-up to Mississippi Free-dom Summer in 1964. The SNCC had been working with the left-wing lawyers' association, the National Lawyers Guild (NLG). NLG lawyers had been providing desperately needed legal assistance and representation for the SNCC field workers in the face of massive Southern legal repression. There were few other lawyers available or willing to provide this assistance. The NAACP and other mainstream civil rights groups tried to put pressure on the coordinating committee to break with the Guild and when they failed the Justice Department joined the fray.

James Forman of the SNCC describes how he and two colleagues from the SNCC were called to a meeting with Burke Marshall of the Justice Department 'ostensibly to discuss the situation in the Third Congressional District [in delta Mississippi].... But when it finally took place, the Lawyers Guild seemed to be the main subject on the minds of our hosts.' Describing the contribution of cold war liberal historian and Presidential aide and hagiographer, Arthur Schlesinger Jr, Forman (1972: 382) goes on:

Suddenly he spoke — and when he did, we knew he spoke with the consent of the government officials present and the elder Bingham [Member of the House of Representatives]. 'There are many of us who have spent years fighting the communists,' he said as if he had made this speech many times. 'We worked hard during the thirties and the forties fighting forces such as the National Lawyers Guild. We find it unpardonable that you would work with them,' he concluded.'... What blindness and arrogance, I thought. He knew nothing about the reality of our struggle in the South.

Forman (1972: 383-4) describes the fundamental re-evaluations that were taking place within the SNCC which were to lead to increasingly open challenges to the dominant ideology.

By the end of the summer, it was firmly established in the minds of the sisters and brothers that SNCC was like an underdeveloped nation, struggling for its own self-determination. We would take help from anyone, always insisting that no one who gave us help had the right to dictate our policies. We knew only too well that there were people who wanted us to 'fight Communism', to engage in their factional struggles. Whitney Young [of the NAACP] was not the first nor would Arthur Schlesinger be the last. These forces would continue to attack us, claiming that by allowing the guild to participate in the Summer Project, SNCC was destroying years of hard work — years of Red baiting, they should have said, and years of character assassination.... Therefore what SNCC had done was crucial. In effect, SNCC was breaking through the circle of fear that had been imposed on people by McCarthyism and which still lingered on. It deserves infinite praise, I believe, for its attitude on freedom of association, because SNCC fought not only for its own friends, but for the civil liberties of all.

This process of challenging the anti-Communist hegemony continued with the SNCC challenging Dr King's decision to fire Jack O'Dell from the SCLC because of pressure from the FBI and Kennedy administration over O'Dell's communist associations. Stokely Carmichael demanded that King and other established civil rights leaders 'stop taking a defensive stand on communism' (Marable 1983: 75).

The challenge the SNCC presented to the status quo was reflected in the pressures Forman described above and in the conflicts between it and the other components of the CRM (see Carson 1981). These were apparent over which priorities the movement should establish, over the seating of the Mississippi Freedom Democratic Party at the Democratic National Convention in Atlantic City in 1964 and in terms of the relationship

between black organizations and liberal and labour organizations and in terms of whether civil rights organizations should
be all-black, which then would form alliances with anti-racist
whites. These divisions were heightened by the nature of the
1963 March of Washington (see discussion below), by the urban
uprisings which raged through the US from the Summer of 1964
through 1968, and by differences over foreign policy (as
discussed above). In these disputes over the direction and priorities of black struggle, access to and control of resources was an
important variable affecting the outcomes of the conflicts.
Herbert Haines made a detailed study of the funding of the
CRM from 1957 to 1970 and found that the total amounts
contributed to the seven groups he studied increased during the
late 1950s and 1960s, and peaked in the late 1960s. He found that
these increases primarily reflected increased funding for the
moderate groups and an injection of new money. His conclusions are worth quoting at length (Haynes 1984: 41-2):

> These findings suggest that positive radical flank effects contributed
> significantly to increases in the outside funding of moderate civil
> rights organizations in the 1960s. The increasing importance of
> corporations, foundations, and the federal government, moreover,
> suggests that a portion of the nation's corporate élite recognized that
> it had a crucial interest in pacifying the black population, particu-
> larly in the volatile cities, and in accommodating certain manage-
> able black demands. It also suggests that many previously
> uninvolved groups were 'enlightened' by the glow of burning cities,
> after years of indifference to non-violent cajoling by the National
> Urban League and the NAACP. Some whites came to realize that
> the integration of blacks into the US mainstream was not such a bad
> idea after all, that it was in their own best interests given the more
> radical alternatives, and that it was something they ought to be
> encouraging with their resources. The prime beneficiaries of such
> changes of heart were the big moderate groups.

The conflict over the nature of the 1963 March on
Washington was indicative of these growing splits. Malcolm X
called it the 'Farce on Washington'. His description was rejected
by liberals in all sections of US society as extremist — though, as
we shall see, it has been validated since then by the writings of
those involved. Malcolm X speaking in Detroit two months after
the March said (quoted in Zinn 1980: 449):

> The Negroes were out there in the streets. They were talking about
> how they were going to march on Washington.... That they were

going to march on Washington, march on the Senate, march on the White House, march on the Congress, and tie it up, bring it to a halt, not let the government proceed. They even said they were going out to the airport and lay down on the runway and not let any airplanes land. I'm telling you what they said. That was revolution. That was revolution. That was the black revolution. It was the grass roots out there in the street. It scared the white man to death, scared the white power structure in Washington DC to death; I was there. When they found out that this black steam-roller was going to come down on the capital, they called in... these national Negro leaders that you respect and told them, 'Call it off,' Kennedy said. 'Look you all are letting this thing go too far.' And Old Tom said, 'Boss, I can't stop it because I didn't start it.' I'm telling you what they said. They said, 'I'm not even in it, much less at the head of it.' They said, 'These Negroes are doing things on their own. They're running ahead of us.' And that old shrewd fox, he said, 'If you all aren't in it, I'll put you in it. I'll put you at head of it. I'll endorse it. I'll welcome it. I'll help it. I'll join it.' This is what they did with the march on Washington. They joined it... became part of it, took it over. And as they took it over, it lost its militancy. It ceased to be angry, it ceased to be hot, it ceased to be uncompromising. Why, it even ceased to be a march. It became a picnic, a circus. Nothing but a circus, with clowns and all.... No, it was a sell out. It was a takeover.... They controlled it so tight, they told those Negroes what time to hit town, where to stop, what signs to carry, what song to sing, what speech they could make, and what speech they couldn't make, and then told them to get out of town by sundown.

In his glorified history of Kennedy's thousand days, Arthur Schlesinger Jr wrote (ibid.: 450): 'The conference with the President did persuade the civil rights leaders that they should not lay siege to Capital Hill.... So in 1963 Kennedy moved to incorporate the Negro revolution into the democratic coalition.'

Manning Marable's analysis (1985: 90-1) of the politics of the 1963 march also supports Malcolm X's contemporary analysis:

Months before Kennedy announced his decision to obtain a new civil rights act, however, [A. Philip] Randolph proposed organizing a second March on Washington DC, both as a means of dramatizing the campaign for desegregation and as a method by which to place 'additional pressure on the Kennedy administration to support equal employment legislation.'... The response within the civil rights front was at best mixed. The CORE's [Congress of Racial Equality'] national steering committee 'eagerly agreed to act as a co-sponsor.' SNCC leaders, particularly chairman John Lewis, and theoretician James Forman, viewed the March as an opportunity to stage demonstrations at the US Justice Department against its abysmal failure to protect civil rights workers' lives. SCLC leaders Clarence Jones and Reverend George Latency projected 'massive, militant, monumental sit-ins on Congress.... We will tie up public transportation by laying our bodies prostrate on runways of airports, across railroad tracks, and in bus depots.' Such rhetoric threw a chill into the NAACP and Urban League bureaucrats. After learning that Kennedy objected to the march, [Roy] Wilkins [of the NAACP] contemptuously dismissed the mobilization before reporters, stating, 'That little baby does not belong to me.' By late June, however, the call for a second march had acquired a life of its own, and it was too late for Randolph, Wilkins or anyone else to cancel.

Marable describes how the moderate leaders worked in conjunction with the Kennedy administration — as Schlesinger has written and Malcolm X stated — and hijacked the march and insured that it would not be confrontational. Randolph, playing the traditional role of the petit bourgeois leader, told Kennedy that blacks were now on the streets and it was 'very likely impossible to get them off. If they are bound to be in the streets in any case, is it not better that they be led by organizations dedicated to civil rights and disciplined by struggle than to leave them to other leaders who care neither about civil rights nor about non-violence?' (ibid.: 92)

Many radicals stayed away from the March — for example, Stokely Carmichael declared that the 'struggle for voting rights in Mississippi was more important than a showy display in Washington' (ibid.). John Lewis attended and prepared a speech which was so threatening in terms of the issues raised that the Catholic archbishop of Washington let it be known that he would boycott the March if it were delivered. After massive pressure, Lewis and Forman redrafted the speech which was still of a different order from the other speeches of the day (ibid.: 95):

> We came here today with a great sense of misgiving.... It is true that we support the administration's Civil Rights Bill in the Congress. We support it with great reservations, however.... In its present form this Bill will not protect the citizens of Danville, Virginia who must live in constant fear of a police state. It will not protect the hundreds and thousands of people who have been arrested upon trumped charges.... It will not help the citizens of Mississippi, of Alabama and Georgia who are qualified to vote but lack a sixth grade education.... We must have legislation that will protect the Mississippi share-cropper who is put off his farm because he dares

to register to vote. We need a bill that will provide for the homeless and starving people of this nation.... My friends, let us not forget that we are involved in a serious social revolution.... Where is our party? Where is the political party that will make it unnecessary to march on Washington? Where is the political party that will make it unnecessary to march in the streets of Birmingham?

The Civil Rights Act of 1964 and the Voting Rights Act of 1965 passed after the assassination of President Kennedy marked the apex of the achievements of the CRM. *De jure* segregation had been swept away and blacks could now enjoy the fruits of their class position — middle class enjoying and the mass going hungry — and could use the ballot box to achieve whatever was possible to achieve. The problems raised by Lewis in his speech, however, remained. The problems faced by blacks in the urban ghettoes, for example, had not been created and were not being maintained by *de jure* segregation. The structures of the political economy have created the ghetto, have determined resource allocations which determine housing, education, health, employment and policing. None of these issues were addressed, or could be addressed, by the civil rights legislation. It was not surprising, therefore, that Northern blacks whose pride had been raised by the CRM's bravery and dignity and whose interests were not being addressed were increasingly angry. The uprising in Harlem in the summer of 1964 began a chain of over 200 uprisings which raged through urban America for the next four years. The consequences of those uprisings were less clear-cut than the legislative victories of the CRM. There were a range of symbolic responses, an increase in welfare rolls, co-optation of activists, and an increase in training, equipping, and intelligence gathering by police forces at every level. What there wasn't was any fundamental change in the social, economic and political conditions which had produced the uprisings (see Kushnick 1981/2).

The achievements of the CRM were real but limited. Spin-off from the movement led to increased and new types of political mobilization in cities such as Chicago. The burden of Jim Crow was removed from the backs of black people in the South. But the class differences in the black community and the commitment to the capitalist economy of the black leadership, and the incorporation of large sections of the black middle class into various levels of the state bureaucracy, continued and increased the isolation of the mass of black people and their needs from the political agenda.

W.E.B. DuBois continued to raise such issues through the 1950s up to his death on the day of the march on Washington in 1963. In 1958 he received an honorary degree at Prague's Charles University and declared that (Horne 1986: 224):

> [During the 1930s] I repudiated the idea that Negroes were in danger of inner-class division based on income and exploitation. Here again, I was wrong. Twenty years later, by 1950, it was clear that the great machine of big business was sweeping not only the mass of white Americans... it had also and quite naturally swept Negroes in the same maelstrom.

In 1953 he had explored 'the economics of racism, he elaborated on the fight involving those fearless enough to go against the prevailing consensus, simultaneously, there was the potential Shangri-La facing those who wished to go along. He predicted the fall of segregation in public accommodation and schools, which would mean blacks 'will be divided into classes even more sharply than now' (ibid.: 225). Marable (1986: 207) argues that:

> In early 1960, Dr DuBois argued that 'class divisions' within Negro communities had so divided blacks 'that they are no longer [one] single body. They are different sets of people with different sets of interests.' At the University of Wisconsin, DuBois indicated that the civil rights movement's strategy of non-violent demonstrations and sit-ins 'does not reach the centre of the problem' confronting blacks. Nearly alone among major civil rights leaders, DuBois urged the proponents of desegregation to chart 'the next step' of their collective struggle. The abolition of Jim Crow meant little if Negroes were unemployed. Blacks must 'insist upon the legal rights which are already theirs, and add to that increasingly a Socialistic form of government, an insistence upon the welfare state.' The demand for civil rights must ultimately check the power 'of those corporations which monopolize wealth.' DuBois now recognized that full equality for Negroes was not possible beneath the capitalist system.

Dr Martin Luther King Jr made a similar progression in his politics. By the time of his murder he had moved not only to open opposition to the war in Vietnam but to a race/class politics. He was organizing a Poor People's March at the time of his death. Fortunately for the US status quo, Dr King, like Malcolm X in 1965, was murdered and, as Paul Robeson, had been turned into a non-person in the cold war period. David Garrow (1981: 214-15) has traced Dr King's trajectory in the following terms:

> By 1967 King was telling the SCLC staff, 'We must recognize that we can't solve our problems now until there is a radical redistribution of economic and political power,' and by early 1968 he had taken the final step to the admission that issues of economic class were more crucial and troublesome and less susceptible to change, than issues of race. 'America,' he remarked to one interviewer, 'is deeply racist and its democracy is flawed both economically and socially.' He added that 'the black revolution is much more than a struggle for the rights of Negroes. It is forcing America to face all its inter-related flaws — racism, poverty, militarism, and materialism. It is exposing evils that are rooted deeply in the whole structure of our society. It reveals systemic rather than superficial flaws and suggests that radical reconstruction of society itself is the real issue to be faced.' ... by early 1968 he publicly was stating, 'We are engaged in the class struggle.' While his emphasis was not purely materialistic, redistribution of economic power was the central requirement. To one audience King stated, 'We're dealing in a sense with class issues, we're dealing with the problem of the gulf between the haves and the have nots.

The position of the mass of black Americans at this time illustrates the validity of these perceptions of Drs DuBois and King. The deteriorating position of the large body of white Americans as capitalism is being restructured at the expense of the working class is further proof of the centrality of class in the US. The failure of the white working class to confront success-fully the systemic causes of its predicament is largely a consequence of its failure to confront racism. The challenge facing progressive whites is to engage in a serious campaign to confront that failure. The challenge facing progressive blacks is to fight for control of black struggle against the traditional petit bourgeois leaders and to create space for the black masses to emerge into establishing their own agenda.

Acknowledgment: I would like to thank the Nuffield Foundation's Small Grants Scheme for the Social Sciences and the University of Manchester Committee on Staff Travel Funds for Research in the Humanities and Social Sciences for their financial assistance. I would like to thank my colleagues at the Institute of Race Relations for their years of education and encouragement. I would also like to thank Benjamin P. Bowser, Pat Kushnick and Jacqueline Ould and the editors of this book for their comments and suggestions. The remaining errors are, of course, mine.

11

Black Power Politics as Social Movement: Dialectics of Leadership in the Campaign to elect Harold Washington Mayor of Chicago

Gerald McWorter, Doug Gills and Ron Bailey

Introduction

The election of Harold Washington was a great victory for the black community. This was a case of successful political protest rather than merely conventional institutionalized political behaviour. The Washington campaign became a crusade in the black community and, therefore, its implication for the future has as much to do with the development of the black liberation movement as it does with the routine organization of behaviour within the established political system. An explosion of black political protest is best understood in the context of a social movement mode of analysis. This is a fundamental issue of perspective, because the absence of the social movement paradigm from much of the current literature can lead one to make false judgments about the nature of black politics.

The social movement paradigm focuses on the social behaviour of an aggregate of individuals mobilized outside formal political institutions to use resources to make a change in the social situation (McAdam, 1982; Freeman, 1983; Oberschall, 1973; Zald and McCarthy, 1979). The electoral behaviour model focuses on how resources are used for formal political participation (voting, office-holding, etc.), and the formal character of this process is the basis upon which the political behaviour of all groups is standardized and can be routinely compared (Milbrath and Goel 1977).

Our social movement approach sets a broad context in which black electoral behaviour constitutes only one of the many forms of possible political action (McAdam 1983). Since protest social movements are regarded as 'normal' by blacks more so than by whites, approaching the Washington campaign in this way can help explain black-white differences in voter registration and turnout (Elsinger 1973). Our analysis focuses on militant protest leadership and how this contributed to the election of May Harold Washington.[1]

Black people have a long history of fighting to get inside the political system, to gain access to 'legitimate political resources' (Walton 1972). After the Civil War, three constitutional amendments established for blacks their freedom, citizenship and right to vote. In the next 100 years, the struggle for voting rights was against *de jure* obstacles in the South (for example, grandfather clause, poll taxes, literacy tests) and *de facto* obstacles in the North (for example, gerrymandering and vote fraud). While a breakthrough in black office-holding occurred during Reconstruction, black elected officials increased in especially significant numbers during the post-Second World War period. In this period, black elected representation has been directly related to enforcement of voting rights and the presence of unifying electoral movements, at least at the local level.

The main basis for black protest has had to be *outside* the formal political system and based on the development of political resources *inside* the black community. The primary base has traditionally been in the black church, the dominant black social institution. However, black colleges, media, social and fraternal organizations, and independent black businesses have all been significant, especially as power brokers for black middle class interests. Each social institution has a stable leadership composed of high status élites, and some sector of the overall black community as its mass base. These élites frequently negotiate the interests of the entire black community (Killian

1965).

There is another aspect of black protest 'outside' the political system which is rooted in the dual traditions of black nationalism and socialist radicalism. There exist a number of small loosely-related organizations which maintain a highly ideological political style of activity. Because of the intense development of cadres in this type of protest politics, there is the latent potential for these groups to provide leadership for relatively large groups of people, such as that which occurs in the mobilization phase of a protest movement. Furthermore, these groups often have a 'vanguard' quality which enables them to start movement activity before it becomes popular, to 'risk' legitimacy by disrupting the existing norms of the political order (Geschwender 1971).

In sum, we can make a distinction between political 'insiders' and 'outsiders', and we can identify 'élites', rooted in institutionalized, high status social positions.[2] This chapter is an investigation of these leadership differences in the campaign to elect Harold Washington s mayor of Chicago. Our analysis will focus on three questions: (1) Did a dual leadership of insiders and outsiders exist in the campaign? (2) How did this develop? And (3) What did the outsiders contribute through the political tactics of black social protest?

Dual Leadership

This model conceptualizes black community dual leadership in the campaign to elect Washington as a development process contributing to three time-specific events: the announcement of candidacy, the primary, and the general election. The significance of these three black political victories can be seen by comparing black and white electoral participation. The degree of difference can be observed by looking at the 1979 and 1983 mayoral results. Table 11.1 demonstrates that black electoral superiority had developed by 1982 and expressed itself in the Washington mayoral votes in 1983. This upsurge in black voting was an expression of black protest leadership. Figure 11.1 depicts the process of movement of dual leadership as it has developed historically in the politics of Chicago's black community and as it directly relates to the three focal events of the 1983 mayoral election. Central to the process is the relative conver

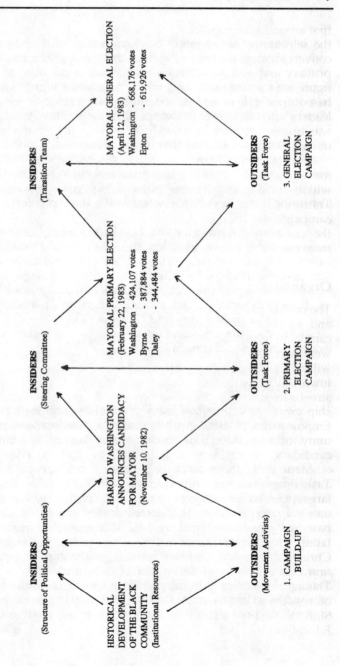

Figure 11.1: Political Process Model of Dual Leadership in the Campaigns to Elect Harold Washington

INSIDERS
(Structure of Political Opportunities)

INSIDERS
(Steering Committee)

INSIDERS
(Transition Team)

MAYORAL GENERAL ELECTION
(April 12, 1983)
Washington - 668,176 votes
Epton   - 619,926 votes

MAYORAL PRIMARY ELECTION
(February 22, 1983)
Washington - 424,107 votes
Byrne   - 387,884 votes
Daley   - 344,484 votes

HAROLD WASHINGTON
ANNOUNCES CANDIDACY
FOR MAYOR
(November 10, 1982)

HISTORICAL
DEVELOPMENT
OF THE BLACK
COMMUNITY
(Institutional Resources)

OUTSIDERS
(Movement Activists)

OUTSIDERS
(Task Force)

OUTSIDERS
(Task Force)

1. CAMPAIGN
BUILD-UP

2. PRIMARY
ELECTION
CAMPAIGN

3. GENERAL
ELECTION
CAMPAIGN

first around identification of the key political issues and second, the selection of a candidate — Harold Washington. Then this convergence of leadership culminated in the victories of the primary and general election in Chicago. Other aspects of the figure are the relative divergence of 'insider-outsider' leadership based upon differences in real or perceived interests of various leaders and their constituencies. When the black community was under racist attack, there was greater and more sustained unity which overcame the divergence of interests.

Also indicated in the model, are the specific organizational forms that the insider-outsider leadership dialectic manifested within the Washington campaign. The Steering Committee and Transition Team organizations are the formal structures of the campaign and the Task Force organization and its networks into the community represent the informal aspects that tie the movement to the formal political system, etc.[3]

Organization of the Campaign

The critical juncture occurred with the establishment of a formal and an informal campaign apparatus — the organization of campaign leadership on an insider/outsider basis. The outsiders were necessary to give the campaign a strike force of activists willing to use militant tactics if necessary. Chicago is a machine town, full of gangsters, including large black institutionalized street gangs. Within the black community, the 'outsider' leadership group came together as the Task Force for Black Political Empowerment (Task Force). Its major role was to defend the unity of the black community in support of Washington's candidacy.

Many of the individuals and organizations that united in the Task Force had been working together for a long time. The largest group of loosely coordinated organizations and individuals is called 'The African Community of Chicago' (ACC). It is based on a black nationalistic/Pan Africanist ideological orientation. They annually sponsor Kwanzaa (a black alternative to Christmas) which draws over 1,000 people, and African Liberation Day in late May, which annually draws over 250 people. This represents the institutionalization of black culture (rituals of resistance) initiated in the 1960s. Typical groups include: Shule YaToto (a black independent school), Institute of Positive Education), and the Association of African Historians.

Table 11.1: Mobilisation of Racial Groups: Registration and
Turnout as % of Voting Age Population, 1979-83

A. Registration

	Date	Black	White	Gap
Primary	1979	69.4	77.4	-8.0
General	1982	86.7	78.3	+8.4
Primary	1983	87.2	82.2	+5.0
General	1983	89.1	83.2	+5.9

B. Turnout

	Date	Black	White	Gap
Primary	1979	34.5	50.6	-16.1
General	1982	55.8	54.0	+1.8
Primary	1983	64.2	64.0	+0.2
General	1983	73.0	67.2	+5.8

Source: Kleppner, 1983.

Leadership of the ACC received control of the Chicago franchise
of the National Black United Front (NBUF, formed in Brooklyn,
1980) and the National Black Independent Political Party
(NBIPP, formed in Philadelphia, 1980). Several key ACC leaders
work together in an inner city Black Studies Program of
Northeastern Illinois University (Conrad Worrill, Anderson
Thompson and Robert Starks). Worrill was head of Chicago
NBUF, and spokesperson for the ACC; Thompson was head of
Chicago NBIPP, and spokesperson for the Task Force (research).
Starks, while holding no public posts in black nationalist organi-
zations, serves as a liaison between mainstream groups and the
ACC through his colleagues at the Center for Inner City Studies
on the near South Side of Chicago.

A second network of organizations and individuals were
reform-oriented community groups and service agencies. These
included the Kenwood-Oakland Community Organization
(KOCO), Midwest Community Council (MCC), Citizens for Self
Determination, Westside Coalition for Unity and Action; Bobby
Wright Mental Health Center, Minority Economic Development

Table 11.2: Organisation of Leadership in the Harold Washington Campaign

Task Force

Date Formed	November 7, 1982 (publically announced January 10, 1983)
Membership	95
Leading Figures	1. Robert Starks, Associate Professor, Centre for Inner City Studies, Northeastern Illinois University 2. Conrad Worrill, Associate Professor, Centre for Inner City Studies, Northeastern Illinois University 3. Lu Palmer, Adjunct Professor, Urban Studies, Associated, Colleges of the Midwest
% Black	100%
Purpose:	To help elect Harold Washington by mobilising Black unity and using tactics that the regular campaign could not carry out.

Steering Committee

Date formed	December 13, 1982
Membership	62
Leading Figures	1. Bill Berry, Special Assistant to the President, Johnson Products Company 2. Warren Bacon, Manager of Community Relations, Inland Steel Company 3. Walter Clark, Vice President, First Federal Saving and Loan
% Black	71%
Purpose:	To provide overall policy and planning, and to develop financial and political resources for the campaign.

Transition Team

Date formed	April, 1983
Membership	90
Leading Figures	1. Bill Berry, Special Assistant to the President, Johnson Products Company 2. James O'Connor, President and Chairperson, Commonwealth Edison 3. Norman Ross, Senior Vice President, 1st National Bank of Chicago 4. Kenneth Glover, Vice President, South Shore Bank
% Black	39.7%
Purpose:	To analyse and prepare recommendations for a new mayoral administration; city budget, administrative structure, policy and key personnel appointments, etc.

Corporation, and Coalition for Black Trade Unionists. In contrast to the city-wide and ideological ACC, most of these groups are based in local neighbourhoods and pragmatically fight for economic and welfare reforms on a step-by-step, incremental basis. The ACC maintains a small group of highly committed ideological adherents, while the reformers deal with material incentives based on the day-to-day needs of their constituency. These reformers are united into working class based, city-wide coalitions that cut across nationality and race. Bob Lucas (KOCO) and Nancy Jefferson (MCC) share leadership roles in service coalitions like the Chicago (housing) Rehab Network, and protest coalitions like People Organized for Welfare and Economic Reform (POWER). These coalitions link black and white 'outside' leadership, especially whites like Slim Coleman and the Uptown Coalition serving the interests of mainly inner city poor whites. A third bloc of community forces evolved around Lu Palmer, the head of Chicago Black United Communities (CBUC) discussed below.

The rest of the identifiable blocs were black ministers, entrepreneurs, politicians, other city-wide organizations, and Marxists. The Ministers and entrepreneurs have small congregations and/or markets, and are openly sympathetic to nationalist causes. The politicians were from 12 wards. They were either independent office-holders or aspiring candidates with no mainstream or 'Machine' (Regular Democratic Party) support. Hence, they were risking little by being in this 'outside' leadership context. After being elected and consolidating a ward organization, one might expect this open affiliation with outsiders to decline. Many candidates stopped participating after the primary election — both the winners and losers. The Marxists were looking for fertile soil in the context of black militancy, but not much happened since the groups were hardly represented by more than one observer/activist. These groups were the Communist Party (USA), the League of Revolutionary Struggle (ML), Peoples Colleges, and two independent black Marxist collectives.

The two other city-wide organizations did as much as the Task Force, though they all worked together so closely that volunteers were often unsure of which group they were *working under*. Everybody seemed only to know what they were *working for*: the election of Chicago's first black mayor, Harold Washington. One organization was the CBUC headed by Lu

Palmer, the other was PUSH headed by Reverend Jesse Jackson. These two were headquartered in the First Congressional District represented by Harold Washington. The critical factor was that each organization had powerful personalities for leaders who had been frequently at odds, between each other, and with Washington. However, in this context, there was a contagious rapprochement spreading because the possibility of a black mayor was something all of them wanted. The nationalists began to unite with Jesse Jackson. Lu Palmer and Jesse made up and Lu began to speak on the PUSH Saturdas morning radio broadcasts. Reformers began working with the nationalists, etc. The historical moment created this militant black unity of 'outsiders,' and this unity helped the moment have a magical quality people could believe in.

The development of 'insider' leadership took place on two fronts. First, a Steering Committee was organized for broad policy planning, development of financial resources, and for establishing legitimacy with the multiple constituencies represented by its 'blue ribbon' members who cut across racial, nationality, class, gender, and geographical lines. A second aspect was the organization of a campaign staff, a campaign manager and office workers who would handle policy implementation and coordinate the day-to-day activities of the campaign. This staff was an interesting combination of movement volunteers with utopian visions of political reform, operatives from machine-style political backgrounds along with reformers who wanted to move from the 'outside' (community) toward the 'inside' (City Hall administration, key board appointments).

The organization of formal campaign leadership began with close associates of Harold Washington being pulled together as staff, led by Renault Robinson as the campaign manager. Robinson had a well-known history of leadership in the Afro-American Patrolmen's League (AAPL) (McClory 1977). More recently (1980) he had been appointed to a term of the Chicago Housing Authority Board by Mayor Byrne as a concession to the black community. However, at that time, the campaign lacked organizational coherence — no research, no media plan and projection. There was a breakdown in internal and external communication, weak office staff coordination and poor space (initially occupying offices of the AAPL in a South Side black community). But within a month after announcing his candidacy, Washington pulled together a 'blue ribbon' Steering Committee and changed campaign managers. Al Raby was retained as campaign manager and by, 7 January 1983, he had developed the framework for running a professional campaign office in the heart of the downtown. The latter move provided readily available access to media outlets, transport outlets, facilities, finance flows and city-wide volunteers. This move facilitated the staffing of district offices across the city.

There were two key groups on the Steering Committee. A civil rights network from the 1960s, and leading reformers from the struggles that led to the campaign from the 1970s and early 1980s. The Steering Committee was headed by Bill Berry who had gained prominence in the 1960s. Berry was the head of the Chicago Urban League when it grew to be the largest chapter in the country. CUL benefited its budget and gained mainstream legitimacy by Berry's rejection of black militants and through his close working relationship to the major Chicago corporations (Strickland 1966). He was a key link between white mainstream leadership and the black élites and, even in his seventies, he maintains a weekly television talk show.

The chief research person, Harold Baron, worked for bill Berry as the Urban League's director of research. Baron was a link of the campaign to progressive intellectuals and university faculty. Al Raby, the campaign manager, was the former head of the Coordinating Council of Community Organizations (CCCO). During the 1960s, it was the largest such coalition in the USA. The CCCO maintained unity with diverse groups (for example, the NAACP and SNCC). It sponsored Martin Luther King, moving his efforts into Chicago, and CCCO led the nation's largest school protests — the two boycotts of Chicago public schools (October 1963 and February 1964) (Rivera, McWorters and Lillienstein 1964). Warren Bacon, a division manager of Inland Steel, was on the School Board during the boycotts. And, as a liberal, he opposed the dominant, reactionary interests on the Board who were under Daley's control. In this period, Bacon worked closely with Berry. Bacon now serves on the Illinois Board of Higher Education.

Washington also selected the two leading blacks in trade union leadership positions. They are part of the 1970s-1980s group of reformers: Charles Hayes, International Vice President of the United Food and Commercial Workers International Union; and Addie Wyatt, Vice President of the Coalition of

Labor Union Women. Others include: Nancy Jefferson, Executive Director of the Midwest Community Council; Artensa Randolph, Chair of the Advisor Council of the Chicago Housing Authority; Danny Davis, an independent City Council member; Juan Soliz, Latino independent candidate for the City Council; and Jorge Morales, Latino minister and community activist.

Other members of the initial Steering Committee group included three representatives from the business community: Lerone Bennett, an internationally famous writer with Johnson Publishing Company; Ed Gardner, President of Soft-Sheen Cosmetic Company; and Walter Clark, Vice President of First Federal Saving and Loan (second largest in Chicago). Clark also served as treasurer for the Steering Committee. Lastly, there were three progressive whites: Robert Mann, lawyer, former state legislator; Robert Hallock, lawyer; and Rebecca Sive-Tomashefsky, Executive Director, Playboy Foundation. Also, a number of the leaders were bankers whose main role was to raise money.

The organization of the campaign was difficult precisely because the leadership had to deal with vastly different sets of expectations. The mainstream demand was that the future mayor and campaign organization be acceptable to all aspects of the Chicago community, especially whites and business interests. This was quite different from the black demand that far-reaching reforms be advocated by aggressively pitting black power advocacy against the white racism and machine dominance of the Democratic Party. In general, this is the contrast between the *insider* rightward pull of mainstream institutional politics and the *outsider* leftward pull of black people mobilized into a protest movement. In this context, outsiders were at 'the point of political production,' fighting for votes, for more status. On the inside, however, people were respected more for their social station in life. Status was fixed to rather stable occupational and political roles. This set the basis for the outsiders' rise and fall in status, because once their 'production' of votes was no longer needed, they experienced a rapid decline in status.

After the primary victory it was necessary to make definite decisions about planning a new Washington administration prepared to take over control of the City Hall. This posed a new problem because running a large government bureaucracy and managing a diverse legislative body requires different skills than those needed for mobilizing voters, especially when black unity might win against a white racist vote, but would not work as the basis for running the entire city administration. Washington organized a Transition Team modelled after the method used to facilitate succession of presidential administrations.

The overall Transition Team was composed of 300 people. Our concern here is only with the composition of leading bodies of the Transition Team and the leadership of the various subcommittees, which number 90 people. The main division of the Transition Team was into a 25-member Financial Advisory Committee (The Fact Force) and a 65-member Transition Oversight Committee.

Table 11.3 summarizes the social character of each leadership group. On the insider-outside axis, the Task Force and the Transition Team demonstrated opposite tendencies in the expected directions. The Transition Team had somewhat more as an insider character, but quite significant was the outsider character of the Task Force (68.4). Both the Steering Committee and the Transition Team were dominated by élites. About three-quarters of these organizations were business, professional or ministerial élites. This diverged sharply from the predominantly outsider (community and labour) composition of the Task Force.

Table 11.3: Social Character of Leadership Organizations in the Harold Washington Campaign

Group	(1)%	(2)%	(3)%
Insiders	14.7%	11.3%	14.4%
Outsiders	68.4%	12.9%	11.1%
Elites	16.9%	75.8%	74.4%

Key: (1) Task Force (N=95); (2) Steering Committee (N=62); (3) Transition Team (N = 90)

Source: Official records and documents from each committee.

Further analysis of these data reveals a clear difference between the Steering Committee and the Transition Team leadership. black ministers are over 20 per cent of the élites on the Steering

Committee, but none are in the Transition Team leadership. black business and professional élites dominate the Steering Committee while white élites dominate the Transition Team.

Table 11.4: Elites in the Leadership Organizations of the Harold Washington Campaign

Type	(1)%	(2)%	(3)%
Blk. Ministers	43.7	3.9	0.0
Blk. Business	56.3	60.9	36.9
White Elites	0.0	15.2	63.1

Key: (1) Task Force (N = 16); (2) Steering Committee (N=46); (3) Transition Team (N = 65).

Source: Official records and documents from each committee.

The Task Force is different in one additional way, namely, the reliance on the more independent small business person and the academic professional. These middle class positions allow for greater relative freedom, both on the job and in getting time away from the job. On the other hand, the Steering Committee was dominated by larger businesses and professionals in large bureaucratic agency settings that discipline the leaders within ideological and political limits defined by the political mainstream.

Overall, there is a great deal of significance in the percentage of black people in each leadership group: Task Force (100 per cent); Steering Committee (71 per cent) and Transition Team (39.7 per cent). This pattern of declining black composition rather accurately parallels the percentage of black people in the relevant reference group being served. The Task Force was for building unity in the black community, so it was 100 per cent black while the steering Committee was for Washington's broad electoral support. His vote in the general election was 77 per cent black, while the steering Committee was 71 per cent black. Washington maintained a proportionate per cent black of all leadership groups in his campaign. This is also reflected in the composition of blacks in the Transition Team leadership. Blacks comprised 39.7 per cent of the leading positions which coincides with their percentage in the city population (39.8 in 1980).

The three groups are quite different in terms of the bureaucratic character of individual resources being organized. The Task Force was a loosely organized group mainly based on an individual's willingness to contribute personal resources to a collective process. As in most social movement contexts, the participants select themselves and gain status in the movement to the extent to which they live up to the expectations of the membership. They lose status when they cease to function. The Transition Team members came from organized institutional contexts and, in a sense, they represented themselves as well as an organization. They derived their status as much from their position as from the performance in the role assigned. The Steering Committee was mixed in this regard. The top leadership of the Steering Committee consisted of institutional élites who were given formal public recognition, while the expanded committee structure (consisting of a number of citizens committees) allowed for a great deal of formal and informal co-optation. The informal co-optation on some subcommittees made them much more like the Task Force where status was a matter of performance: 'What have you done lately?' is the question asked in these contexts.

The general interconnection between these three leadership groups is based on overlapping membership as is shown in the following box:

Task Force: 48.4 per cent outsiders (N = 95) sent five members to the Steering Committee, three of whom are outsiders.

Steering Committee: 75.8 per cent élites (N = 62) of which 60.9 per cent are black (N = 46) professional/business people sent 17 members to Transition Team, and 70.6 per cent are élites of which 58.2 per cent are black professionals/business people.

Transition Team: (N = 90) 73.8 per cent are élites of which 62.9 per cent are white.

Nancy Jefferson was the only person on all three leadership committees. She combines her position in community work with memberships on the Chicago Police Board and the Board of First National Bank.

Historical Development of a Dual Leadership

The dual leadership of the Washington Campaign developed in the historical context of black Chicago. On the one hand, the black community grew and developed a diverse set of institutional resources within segregated geographical limits and, on the other, a pattern of electoral activity emerged that resulted in a form of proportional representation as far as city council representation is concerned.

The fundamental resource of the black community of Chicago is its population size. Its proportional growth is indicated in Table 11.5.

Table 11.5: Chicago Population: Per Cent Black, 1890-1980

Years	% Black	Total Population
1890	1.3	1,099,850
1910	2.0	2,185,283
1930	6.9	3,376,438
1950	14.0	3,620,962
1970	34.4	3,366,957
1980	39.8	3,005,072

Source: City of Chicago, The Negro Population in Chicago. Department of Planning, 1978, US Census of Population 1980.

Based on the *Index of Residential Dissimilarity*, Chicago is one of the most segregated cities in the USA. This score was 92.1 in 1950 and it has slowly increased to 93.0 by 1980.

Out of this segregated social world, developed a black middle class in control of increasing resources (for example, education and skills, income, businesses, access to facilities and personnel, organizations and associations). Those resources were used to fuel the black liberation protest movement. In 1950 there were 10,065 blacks in Chicago with at least a college education and, by 1980, this number had increased to over 47,000. But blacks did not make great gains in positions of power. The Chicago Urban League carried out a study of blacks in top decision-making positions in 1967 and 1977. The overall pattern is found in Table 11.6 (Fox et al. 1980).

Table 11.6: Blacks in Decision-Making Positions in Chicago: 1965 and 1977

Date	Item	Public	Private
1965	Total	1223	9900
	Black	75	226
	% Black	6.1	2.3
1977	Total	1619	12013
	Black	204	364
	% Black	12.6	3.0

Source: Fox et al. (1980)

It is obvious from Table 11.6, that blacks are overweeningly under-represented in both the public (government) and private sectors, but greater representation and improvement has taken place in the public sector. The public sector is much more sensitive and responsive to the demands of the black protest movement since it needs the potential political resources of that movement — votes. It needs votes to continue to maintain legitimacy. The pattern seems to be that small electoral districts with large black populations tend to be represented well. This is born out by the 'Black Power Batting Average' for City Council representation (Figure 11.2).

The Black Power Batting Average is computed by dividing the percentage black of the City Council by the percentage black of the voting age population. Elsinger calls this a 'black representation ratio' (Elsinger 1973) and Karnig and Welch call it a 'black council equality ratio' (Karnig and Welch 1980). Figure 11.2 presents the Black Power Batting Average for Chicago, 1923-83.

The increase in the number of black representatives in the City Council is a major indication of the developing capacity of the black community to mobilize resources to elect blacks to political office. Given the racial character of many public policies in the City of Chicago, it would be expected that black council members would form voting blocs, particularly with regard to issues of high salience for the black electorate.

Figure 11.2 graphically portrays the pattern of post-First World War black political representation. There are three

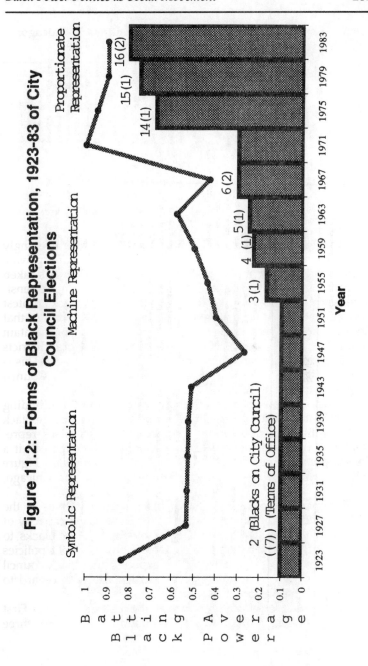

Figure 11.2: Forms of Black Representation, 1923-83 of City Council Elections

Table 11.2: Resurgence of Mass Protest During Mayoral
Administration of Jane Byrne, 1979-83

Issue	Problem	Affected Population	Protest Leadership	Protest Action (Date of Greatest Intensity)	Outcome of Protest
1. Health	Deteriorating health services and facilities. Problem becomes more critical as cuts in health service increase.	Most working-class blacks, and large segments of general assistance recipients. Over 250,000 in-patients are treated at Cook County annually.	Committee to Save Cook County Hospital. Black community leaders and health professionals and health activists.	Spring 1980 mass demonstrations. State officials are brought in to hear local community testimony 1979, 1980.	Hospital is saved temporarily; fight becomes part of the increasing anti-Regan, anti-Thompson fiscal policy resistence.
2. Education	Black representation on Board of Education struggle for democratic control over education.	Over 5000,000 students students are in Public School System of which 61% are black, 20% lating. Chicago district has largest enrollment in country.	Parent Equalisers CBUC-led mass struggles. SUBS coalition provided popular exposure through newspaper.	1979-80, mass protests petition drives are launched. During 1982 CBUC leads opposition to Byrne's appointment of two whites to Board replacing blacks.	Successfull in opposing Tom Ayres selection by School Ed. President Palmer becomes a leading advocate and adviser in Washington's campaign. Tillman runs for alderman's placing second in 3rd Ward. Plamer runs unsuccessfully for Congress in First District.
3. Public Housing	Black representation diluted by Byrne on CHA Board. Conditions in public housing worsening.	150,000 families reside in CHA housing developments. Over 90% are black. 75% of families are headed by women, 2/3 are on public assistance.	Chicago Housing Tenants organisation and other tenant/ community activists.	Stormy series of protest actions escalate during spring/summer 1982 leading to arrest of many leading activists.	C. Swibel is forced to resign as Chairperson. Replaced by Mooney. A.Swibel, Byrne protege. Community leaders call for boycott of Chicago Fest. Marion Stamps runs for alderperson in 43rd Ward. Robinson becomes campaign manager for Washington, appointed CHA Chairman after election.

4. Streeter Campaign: 17th Ward (Politics)	Byrne attempted to unseat Streeter for opposing her appointment of Janus-Bonow to school board.	The 17th Ward is 97% black and voting against machine positions and opposed to "plantation" Politics.	CBUC joined forced with other Westside community groups to oppose Byrne. They were joined by other white reformers.	(May-July 1982) With the support of a black-led citywide coalition. Streeter defeated Byrne's candidate in the primary and runoff.	The Streeter victory was termed a "people's victory" and a defeat for Byrne and the Regular Party. Served to further weaken the machine in the black community.
5. Black Businesses and Jobs.	Underpinning the status issue of black representation were issues of inequality of job and contract opportunities for blacks.	Blacks are 40% of population, yet have only 27% of the policy positions and 27% of total jobs. Blacks get less than 20% of City contracts.	Supporting the Chicago Fest protest was a broad coalition both within the black community and citywide. Key organisation was PUSH, CBUC.	(August 1982) A 14 day boycott of Chicago Fest led by Coalition to Stop Chicago Fest and supported by by a white-latino "Committee of 500".	Led directly into mass voter registration push. The leadership became key supporters of Washington's mayoral bid.
6. Unemployment. Welfare	The economic crisis and the Reagan-Thompson budget cuts represent a direct attack on the standard of living.	Over 600,000 people in poverty: 200,000 GA recipients. Unemployment is over 12.4%. The overwhelming majority are blacks.	POWER spearheaded by community activists across the city. An all-Chicago Summer Congress held in August 1982.	(August-September 1982) Led exposures of Reagan-Thompson-Byrne link to domestic cuts and diversion of public resources into politicians coffers.	Led to mass voter registration drive that was based upon mobilising and disenfranchised among blacks, latinos and poor whites.
7. CD Fund Reprogramming (Private Housing)	A large percent of Federal Community Development Funds were retained to support machine politicians and patronage as well as investments in Central Business District.	City receives over $110 million in Block Grant funds to support housing rehab. neighborhood development and revitalisation.	Chicago Rehab. Network, a coalition of housing development organisations, was joined by other community-based organisations.	(August-September 1982) Made administrative complaints; protested at Mayor Byrne's office and launched media campaign against repealed funds to meet other political objectives of Byrne's administration.	Led to a general and widespread anti-Byrne motion that had developed in the neighbourhoods. It served to undermine Byrne's base of support. HUD ruled funds had to be restored.

definite periods: (a) *Symbolic representation* (1923-47) represents seven terms of office when two blacks were on the Council. These two blacks were symbolically the representatives of all blacks in the city. The declining Black Power Batting Average reflects increases in black population while council membership stayed the same. (b) *Machine representation* (1947-67) represents five terms of office but an incremental increase on representation from three to six black members of the Council. These politicians were loyalists in the Daley machine. (c) *Proportionate representation* (1967-83) characterized by an increase to 16 black members of the council. Black council representatives are divided into machine regulars and independents. Currently there are 19 predominantly black wards in Chicago. Two of the wards have white alderpersons who are machine loyalist, while one is an independent.

Pre-Campaign Build-Up

The basic resources of the black community had to be mobilized if this change in the structure of political opportunity (increased representation) were to be taken advantage of by effective social protest. Mobilization can be effective to the extent that sufficient black unity exists to focus the mobilized resources on one key objective. These two political conditions of social protest — mobilization of resources and unified political focus — were developed in Chicago by insurgent forces, especially the black militants who became the Task Force for black political empowerment. There were three aspects of this pre-campaign build-up:

1 building a consensus of issues, especially the mayoral election, with the unifying political objective to defeat Jany Byrne;

2 building a consensus of leadership, by agreeing to support one major black candidate — Harold Washington; and

3 building basic political resources, voter registration, education, and turnout to accomplish the defeat of Byrne and the election of Washington.

Table 11.7 describes the major aspects of the overall social protest movement in Chicago during the pre-campaign period 1980-2. All involve the 'bread and butter,' standard of living and against discriminatory practices by the Byrne city government. The issues are: quality of services (numbers 1, 6 and 7) representation (numbers 2, 3 and 4), and economic distribution (number 5). Large sectors of the overall city population were affected by these issues and, therefore, had an interest in the success of the protests.

There was significant media support for protest action. In the black community, there was a major daily newspaper (*Defender*), a weekly press (*Metro News* and *Chicago Observer*), several black-oriented radio stations, and a Black Press Institute which provided general access to all black newspapers as a clipping service. This was supplemented by black journalists in the mainstream media (for example, Vernon Jarrett and Monroe Anderson at the *Tribune*) including at least one black show on every TV station. A critical role was played by a newspaper started by radical white militants operating 'outside' the political mainstream (*All Chicago City News*).

But the critical media dynamic was provided by Lu Palmer who coined the phrase 'We Shall See in '83.' This became his slogan in 1981:

> Well in '81, we held a city-wide political conference... 'Toward A Black Mayor'. You know it is really kind of revolutionary for black folks to start doing something in '81 and looking toward a goal of '83.... So we said at Malcolm X College, first thing we are going to have to do is change the mind-set of our people. So we coined a slogan 'We Shall See, in '83.' And we printed that slogan on every piece of literature that went out. I was on the air with *Lu's Notebook* on four black radio stations sponsored by Illinois Bell, and I just laid on my family of listeners 'We Shall See in '83.' I do a talk show at night, two nights a week, *On Target*. I signed off, 'this is Lu Palmer reminding you that "We Shall See in '83." Slowly, agonizingly slowly, it began to catch on and people in the community began at least to think about the fact that we *could* see in '83. And, over a period of time, brothers and sisters, we shall see in '83 became an institutionalized rhythm in the hearts, minds and the souls of black people to the point that when Harold Washington finally announced, November 10, 1982, the first words out of his mouth were 'We Shall See in '83' (Palmer 1984).

This media context that promotes Chicago movement protest is the weekly hour broadcasts on three radio stations from Operation PUSH. For over a decade the PUSH microphone has been open to virtually every progressive black political candidate *and* protest cause. As issues developed, the black community knew resistance was yielding results and people were getting excited. The machine backed Byrne administration became the central political target of a pro-reform anti-machine movement.

The transition was made as struggle proceeded from these various 'economic' issues into a political protest movement with one concrete 'political' target.' In symbolic and concrete terms, the signal that a new politics was imminent in Chicago was the death of Mayor Daley. As a monolithic structure, the political machine Daley left his successors was apparently not prepared for this eventuality. Subsequent events seemed to reflect the weakness of an outdated structure unable to adapt to new conditions, but tenaciously reluctant to transfer power to new political forces.

But what makes this instance of black political protest unique is not that there was unity about who black people were against, but that there was such unity about who black people were prepared to support. Table 11.3 presents the top ten names identified in three different surveys of the black community that tried to find out who could draw the most black support as a candidate for mayor.

Black politicians began to meet regularly and black business leaders were being regularly sounded out by political insiders trying to identify the material resources required to fight in the campaign for a black mayor if a consensus candidate were found. The black élites saw the possibility of running Washington, but he did not have their full support. By 1982, this relatively weak consensus of black élites was taken to the grassroots level. As one of the early militant leaders working for a black mayor, Lu Palmer was well aware that victory was possible only if a rather high level of black unity could be developed. Palmer took the polling of black public opinion as a research project and as a way to organize people for the 'possibility' of a black mayor. By his account, CBUC and friends distributed over 25,000 ballots and got back over 13,000. The responses included over 54 names. The top names on the ballots were asked if they were interested and a final list of 20 interested individuals was to be presented to a mass community meeting as what he called a 'plebiscite.' About 1,500 people attended a mass meeting at Bethel AME Church and voted on the candidates (see Table 11.8 for results). The mass list developed by CBUC is slightly different in that there are three

Table 11.8: Selection of a Black Mayoral Candidate:
Three Citywide Surveys, 1980-1893

ELITE*	ELITE**	MASS***
1. Harold Washington (1) (US Congressman)	1. Cecil Partee (1)	1. Harold Washington (1)
2. Roland Burris (1) (State Comptroller)	2. Harold Washington (1)	2. Lu Palmer (0) (Chair, CBUC)
3. Richard Hewhouse (1) (State Representative)	3. Roland Burris (1)	3. Danny Davis (1)
4. Wilson Frost (1) (Alderperson)	4. Jesse Jackson (0)	4. Roland Burris (1)
5. Cecil Partee (1) (City Treasurer)	5. Richard Hewhouse (1)	5. Jesse Jackson (0)
6. Warren Bacon (1) (State Board of Human Education)	6. Wilson Frost (1)	6. Lenora Cartwright (1) (City Commissioner Human Service)
7. Clifford Kelley (1) (Alderperson)	7. Tom Todd (E) (Attorney)	7. Renault Robinson (1) (CHA Board)
8. Earl Neal (1) (CHA Board)	8. Clifford Kelly (1)	8. Anna Langford (E) (Lawyer)
9. Kenneth Smith (E) (Minister)	9. Manford Byrd (1) (Deputy School Superintendant)	9. Manford Byrd (1)
10. Jesse Jackson (0) (PUSII Executive)	10. Danny Davis (1) (Alderperson)	10. Margaret Burroughs (E) (Director, DuSable Museum)
11. Clark Burrus (E) (Corporation Executive)		

* Survey by the Chicago Reporter Newsletter - 9 insiders (1), 2 elites (E), and 1 outsider (0)
** Survey by AIM Magazine (Summer 1981) - 8 insiders, 1 elite, and 1 outsider
*** Community Vote organised by CBUC (May 1982) - 6 insiders, 2 elites, 2 outsiders; also 3 women

Note:

The Chicago Reporter is a monthly civic newsleter with a race relations improvement focus;
AIM Magazine is published monthly as a racial harmony and peace-orientated Black publication.

"CBU" the Chicago Black United Committees is a leading activist organisation headed by Lu Palmer.

"CHA" is the Chicago Housing Authority.

outsiders, and three women. Further, most of the insiders are
independents. The CBUC polling process more adequately
reflected the popular independent character of the movement
fuelling the Washington campaign.

Included among Washington's friends, were the militants of
his generation who were high achievers and fought inside
Chicago politics. Washington had been careful to maintain
strong inside political ties, receiving his apprenticeship training
in the Dawson and Metcalfe ward organizations. So now
Washington was being selected by this more recent generation
of protest leaders, and at least given a chance by the black élite,
though without their strong material encouragement. He had
run for mayor before, in 1977, and he had good name recognition. By the autumn of 1982 a consensus had developed that the
best black candidate for mayor was Harold Washington.

When Washington was approached by the militant outside
political leaders, he responded as a political insider would to
outside protest leadership. He made his candidacy contingent
upon the movement being able to register 50,000 new black
voters and upon turning them out in the autumn (state-wide)
1982 election. He later increased his demand to 100,000 new
voters.

The militant movement responded to his challenge. A suit
was filed in court to open up the registration process and, for the
first time in the political process, it was opened up in employment offices, churches and public housing projects. As it turned
out, the registration centres were located in places where local
struggles had been taking place and were being operated, in
part, by the militants who had been leading these protest struggles. It was not hard for people to connect the two aspects —
economic reform for their own narrow interest with a political
target that united people throughout the city. This set the stage
for the key material support from the black élites. Ed Gardner,
founder and president of Soft-Sheen Cosmetics Company,
provided at least $50,000 for an advertising campaign to
popularize the voter registration drive: 'Come Alive, October 5'
was promoted in the autumn of 1982 as the action slogan to
implement the theme 'We Shall See in '83.' By 5 October, over
160,000 new registrants had been placed on the rolls. Over
100,000 of these new registrants were black.

Thus, the immediate build-up of political resources (issues, a
candidate and votes) was to a great extent initiated and carried

out by black protest movement leadership.

The Task Force

As a militant coalition of organized forces, the Task Force was based on previous networks developed in the movement and forged in the community-based fights for reform during 1982. In October (1982), Joe Gardner (then a top executive in PUSH) called a meeting of about 100 people to discuss a black candidate for mayor. This gathering at Roberts Motel (largest black motel in town) decided that were such a campaign to develop, it would be necessary to have a militant organization that would be a parallel force to the official campaign. The emerging strategy required a free wheeling coalition operating outside the conventional limitations that define political insiders and institutional élites. Robert Starks was asked to develop a definite plan and, on that basis, the Task Force for Black Political Empowerment was formed.

The climate of unity was set, but its implementation in a context of militant political outsiders required movement skills, and not the bureaucratic logic of rule-governed behaviour. At the very beginning, insurgent styled insiders were dominant inside the Task Force. Danny Davis, one of the most independent of the black members of the City Council, acted as chairperson for the first few meetings, and was joined by virtually every new political aspirant. However, this was at odds with the more 'movement' oriented masses who began to attend the meetings in increasing numbers. The main struggle was over whether to focus on the election exclusively or to include other issues of struggle as well. A committee led by Bob Lucas developed a coalitional leadership slate and from that emerged the Starks/Worrill leadership.

The main thrust of the Task Force in the early period was to develop political resources. Washington's first goal was to get on the ballot, and this required 3,505 signed petitions. While he was reported to have got 100,000, the Task Force leadership announced that they had collected 20,000. Washington had just received 172,641 votes in his successful re-election to Congress, so he already had a mass base. But the issue of building resources was not only one of getting petitions signed, it was one requiring the mobilization of voters.

CBUC organized four voter clinics (on 3, 10, 23 and 30

December) and the Task Force joined with POWER and filed suit to open up the registration process. They won the suit to take the registration out to unemployment and welfare offices, schools, and churches and libraries. A plan for the participation of the Task Force was suggested by Bon Lucas of KOCO. His first involvement in the movement came when he joined CORE in 1959. He was the functional link between the POWER forces and the Task Force in the coordination of a city-wide voter registration drive. Lucas used his movement experience and his pragmatic grounding as a community organizer to feed the enthusiasm of the Task Force volunteers into a coherent timetable and division of labour.

Movement participants were attending many meetings. In fact, a movement 'industry' developed around this process (Zald and McCarthy 1979). A full week of meetings included: the PUSH Saturday morning sessions, Saturday afternoon campaign worker sessions at the Charles Hayes Labor Center, Tuesday night Task Force meetings, and Wednesday night CBUC meetings. The most committed had subcommittee meetings, and everyone had assignments to carry out. It is hard to determine the relative importance of these different settings for resource development because it was not unusual for the same person to attend more than one meeting and report the results of the same community work in each setting. Further, the organizations were in competition with each other to the extent that several of them went on membership drives in the midst of this mass effort, including PUSH, CBUC, and NBUF.

The general political climate was decidedly in favour of Byrne and Daley as they had the backing of the mainstream media. This was raised to a national level when presidential politics invaded the city: Mondale supported Daley, and Kennedy supported Byrne. This outraged the Congressional Black Caucus (CBC). The CBC, mindful that three of its members were from Chicago (including the black candidate Washington) and that Jesse Jackson might well run for the presidency, had to act. It had avoided getting involved because it seemed that the general trend was against a Washington win, but the national attention was too great a status threat — it challenged their claim to national political leadership of the black community. The CBC took the national white leadership of the Democratic Party to task and placed its support firmly behind Washington. In fact, Congressman John Conyers from

Detroit moved to Chicago with his staff to be an on-site national adviser to the campaign, and to help unite the black élite leadership behind Washington.

Three Campaign Tactics

Locally, there were three major developments that opened up the political climate and set the stage for a rapidly expanding social movement.

(1) During January (18th, 23rd, 26th and 30th), a series of four debates was organized and broadcast on radio and television. This gave Washington his greatest public exposure to date. And, for the black community, he was cast in the role of a gladiator. More than Byrne and Daley, Washington was an orator who combined the rhetorical flair of the black ministerial tradition with the polysyllabic acumen that a law degree brings. He 'turned the black community on.' He became viable within and outside the black community. His coffers began to swell as local and national money came pouring into his headquarters in the final weeks of the Primary.

(2) One week after the last debate, Washington's campaign held the largest rally for any candidate, when over 15,000 people came out on a 'hard' winter day in Chicago. An earlier rally had not really worked (2,500 turned out when 10,000 were expected). This rally had to work if the momentum generated by the 'Debates' was going to continue. The people came from throughout the city. The committed base of the campaign was there for all to see. There was increased participation from the mainstream black élites and insiders, but they had to witness the emergence of a black social protest movement that they did not and probably could not control. This led to increased interest in Washington since he might be able to control them and, certainly, it increased the amount of attention paid to the Task Force because that is the precise reason for its being.

(3) The development of the basic button led to mass identification with the campaign. POWER made a simple 'blue button' with a rising sun stating, 'Washington for Chicago.' This slogan was adopted by the time of the general election and over 1.25 million buttons were distributed. In sum, a positively charged climate had emerged which had as its main aspect greater candidate credibility (debates), greater visibility of mass and élite support (rally), and the movement had a public symbol of

identification and a statement of solidarity (the button).

Our general thesis was stated in part by Nate Clay (1983), a local black journalist, in his analysis of the major rally on 6 February:

> It had all the flavour of a civil rights movement rally of the 1960s. The overflow, enthusiastic crowd that filled the cavernous University of Illinois Pavilion at an 'All Chicago' rally for mayoral candidate Harold Washington was deep testament to the fervour in the black community around his candidacy.
>
> Amazed white commentators admitted that it was the biggest political rally either of the three major contenders has held. I have no doubt that Congressman Washington can become Mayor Washington if, within the next two weeks, his operation evolves from a campaign to a movement. Black people are turned on by movements, not campaigns.

Significance of the Task Force

In general, there were three instances in which the Task Force played a key role in defending black unity: ministers, media, and the gangs. The black minister, as the main institutional élite in the black community has long been a broker of political influence. Many ministers had declared support for Byrne and Daley, including inviting them to speak in their churches. The Task Force countered this motion by forming an alliance of 300 ministers, under Reverend Al Sampon's lead and they took out an advertisement in the *Defender* in order to identify the black Church with Washington. As outsiders, the Task Force formed squads to picket the endorsement meetings of black ministers with Daley and Byrne (for example, 19 January at the Hyde Park Hilton when 75 ministers met to endorse Daley). This created an interesting contradiction as some of these ministers felt so much pressure from their congregations that they had to pull back and get on the Washington bandwagon. One of the major 'race defectors' was Reverend J.H. Jackson, former head of the National Baptist Convention. Yet, his importance had greatly diminished since he had joined with Mayor Daley in his opposition to the Civil Rights Movement of the 1960s. He even opposed Martin Luther King. It appeared that race loyalty in the midst of this movement was greater than the traditional hold that black ministers had on their congregation in Chicago. It was time to fight back against the 'white folks and win,' rather than follow the leader so characteristic of past practices of the black Church.

Another instance of the Task Force defending unity emerged when it was learned that the *Defender* newspaper was likely to withhold its support from Washington. A committee of the Task Force leadership met with the newspaper editors and threatened a counter-attack, even a boycott. The *Defender* subsequently changed its orientation and supported Washington.

Lastly, there was the gang problem. The Task Force was so committed to its goals that it opened the doors to everyone in the black community, even to street gangs such as the El Rukins (formerly the Blackstone Rangers). However, it appears that Byrne and 'Fast' Eddie Vrdolyak, out of their respective war chests of $10 million and $1 million, appropriated money to buy the gangs' support. They stopped coming to Task Force meetings and began to harass campaign street workers, including anybody wearing a blue button. Several Task Force leaders led groups to confront the gangs. But it is interesting to note that these confrontations were initiated by the community reformers more than by the ACC leadership, since the former were used to defending the rights of community people. The ACC leadership found it possible to include the gangs in their definition of black unity, which set up people in the Task Force for attack.

Resource Mobilization

The Task Force raised little money for the campaign itself. However, it did manage to gather enough resources to sustain a temporary office on 47th Street, to maintain a part-time office manager and a bank of telephones. The phone lines were handled by staff volunteers who called registered voters in the 19 black wards to recruit volunteers for the movement and to encourage a high turnout for Harold Washington.

The Task Force did produce two mass leaflets ('Our Future is in Your Hands' and 'We Discovered It [Chicago], We Should Govern It'). The Task Force developed its own button (red, black and green, the symbolic colours of black nationalism) which was distributed through networks primarily on the South Side. The Task Force recruited several hundred people to distribute leaflets door-to-door and at shopping centres during the last two weekends of the Primary.

The Task Force leadership reports that there were hundreds of workers on the streets passing out 'one million pieces' of pro-Harold Washington literature during the weekend of the Primary. Working through CBUC, and the Near South Side Campaign office, the Task Force played a key role in training, perhaps, several hundred election day workers, many of whom had never before done anything other than vote in an election. Task Force personnel provided workers for Washington's public appearances at public transport stops and at public housing developments. On election day the Task Force recruited a fleet of cars to transport voters to the polls and to provide logistics, and 'troubleshooting' functions.

Crisis of Victory

Harold Washington's primary victory was a people's victory. It generated a community-wide 'high' with effects upon subsequent mass organization, particularly upon the Task Force. The crescendo effect of a significant social protest is often followed by a down turn in the level of effort and organizational discipline. The loss of focus within the Task Force came precisely at the point when another upswing or upsurge in activity was required. The general election was seven weeks away. There was a loss of orientation and momentum. This occurred simultaneously with the campaign organization being forced to adjust to the new conditions of success and to the need for an expanded (city-wide) movement. The new political tasks of the campaign required that political resources be redirected and concentrated outside the black community. This was indicated by the increased level of effort being expended in trying to reach Latinos and white voters. Second, there was new emphasis on 'top-down' coalition development which contrasted sharply with the 'bottom-up' thrust of the primary and the pre-campaign build-up: (1) the Steering Committee was expanded to include more black élites, whites and Latinos in formal and functional campaign roles; and (2) there was the formation and announcement of a 'blue ribbon' transition team composed of mainly white business and professional élites.

The effect of these readjustments in campaign orientation and activity led to the loss of status of (and a role shift for) the Task Force: there were new needs for the general election. This was possible because it was no longer necessary to use militant tactics to defend black unity. The pervasive racism generated by Epton's campaign, and the racist reaction of the machine's defeated leadership was sufficient to ensure unity in the black community. Washington took on all the traits of a gladiator who could do no wrong in the black community. When white Chicago Democrats decided to vote Republican, Chicago was put on war alert.

However, the Task Force leadership resisted preparing a plan on how to stay out in the face of the spontaneous mass energy unleashed by the Primary victory. Hence, the Task Force's role became focused on campaign literature distribution and advance street work for Harold Washington. It raised no new demands and no programme. An important distinction between the role of the Task Force in the primary and the general election periods is that it had lost its capacity to innovate tactically. (Or, as Al Sampson, a leading member of the Task Force stated, 'We haven't busted any new grapes since the Primary.')

Thus, the effect of the primary victory (and the transition in strategy on the part of campaign leadership in the face of an expanding movement) significantly altered the social character of the leading bodies of the campaign organization. We saw earlier that the composition of the insider organizations was predominantly institutional élites. The Transition Team was composed of professionals with technical and bureaucratic skills, while the Steering Committee was expanded to include more black ministers and Latino and white professionals.

The orientation and outward thrust of the campaign were altered. Simultaneously, this development produced a role-shift in the relative importance of the Task Force. The Task Force had given the campaign a militant character that was no longer required. The role redifinition of the Task Force was reflected in its demise and fall in status relative to other bodies and activities in the campaign organizations. Included in this was the expanded use of television and radio advertising supplanting the need for door-to-door street workers. The campaign's attempt to reach into the black community was only very intense during the last two weeks leading up to the general election.

Conclusion

Since 1982 the *Western Journal of Black Studies* has been reporting
the results of scholarly research in the area of black political
representation (Dennis and Moeser 1982; Foster 1983); political
organization and leadership (Murray and Vedlitz 1982; Tryman
1977); and leadership style, decision-making and performance of
black office-holders (Goldstein 1981; Uzzell 1981; Lowenstein
1981). This chapter is a contribution to this emerging area in the
scholarly literature on black urban and mayoral politics and its
interface with the broader black liberation movement. We have
focused on the social character of the leadership which emerged
or was recruited in the Harold Washington mayoral campaign.

The Harold Washington electoral dynamic represents an
instance where a mass political protest movement was directed
into the electoral arena. It has, as such, important implications
for the future and direction of urban black politics and the
struggle for black liberation on a number of fronts.

We have focused this analysis on the leadership of the
Washington campaign for mayor of the city of Chicago. We have
argued that this was a dramatic case of social protest being
expressed within the electoral arena. Therefore, we have
demonstrated that the social movement mode of analysis can
best explain what happened. The Washington campaign was a
particular instance of the black liberation movement using
legitimate means to gain control over the administration of city
government through the electoral processes. We have drawn
three major conclusions:

1   At the core of black politics in Chicago, there is a dual leadership
    composed of 'political insiders' and 'movement outsiders.' This
    dual structure is held together through relationships with élites in
    the black community who occupy leading positions within its
    social institutions.

2   The Washington campaign's dual leadership was developed
    through local community struggles. Further, in the primary it was
    the outsider leadership that played the decisive role (Task Force)
    but toward the general election the élites took over, first the black
    élites (Steering Committee) and then the white élites (Transition
    Team).

3   Overall, this political event reflects the special conditions created
    by mass mobilization, clear political focus, and a united black
    leadership (outsiders, élites, and insiders).

We do not believe that the future will merely repeat this process in Chicago or any other city. However, what we can learn is that when a community is oppressed and exploited, an explosion of political protest is probably more normal than acquiescence and submission and, in the final analysis, the outcomes are influenced decisively by the qualities of leadership.

Notes

1   This article is part of a larger project dealing with the election of
        Harold Washington. A great mass of data was collected through
        the 'involved' observation of activist fieldwork, extensive clipping
        of a nearly complete collection of official campaign documents. A
        full book-length study is being prepared. See our article 'Chicago
        History and Mayoral Politics' in Bush (1984).

2   A relevant theoretical summation of black leadership in Chicago
        has been undertaken by Wilson (1960). He makes a distinction
        between the political leader and civic leader, a categorization
        similar to our insider-outsider distinction. He further goes on to
        describe three periods in the development of black leadership:
        compatible élites (black political and civic leaders working
        together for common ends), diverging élites (same black
        leadership groups working at odds), and a new merger (the
        coming together of black and white élites for new reforms).
        Wilson identifies compatible élites with the 1920s and the
        diverging élites with the 1950s. He said that the third stage had
        not reached Chicago by 1960. It is interesting that as late as the
        early 1980s, political analysts predicted it would remain this way
        because blacks were going to follow and repeat the pattern of
        white ethnics. This meant simply that blacks would take their turn
        at the helm of the machine (Rakove 1982) or remain subservient to
        the machine through weak political leadership (Preston 1982).
        This incorrect perception of social and political reality in the black
        community results from having the wrong set of assumptions
        about black politics, limiting our capacity to explain and to predict
        social change. Only by understanding the continual dialectic of
        black leadership, being pulled inside to institutional politics and
        outside into social movement politics, can one understand black
        protest.

3   In Figure 11.1 our political leadership categories are based on
        judgements about the political resources represented by the
        individual member of the leadership group. (a) Task Force: in this
        group each person was formally listed in the organization's
        minutes and, on at least two occasions, observed by a researcher
        making a contribution in a weekly planning session. The
        outside/insider measure was based on their self-report main
        organizational role that brought resources to the Task Force. (b)
        Steering Committee and Transition Team: these two groups
        released official lists of leadership along with their main
        occupational or political role. We assumed that these affiliations
        represented the key resources of use to the campaign.

12

Race, Class and Polarization in Los Angeles

Julia Maxted and Abebe Zegeye

The operations of the social and spatial structures which sustained and shaped expansionary post-war capitalist accumulation in the United States have become increasingly disarticulated over the past twenty years. The bipolar arrangements that characterized this structure, the segmentation between primary and secondary labour market employment, and suburban and inner city residence are undergoing a profound restructuring. They are giving way to a broad polarization of the labour market cut across by fragmentations based on race, ethnicity, immigrant status and gender. As Soja (1989: 178) suggests:

> In its most general sense, restructuring is meant to convey a break in secular trends and a shift towards a significantly different order and configuration of social, economic and political life. It thus evokes a sequence of breaking down and building up again, deconstruction and attempted reconstruction arising from certain incapacities and weaknesses in the established order which precludes conventional adaptation and demands significant structural change instead.

The emergence of a new regime of accumulation out of this restructuring is not written into the fate of capitalist development. Regimes of accumulation and modes of regulation are outcomes of human struggles, outcomes that have succeeded because they have ensured some regularity and permanence in social reproduction (Lipietz 1986). We are at present witnessing a continuum of situations, of local regimes and modes of insertion into national and global economies. What is particularly pertinent to the question of the articulation of race and class in these emerging arrangements is Poulantzas's suggestion (1975: 13) that every social formation or historically existing society has consisted in the overlay and structural coexistence of several modes of production at once. Thus each social formation includes vestiges and survivals of older modes of production, now relegated to structurally dependent positions within the new, as well as anticipatory tendencies which are potentially inconsistent with the existing system.

The Los Angeles metropolitan region exemplifies the many different patterns and processes associated with the societal restructuring of the late twentieth century. Seemingly paradoxical but functionally interdependent juxtapositions such as the expansion of firms with hitherto peripheral, paternalistic forms of labour organization, and of high technology industrial complexes are the epitomizing features of contemporary Los Angeles. In a paper entitled 'The Devaluation of Labor Power', Gould (1981) has brought a new coherence to the analysis of the current restructuring process. His identification of the pressure for the devaluation of labour power as an integral part of this process has informed our approach to examining the changing social relations and the continuing salience of race in late twentieth century United States society.

Labour Market Segmentation and the Post Second World War Structure of Accumulation

The pivot of structural cohesion of the post-war intensive (Fordist) regime of accumulation was the articulation between production in Department I, the sector of producer goods, and Department II, the domestic sector of consumer goods (Aglietta 1979). This entailed a transformation of the conditions of reproduction of labour power, resulting from changes in the modalities of class struggle. The consolidation of Fordism was predicated on the long struggle of the new industrial CIO unions during the depression to force their way for union recognition in large corporations and the codification of a collective bargaining agreement (Davis 1986).

The Second World War had set the stage for the restructuring of the historical relations between organized labour, capital and the state. The rapid centralization, mechanization and speed up that had taken place in wartime had been smoothed by the National War Labor Board's intervention in the arbitration and grievance procedure. Large corporations acquiesced to collective bargaining in the face of booming production, soaring profits and the purge of the more radical unions from the CIO. The state moved towards the containment of industrial unionism within institutional constraints that harmonized managerial control over the labour process.

Collective bargaining agreements were not inscribed in state legislation. They were based instead on the precedent set by the so-called 'Treaty of Detroit', signed by the United Auto Workers and General Motors in 1950. This instituted a dynamic wage system that synchronized mass consumption with labour productivity. The core of manufacturing industry became relatively immune to the cyclical lay-offs and capital devaluation which had characterized the prevailing movement of accumulation.

The emergence of the large corporation as the decisive institution in the economy imposed a re-ordering of work relations. A systematizing and normalizing of production relations went hand in hand with the gaining of oligopolistic positions in national and international markets (Baron 1975). These core corporations typically exhibited large levels of industry concentration, higher profits and were in relatively protected sectors with reduced risk of failure. As part of the ordering of large firms the working conditions of many employees were stabilized.

In contrast many of the medium and small employers made up a secondary sector of less desirable jobs still largely administered by conditions of less complex, competitive organization of the work process (Edwards 1979). The peripheral firms upon which the secondary labour market was based were necessary for the overall operation of the economy and often functioned to the long run advantage of large corporations (Averitt 1968). The existence of the periphery enhanced the profitability of corporations at the centre in product areas where it was least possible to stabilize business risks. These were transferred to peripheral firms and to peripheral workers. The option of subcontracting work to these firms increased the potential for corporate flexibility, especially when unionized sections made substantial gains in the post-war period. Peripheral firms were a low cost alternative to the maintenance of existing productive capacity in slack periods. They also provided the opportunity to circumvent potential union problems. Furthermore, while the Taft-Hartley Agreement had provided the legislative foundation for the consolidation of the existing frontiers of union organization, it also circumscribed and rendered increasingly difficult any advance of organization, particularly in the South or in low wage industries.

Within metropolitan labour markets this emergent segmentation of employment between a primary sector with decent paying jobs and steady employment and a secondary sector of marginal jobs in the competitive sector began to interact with the prevailing racial demarcation of jobs. This was an outgrowth of the old plantation based caste like status of black workers, which defined 'black' jobs as the most menial ones (Baron 1975). This system had been incorporated into wartime production. Black workers in Los Angeles were not employed in large numbers until 1942 in spite of critical labour shortages (Collins 1980). When employed they were concentrated in more technologically backward sectors of production such as shipbuilding and struggled to obtain places in the more advanced sector of aircraft production (de Graaf 1962). Furthermore they were often denied union membership or placed in segregated locals.

After the war black workers lost their jobs in numbers disproportionate to their percentage of the work force. The combination of historically constituted racial divisions in the metropolitan labour market and the primary-secondary labour market compounded the immobility of black workers in the secondary labour market. In the primary sector where jobs existed they were identified as 'black' jobs. Others became separated from normal promotion ladders, subject to speed up or lagged in wage increments taking on the characteristics of the secondary labour market.

Primary sector workers were able to define quasi-guild restrictions for entering certain occupations which functioned to exclude many minorities and women, while at the same time successfully upgrading for primary sector workers the package of commodities defining the socially acceptable subsistence standard of living for the primary sector. Monopoly capital was dependent upon a relatively steady product demand, requiring control over demand that entailed the coordination of mass consumption with continuous productivity increases. The process of individual consumption had to be organized and stable.

The individual ownership of commodities governed the concrete practices of working class consumption (Davis 1986). The two most striking indices of the advance of this intensive regime of accumulation were the growth of higher education and suburban home ownership (Pollenberg 1980). The expansion of higher education had a dramatic effect on the consumption levels of the skilled strata of the working class and provided for effective entry into expanding white collar and technical employment.

There were two levels of working class inclusion into these new structural arrangements. The historical standard of labour power for large sections of the white working class came to encompass suburban home ownership and a college education for their children. Minorities, young people and women underwent a status degradation in that the new social norm of consumption was not recognized in the wages of the workers affected. The exclusion of blacks from access to suburban housing, their subordination into low wage and unstable employment areas provided a strong representation of the status differences between primary and secondary labour employment. Minorities were being excluded from the commodification of civil society.

However, part of the historically high value of labour power obtained in core Fordist organizations was based on a process of credentialing. Credentialing involved the requirement of higher educational and craft qualfications and, in consequence, more costly labour than was necessary for particular jobs. This inflated value of labour was not accompanied by a commensurate increase in productivity (Gould 1981). In sectors of the economy characterized by attenuated competition this process functioned to the advantage of both capital and labour. But any slowing of mass consumption or import penetration would directly undermine or destabilize this process.

As United States' international hegemony waned and was transformed in the late 1960s, an integrated economic system grounded in increasingly competitive production relations emerged. The 'monopolies' of most efficient production of certain American industries was challenged by competitive pressures from Japan and segments of the Third World in which American capital had invested.

The opening of the US economy to import integration was also encouraged by a coalition of forces led by the largest US banks and science based industries. Together with the traditional export interest of the most technically advanced corporations, they saw the opening of the economy as a necessary extension of their own evolution into globally integrated industries. These industries had to reorient cost calculations based on traditionally oligopolistic home markets to an increasingly competitive international system of production.

Credentialing, which had signified an increase in the value of labour power without a commensurate increase in productivity, became a liability. The amount of labour in value terms socially necessary for the production of an increasing number of American commodities came to be defined by the international system. Within this context American commodities were over-valued. As American advantages in the efficiency of other productive forces beside labour declined, the significance of the now over-valued labour power was exacerbated into crisis conditions (Gould 1981). While a high value of labour power was beneficial in the relatively non competitive circumstances of the post-war period, from the late 1960s this became a serious disadvantage for American capital.

The recompense of wages for a certain strata of American workers emerged as high wages, as wages above the socially defined value of labour power as this became increasingly defined within a world capitalist system. Lowering prices under these circumstances to meet competitive pressures would result in diminished profits. In consequence there has arisen tremendous pressure for the devaluation of labour power (Gould 1981).

The pressures for devaluation have focused most strongly on American corporations that were in relatively non-competitive situations in the post-war period where credentialing was strongest, and hence on workers who were most heavily organized by unions. Throughout the core of manufacturing production industry, where unions had previously stabilized the wage component, labour costs are once again becoming the decisive variable in corporate balance sheets (Aglietta and Oudiz 1983).

The cause of the crisis of Fordism is, however, only partially located in the internal contradictions of the labour process and profit cycle. As important as the gradual exhaustion of the source of productivity and profitability have been politically imposed limits on both geographical expansion, and under segmented labour conditions, to the domestic deepening of consumption. The consumer durable market which had been the primary engine of coordinated expansion of Fordist accumulation had also reached relative saturation. During the 1960s car markets continued to grow at rates of 12 and 13 per cent per annum. By the 1970s these had fallen to 2-3 per cent. Consumer durable industries reacted in classic fashion to market saturation and growing foreign competition by undertaking rationalization of existing productive capacity. The range of options open to such industries has differed according to such factors as structure of ownership, strength of union organization and regional location. A number of strategies are being pursued in the attempt to restore profitability and the changing conditions of production in core manufacturing industry are having ramifications throughout the social structure. The following sections will examine the racial and class consequences of these emerging conditions in the Los Angeles area.

The maturation of Fordism under American hegemony has thus produced a constellation of crisis that interlaces contradictions, among others, at the level of the composition of capital, the domestic class structure and the international division of labour. These trends seem to coalesce in cities such as Los Angeles and New York. The structure of production and consumption is changing in these large world cities feeding increasing inequalities and constraints on groups and individuals.

Racial and class inequality is being reproduced in changing conditions that have involved the limited inclusion of a minority of blacks and the continued exclusion of the majority. Likewise the new structures have entailed the inclusion of women but under very different forms of labour organization. The continued presence of pervasive racial and sexual typfications, sustained and fuelled by segmented labour markets, are playing a significant role in the structuring of opportunities as the older structures are being disengaged. Citizen status is producing increasing fragmentation of the Caribbean Basin and Mexico into the dynamics of accumulation. The economic and organizational attractiveness of non citizens as labour market participants has been heightened by the increased political and economic claims associated with citizenship following the civil rights movement and urban protest in the 1960s.

The Composition of Capital and the Polarization of Labour Markets

The attempts to downgrade manufacturing production have led to a polarization of wages and increased wage inequalities in manufacturing as a result of a combination of movements. These include the absolute loss of unionized blue collar jobs through plant cloosures and the replacement of more labour intensive processes by contracting out. Furthermore, growth in manufacturing has been in low wage areas even in high technology industries.

Corporate capital has embarked on a series of strategies to restore profitability closing. These include shutting down plants and moving production overseas, the increased use of subcontracting and forced pay-backs of concessions by unions. Union busting and plant closure have centred on monopoly corporations which have previously sought to reach accommodation with their unionized workers. The most powerful unions have been blackmailed by the threat of plant closure into yielding concession on wages and work rules. These presage the destruction of national pattern bargaining and the creeping fragmentation of industrial unionism. Union busting in construction and in non durable manufacturing has led to meat packing, wood products and tyre production being converted from former high wage industries into low wage, non-union sectors.

California has been quicker than most in shedding old manufacturing business. In the 1982 recession 100,000 jobs were lost in heavy manufacturing (*The Economist*, 19 May 1984) Durable goods industries outside the Southern California military/defence contract sector have been subject to the same pressures as in other parts of the country. Peaking in the early 1980s, plant closures left a trail of unemployment and shattered tax bases across the industrial heartland of Los Angeles County. By 1980 the car industry which had employed 28,000 in 1975 was reduced to less than 9,000. With the closure of Goodyear, Firestone, Goodrich and Uniroyal, the tyre industry was virtually destroyed. What has remained is concentrated in smaller secondary labour market operations unable to diversify or move abroad, increasingly reliant on illegal labour (Morales 1983). Many of the steel plants have closed. The long established metal industry in Los Angeles is now concentrated in small foundries and scrap processing plants. The car industry has been reduced to a single plant in suburban Van Nuys, kept open by Japanese investment.

From 1978-82 an estimated 75,000 jobs were lost in Los Angeles County due to closure and indefinite lay offs (Soja 1989). These have affected primarily a segment of the labour force that was highly unionised. These jobs represented a significant proportion of good jobs available to minorities and females. As the result of federal pressure and the movement away of younger white workers from both the area and manufacturing employment, blacks and Hispanics had begun to enter these plants in the late 1960s. These closures have had an enormous impact on the community. The loss of 8,235 jobs at an average wage of ten dollars an hour resulted in an estimated loss of 138 million dollars in wages.

Hill and Negrey (1989) have found that black workers have been disproportionately affected by plant closure during the 1980s. A Bureau of Labor Statistics survey found that black workers took longer to find work than white at comparable pay and over the course of four years about one fifth dropped out of the labour force altogether (Flaim and Sehgal 1985). Black workers have suffered considerably higher rates of industrial job losses over the 1980s with black job losses due to plant closures affecting 26.7 per cent of the work force, compared to 18.5 per cent of whites and 15 per cent of Hispanics (Hill and Negrey 1989). From 1979-84 nationally one third of all black men working in durable goods manufacturing lost their jobs. Women have experienced lower rates of job losses than men; 11.8 per cent of the work force being affected compared to 20.9 per cent of male manufacturing workers. Non union part time, low wage jobs have overwhelmingly been filled by women. White women in turn gained at higher occupational levels while black women increased at lower occupational levels (Landry 1987).

Plant closures have played a decisive role in the recomposition of capital. They are being used as a deliberate strategy to divest of a relatively unprofitable manufacturing base (Davis 1986). Firms that shut plants in South Los Angeles either moved to the South, or overseas including the Mexican border zone. Litton Industries, Motorola, General Motors, Chrysler and Transitron moved to Mexico; Max Factor to Tennessee and Uniroyal to Brazil and Turkey.

Those major industries least advantaged by restructuring their production internationally have divested of their old capital base to become conglomerates in search of new profits in oil production, financial services and military production. Work forces threatened with plant closure have granted wage concessions only to find the cash flow used for diversification. For example, US Steel having bought Marathon Oil shifted steel production to the South Eastern states and overseas.

There has been a reorientation of mainland US corporations away from consumer durable and mass production markets towards highly profitable and volatile sectors like military production and financial services. The liquid assets gained from wage concession are not put into capital investment but used to enhance stock values through buy-backs and high divided pay-outs. Increasing the turnover time of capital is central to this strategy and contrasts sharply with post-war circuits of capital with their heavy investment in fixed capital and infrastructure.

With stagnation in the mass production sector manufacturing capital has moved towards highly profitable technology and defence industries. The Pentagon is a chief agent in the restructuring of manufacturing employment especially in Southern California. General Tires, Aerojet International, Ford and General Motors have all moved into military and defence production. Military technology now accounts for 13 per cent of all durable goods production in the US. These industries display extreme segmentation in their labour demand. In the electronics and semi-conductors industries employment exhibits a high degree of polarization between high paid technically skilled and low wage assembly workers (Bluestone and Harrison 1982).

From 1970 to 1980 when the entire country experienced a relative increase of less than one million manufacturing jobs, the Los Angeles region added 225,000 manufacturing jobs (Soja et al. 1983). This was more than the next two growth areas, San Francisco and Houston combined. Most of this new employment growth was contained in two very different segments of the manufacturing economy. The first is a cluster of technically advanced manufacturing based in electronics aerospace and massive defence contracting. The second includes low wage industries such as garment, furniture and leather goods production.

High technology employment grew by 65 per cent from 150,000 to 250,000 accounting for 50 per cent of the increase in manufacturing jobs from 1970-80. Southern California now accounts for one quarter of all US employment in aerospace (SCAG 1984a). One third of jobs in this cluster are in technical and management positions and two thirds in operative and assembly work. Firms are increasingly subcontracting out less skilled labour intensive aspects of production to smaller competitive firms.

The apparel industry was responsible for adding 19 per cent of all new manufacturing employment from 1970-80. This growth was concentrated in Los Angeles County while new high technology and biotechnology is becoming increasingly concentrated on Orange and Riverside-San Bernadino Counties. Among the emerging industries two categories of growth industry can be identified; those contributing the most new employment in absolute terms and those with highest growth rates (Morales et al. 1982). Making up the first category are apparel, fabricated metal, rubber, plastics and furniture. The second group consists of apparel, furniture, leather and miscellaneous manufacturing (toys, sports goods).

In both groups every industry is characterized by having an hourly wage that is well below the average for manufacturing in Los Angeles. It is not the high wage industries that are expanding. Furthermore the greatest gains are in apparel which has one of the lowest average hourly wages and a shorter week (34 hours as opposed to 40 for average full time jobs). With the rise of low wage jobs the average hourly wage for production in manufacturing had dropped below the national average since 1977.

The supposedly marginal periphery of non-union production has been the place from which a major assault has been launched against wage levels and bargaining patterns. This has coincided with the stagnation of public employment, which during the 1950s and 1960s was the single largest provider of new high wage jobs (Ginzberg 1979) and the proliferation of the tertiary sector with its pervasive gender and/or racial typifications of particular occupations as less skilled regardless of content or comparability. The job supply in Los Angeles is thus increasingly shaped by several key trends. These include the growth of the advanced service sector including the financial system, the shrinking of traditional manufacturing industry and its replacement with a downgraded manufacturing sector, and the growth of high technology industries with high levels of occupational polarization.

The evidence from the manufacturing sector reveals a shrinking of middle income and unionized blue collar jobs and the expansion of high and low wage jobs. A similar pattern is characterizing the employment profile of the service sector. The response of capital to the crisis of profitability by downgrading manufacturing, internationalizing production and shifting into speculative capital has increased the need for centralized control (Sassen-Koob 1984). Los Angeles is consolidating its position as a new economic centre, as a producer and exporter of advanced services including finance, management and control functions. This consolidation in turn has generated a restructuring of labour demand with the expansion of both low wage level jobs that service the high income lifestyles of the top level professional work force, and in this work force itself (Sassen 1988).

Moreover, great differences of employment exist within the service sector. While professional workers make up 36 per cent of jobs in non profit services, only 3.3 per cent of distributive and 1 per cent of retailing jobs are professional. Some industries such as consumer services have low average pay across occupations and a high incidence of low paying jobs. In contrast distributive and public administration have few poorly paid jobs (Stanback and Noyelle 1982).

In Los Angeles the largest increases have taken place in producer services which accounted for 30.4 per cent of the increase in service employment from 1977-81. In 1981 the total percentage of workers in producer services was 24.9 per cent (Sassen 1988). Employment in finance, insurance and real estate increased by 47 per cent from 1970-80 (SCAG 1984a). The fastest growing service jobs are those with larger than average concentrations of low and high paid jobs, i.e. producer services, banking and management. Producer services have 50 per cent in the next to lowest earning class, and 50 per cent in the two highest. The proliferation of the tertiary sector is characterized by a polarization between a white male dominated sector of professionals and a large pool of low paid labour, overwhelmingly female and minority (Stafford 1985).

Over the ten years from 1970-80, employment in Southern California grew by one and a quarter million jobs. One quarter of this was in manufacturing which now accounts for only 30 per cent of employment. Services grew by 64.4 per cent, becoming the largest sector of employment in 1981. A dual labour market long familiar in manufacturing employment is emerging in services as well (Tyler 1987). The hour glass image of current jobs markets is likely to be accentuated in the growth trends of the 1990s with a small sector of high paying jobs, a large sector of low paying jobs and a shrinking middle.

By the mid-1970s a number of black Americans had been included within a number of middle strata occupations in corporate industry and the public sector. Black women with high levels of educational attainment accounted for most black gains in the 1970s. There was a rapid rise in the 1970s in the number of black women employed in public service. One third of all job gains for black women and one quarter for men in California were in the public sector (Muller 1984). As a consequence in 1984 one out of every three black women, and one out of four black men were employed in the public sector, compared to 1 in 7 white women and 1 in 10 white men. In Los Angeles 22 per cent of all public administration employees were black in 1980.

In comparison with the white middle class the black middle class is concentrated in very distinct occupational segments. One quarter of all employed black men work as social workers, secondary school teachers, postal clerks, in clerical support jobs and the police. black men work in these occupations. Half of all black employed women are registered nurses, elementary school teachers, secondary school teachers, in retail sales jobs or secretaries (Collins 1983). The black middle class consists of a large stratum of clerical and sales workers, a smaller stratum of professionals, and an even smaller stratum of managers and small business owners.

The black middle class is very much occupationally based. It has very little ownership of wealth. From 1970-80 the increase in the black middle class slowed down, especially among black men, even though middle strata jobs continued to grow. Most middle strata growth depended on the ability of black women to find pink and white collar jobs. The growth rate among black professionals declined by two-thirds from 1970 to 1980 (Landry 1987). This was not due to the unavailability of work. White collar work increased by 2 per cent for white males and 3 per cent for white females.

These various gains for black Americans have been severely qualified by growing hopelessness at the bottom levels. The combination of unemployment and labour force statistical data more accurately reflect the status of black men than either alone. In 1960 three out of four black men included in US Census data were working. Today (1991) only 55 per cent are working and an estimated 925,000 working age black men are missing in the census. For each black man counted as unemployed two are out of the labour force. Out of 8.8 million working age black men, 4 million or 46 per cent are without jobs. In 1981, 78 per cent of all working age white men were employed compared to 54 per cent black men.

The trend in black employment is tending towards stable participation in higher level occupations (though pressure for balanced state budgets could well undermine this position) for the minority, and a decreasing rate of participation for the majority. This is accentuated by a sharp decline in the labour force participation rate of young minority workers, especially those with less than 12 years of education (SCAG 1984). Black women in the Southern California region continue to have above average participation rates. Though the number of non white workers increased because of a smaller decline in non white birth rates, the declining participation in low level occupations that began in the early 1960s will continue. There has been a dramatic increase in the number of blacks dropping out of the labour market or never entering. At lower levels of educational attainment black males in particular have labour force participation rates some 10 per cent less than the regional average. Their participation in the national labour force has fallen from 80 per cent in 1945 to less than 60 per cent today. In Southern California the labour force participation rates of black men aged between 55 and 65 is 15 percentage points below the regional average (SCAG 1984).

Despite the long boom of the 1960s the private economy has failed to generate decent paying jobs, if any at all, for millions of former farm tenants and labourers displaced to the cities in the 1950s and 1960s. A much greater proportion of black men hold low wage jobs rather than high wage compared to white men. Black adult men do have lower participation rates than white men, as in Los Angeles they respond to a labour market in which immigrants, and in particular illegal immigrants have become the preferred work force. In 1980 the Latino work force in California outnumbered blacks by 3 to 1 in durable manufacturing and by 7 to 1 in non durable manufacturing. But the main economic disadvantage is higher unemployment and lower wages. Because male earnings are so much greater than female ones the continuing interracial gap in male earnings militates against an improved economic situation for the entire black population. Even though black women have higher labour force participation rates than white women, and nearly comparable wages, their low earnings in women's work are insufficient to improve the real income position of black families. In 1980 one third of full-time women workers earned less than $7,000 while the white male median was $17,000 (Rytira 1982). According to the 1988 US Bureau of Census 11 per cent of black families lived on incomes below the poverty line compared with 5 per cent of white families.

The Internationalization of the Labour Market

The rapidly industrializing and urbanizing sunbelt is converting much of Mexico and the Caribbean Basin into its own domestic hinterland. The flow of undocumented workers is part of an irreversible structural assimilation of adjacent economies and labour markets. With about half of its work force unemployed or underemployed and with real wages plummeting, Mexico alone has almost infinite reserves of labour.

Around the 1960s previous sources of cheap labour, such as rural reserves of southern blacks began to dry up and urban minorities became increasingly politicized. Black workers became increasingly militant as the blocked aspirations of second generation black migrants to the city, along with glaring racial discrimination and political isolation, led to a series of mobilizations and protests. It also led to the progressive withdrawal of second and third generations from the low wage labour market.

The resistance of young blacks to continue filling low wage and menial jobs in the aftermath of the urban rebellions and the absence of another ready source of domestic labour underlies the progressive reliance of employers in the low wage sector on clandestine immigrant labour. Since the 1960s immigration has increased markedly and the composition changed towards a domination of nationalities with large shares of low wage labour.

Immigration entry levels since the late 1960s are among the highest in US immigration history. Legally admitted immigrants numbered 265,000 in 1960. By 1970 this number had reached half a million. By 1980 this reached one million and continued to rise through the 1980s (SCAG 1984). The number of immigrants in Southern California increased by 782,000 from 1970-80. From 1980-3 this number had increased by 730,000. New immigrants may have accounted for up to 45 per cent of the increase in the labour force during the 1980s. Six out of every ten new workers in Los Angeles from 1970-80 were immigrants (SCAG 1984). The largest numbers are from Mexico, the Philippines, Korea, China, India and the Caribbean Basin.

The contemporary high levels of immigration were stimulated by a combination of demographic and socio-political factors which led to a decline in availability of cheap, pliant labour at a time when demand for this type of labour was intensifying. Now the presence of this work force with a peculiar status is producing its own dynamics in the production and consumption patterns in the city. It is the expansion of the low wage job supply that contains the conditions for the absorption of the immigrant influx. Immigrants can be seen as providing labour for low wage service jobs, including those that service both the highly specialized export oriented service sector, and the high income lifestyle of professionals employed in that sector. But immigrants are also an important labour source for the expanding downgraded manufacturing sector, including, but not exclusively, declining industries in need of cheap labour for survival as well as dynamic high technology sector.

A third source of jobs for immigrants is the immigrant community itself (Light 1972; Portes and Bach 1980). These jobs include not only those that are a temporary arrangement until a new job can be found, but also a large array of technical and professional jobs that service the expanding immigrant community in the city (Sassen-Koob 1984). As they include jobs that provide services and goods for the subsistence of members of the community they contribute to lowering the costs of survival both for themselves and ultimately their employers (Sassen 1988).

There is an abundant supply of low wage workers for some

major growth industries. Undocumented immigrants, mostly Hispanics comprise 68 per cent of the work force in the expanding garment industry (Cornelius et al. 1982). In addition to the low wages paid to these workers it is the flexibility of this supply that is also important, i.e. the ability to expand employment in times of growth, and an equal ease of firing with few penalties in downtowns. The powerlessness of these workers has led to a revival of paternalistic organization of the work process, utilizing immigrant networks for recruitment and for the organization of the work process itself within firms. The peer pressure resulting from this form of recruitment works towards disciplining labour within the factory. Citizenship status is emerging as a key component in the segmentation process as the labour market has become transnationalized.

The occupational and industrial distribution of immigrants is characterized by a higher concentration in manual jobs and transformative jobs than the resident population. In 1980 in Southern California, immigrant women were concentrated to an even greater degree than native women in a limited number of menial and operative occupations, in transformative industries such as food, textiles and garments (SCAG 1984). In California as a whole 25 per cent of immigrant women held operative jobs compared to 7 per cent of native women in 1980. Thirty per cent of immigrant women were in transformative jobs, compared to 15 per cent of native women (Bach and Tienda 1984). Almost 50 per cent of immigrant women were concentrated in two areas, operatives and services.

Allowing illegal immigrants into the US not only expands the pool of available labour but more importantly brings into the country workers who feel they must be subservient to capital for fear of being deported. The maintenance of their illegal status serves as a vehicle for the maintenance of artificially low expectations and in addition implies that their very presence will serve as an instrument to attack the value of American labour. In sectors of the Los Angeles economy where lower levels of immigrants were employed wages rose as fast or faster than the national average. Where large numbers of immigrants were employed, wages declined relative to the national average (Muller 1984). The use of immigrant labour by employers not only reduces costs directly through lower wages but also directly by lowering costs for the organization of production.

Conclusion

Within the emerging class structure of the 1990s both the modal
Fordist working class and the traditional mass market which
this sustained may well lose their centrality (Davis 1986). The
economics of class will increasingly be amplified by the gender
and demography of class as economic restructuring reshapes the
traditional income pyramid into a new income hourglass.
'Middle class families, truly in the middle are disappearing
displaced by two income two person households on the top of
the hourglass and single earner blue collar families, clerical
singles women in many jobs the welfare poor and the retired at
the bottom' (Parker 1981: 11).

There is a dialectical relationship between middle class over-
consumptionism and increasing degradation of new job
creation. The tertiarization of the economy has been harnessed
to   the   distributive   advantage   of   an   expanded
managerial/professional strata as well as opening up new
frontiers of accumulation for small and medium sized
entrepreneurs. The managerial/professional strata in US society
continued to expand during the 1970s even as the recession was
wiping out manufacturing jobs. As blue collar employment fell
by 12 per cent from 1980-2 the number of managers and
administrators increased by 9 per cent (*New York Times*, 14 April
1983). These strata, faced with the declining organization of the
working poor and of minorities in the 1970s, have been
successful in benefiting both from inflation and expanded state
expenditures.

The explosive growth of privatized consumption during the
1960s and 1970s imposed unprecedented strains on the fiscal
resources available for collective infrastructure (such as roads,
schools, fire and police). Public spending and taxes became
increasingly a terrain for division between suburbanized
workers and middle strata, predominantly white but including a
small proportion of black Americans on the one hand, and inner
city and non waged workers on the other.

Runaway inflation has further polarised the consumption
defined positions that developed in the 1950s and 1960s. For
example, working class home owners have simultaneously
become beneficiaries of inflated equities and victims of higher
property taxes, tempting the more advantaged sections of the
working class to abandon traditional solidaristic political

alliances to join new interclass 'haves' blocs against collective 'have nots' (Davis 1986). Distributional struggles have thus acquired at times a greater political salience than 'old' class defined alignments.

At least one third of the US work force, however, consists of wage labourers trapped in low income ghettos. During the 1970s new jobs were being created at twice the rate of the previous decade amounting to some 20 million jobs. But the composition of the work force between 1972 and 1980 changed dramatically. Women accounted for 65 per cent of the employment rise. As women's labour force participation rates doubled their relative earnings declined from 65 per cent to 59 per cent. As real wages stagnate and decline across the working class, families have felt the pressure for the inclusion of women, most notably married women within the labour force. Labour power can then be devalued when measured for each individual even as its value rise then measured for the working class family. The normal definition of the value of labour power presumes two wage earners generating severe pressures for many single parent families (Gould 1981). In 1981 the median income of a dual wage earning family was $31,600, a male headed household $25,000, and a female headed household $18,900. Since 1975 real income has hardly changed at all, but a greater proportion of the working age population has been employed. As a result real wages per worker declined (Fainstein 1986/7).

Race is increasingly salient and significant in the emerging economic and political structure. The limited inclusion of blacks within American society has not resulted in the equalization of wages for black and white workers. Instead the absolute gap between blacks and whites of otherwise similar social attributes, ignoring the skewed distribution of these attributes remains approximately the same as 20 years ago (Featherman and Hauser 1978).

The inclusion of blacks in American society under current conditions will raise the status of the individual men and women but is leading to a devaluation of the labour power of those people who normally assume these positions. The inclusion of black Americans has been skewed in the direction of the public sector, an area capable of significant devaluation without impinging on mainstream American capitalism.

The continued exclusion of the majority of blacks also has a function. It has the double consequence of maintaining an important segment of the domestic reserve of the unemployed, here a segment that will be continually used in the future as in the past as a threat to employed black and white workers. The existence of this group is also essential for the successful devaluation process via the mechanism of inclusion. The random absorption of blacks within the work force in every occupation at their percentage in the population would undermine an important weapon for extracting surplus value, the stigmatization of race. It is only while certain racial characteristics remain stigmatized and while this racism is justified by the 'failure' of most blacks to advance that the process of inclusion leads to devaluation of all labour power within a specific occupation (Gould 1981).

Poverty is thus being produced not only by the continuing exclusion of minority males from primary labour markets, but especially through the dynamic incorporation of women and immigrants into low wage sectors of the economy. The economic situation of blacks is increasingly rooted in the character of employment opportunities in growing industries, and the loss of well paying blue collar jobs. Low wage employment in the emerging structure of accumulation, far from being the periphery to a high wage core as under Fordist organization, has become the job growth pole of the economy. This chapter has sought to begin to relate some of the seemingly discrete phenomena and paradoxical juxtapositions emerging in the new spatial and social configurations to the structure which generates them. These new arrangements are challenging the bipolar constructions that have dominated the analysis of post Second World War United States society.

References

Adler, Leslie K. (1970) 'The Red Image,' Ph.D. thesis, University of California

Aglietta, Michel (1979) *A Theory of Capitalist Regulation: The US Experience*, London, New Left Books

Aglietta, M. and G. Oudiz (1983) 'Configurations de l'Economie Mondiale et Régulations Nationales,' Paris, Centre d'Etudes Perspectives et d'Information

Aigner, D. J. and G. C. Cain (1977) 'Statistical Theories of Discrimination in Labor Markets,' *Industrial and Labor Relations Review*, 30, 175-87

Akerlof, George A. and Janet L. Yellen (eds) (1986) *Efficiency Wage Models of the Labor Market*, Cambridge, Cambridge University Press

Alkalimat, Abdul et al. (1986) *Introduction to Afro-American Studies: A People's College Primer*, Chicago, Twenty-First Century Books

Allen, V. (1969) 'Teaching Standard English as a Second Dialect,' *Florida Foreign Language Reporter*, 123-9

Alleyne, M. (1981). *Comparative Afro-American*, Ann Arbor, Karoma

Appiah, Kwame Anthony (1986) 'The Uncompleted Argument: Du Bois and the Illusion of Race,' *Critical Enquiry*, 12 (1), Autumn, 21-37

Appiah, Kwame Anthony (1989) 'Racisms,' in Goldberg, q.v.

Arnauld, A. and Lancelot, C. (1975) *Port-Royal Grammar*, The Hague, Mouton

Aronowitz, Stanley (1981) *The Crisis in Historical Materialism*, New York, Praeger

Arrow, Kenneth (1985) *Allied Economics: Collected Papers*, Cambridge, Mass., Harvard University Press

Averitt, Robert T. (1968) *The Dual Economy: The Dynamics of American Industrial Structure*, New York, W. W. Norton

Bach, R. L. and M. Tienda (1984) 'Contemporary Immigration and Refugee Movements and Employment Adjustment Policies,' in V. M. Briggs Jr and M. Tienda, *Immigration Issues and Policies*, Salt Lake City, Olympus, 37-82

Baier, Kurt (1978) 'Merit and Racism,' *Philosophia*, 8 (2-3), 121-51

Balibar, Etienne (1989) 'The Paradoxes of Universality,' in Goldberg, q.v

Banton, Michael (1989) 'Sociology: Colour us Poor,' *The Times Higher Education Supplement*, 12 December

Barker, Martin, (1981) *The New Racism*, New York, Aletheia Books

Baron, H. (1975) 'Racial Domination in Advanced Capitalism: A Theory of Nationalism and Divisions in the Labor Market,' in Richard Edwards, Michael Reich and David Gordon (eds) *Labor Market Segmentation*, Lexington Massachusetts, Lexington Books

Becker, Gary S. (1971) *The Economics of Discrimination*, Chicago, University of Chicago Press

Berger, P. L. and Luckmann, T. (1966) *The Social Construction of Reality: A Treatise in the Sociology of Knowledge*, New York, Doubleday

Bernstein, Victor H. (1943) 'The Anti-Labor Front,' *The Antioch Review*, 3, 328-40

Blau, Francine D. (1984) 'Discrimination Against Women: Theory and Evidence,' in William Darity (ed.) *Labor Economics: Modern Views*, Boston, Kluwer-Nijhoff, 53-89

Blau, Francine D. and Lawrence Kahn (1981) 'Race and Sex Differences in Quits By Young Workers,' *Industrial and Labor Relations Review*, 34, 563-77

Blau, Peter (1964) *Exchange and Power in Social Life*, New York, John Wiley

Block, W. and M. Walker (1982) *Discrimination, Affirmative Action and Equal Opportunity: An Economic and Social Perspective*, Vancouver, BC, The Frazier Institute

Bloom (1987) *Class, Race and the Civil Rights Movement*, Bloomington, Indiana University Press

Bluestone, B. and Bennett Harrison (1982) *The De-industrialization of America*, New York, Basic Books

Boggs, Carl (1986) *Social Movements and Political Power: Emerging Forms of Radicalism in the West*, Philadelphia, Temple University Press

Bosmajian, H. (1984) 'Reagan's "evil empire-virus-cancer-mickey mouse" phantasmagoria,' *Quarterly Review of Doublespeak*, 11 (1) 5-6

Boston, Thomas D. (1988) *Race, Class and Conservatism*, London, Unwin Hyman Ltd.

Boston, Thomas D. (1991) *Hope and Despair: The Economic Drama of African America*, London, Unwin Hyman Ltd.

Botan, C. and Smitherman, G. (1983) 'White Faces, Black Tongues: Black English and the White Worker,' paper presented at the Speech Communication Association Convention, Washington DC

Bowles, Samuel and Herbert Gintis (1981) 'Structure and Practice in the Labor Theory of Value,' *Review of Radical Political Economics*, 12 (4), Winter

Bowles, Samuel and Herbert Gintis (1983) 'On the Heterogeneity of Power,' unpublished ms

Bowles, Samuel (1985) 'The Production Process in a Competitive Economy: Walrasian, Neo-Hobbesian, and Marxian Models,' *American Economic Review*, 75, 16-36

Bowser, Benjamin P. (1985) 'Race Relations in the US,' *Journal of Black Studies*, 15 (3) March, 307-24

Bowser, Benjamin P. (1985) 'Race Relations in the US,' *Journal of Black Studies*, 15 (3) March, 307-24

Boxill, Bernard (1979) 'The Morality of Reparation,' in Richard A. Wasserstrom (ed.) *Today's Moral Problems*, New York, Macmillan Publishing

Boxill, Bernard (1983) 'The Race-Class Question,' in L. Harris (ed.) *Philosophy Born of Struggle*, Iowa, Iowa University Press, 107-16

Boxill, Bernard R. (1984) *Blacks and Social Justice*, Totowa, Rowman & Allanheld

Boyer, Richard O. and Herbert M. Morais (1965) *Labor's Untold Story*, New York, Marzani & Munsell Publishers

Bracken, Harry M. (1978) 'Philosophy and Racism,' *Philosophia*, 8 (2-3), 241-60

Brown, G. (1851) *Grammar of English Grammars*, New York, W. Wood

Buchanan, Allen E. (1982) *Marx and Justice: The Radical Critique of Liberalism*, New York, Roman & Littlefield

Bulow, Jeremy and Lawrence H. Summers (1986) 'A Theory of Dual Labor Markets with Application to Industrial Policy, Discrimination, and Keynesian Unemployment,' *Journal of Labor Economics*, 4, 376-414

Bush, Rod (ed.) (1984) The New Black Vote, San Francisco, Synthesis Publications

Carleton, Don E. (1985) *Red Scare: Right-Wing Hysteria and Fifties Fanaticism and their Legacy in Texas*, Austin, Texas Monthly Press

Carson, Clayborne (1981) *In Struggle: SNCC and the Black Awakening of the 1960s*, Cambridge, Harvard University Press

Cartwright, N. (1983) *How the Laws of Physics Lie*, Oxford, Oxford University Press

Cassidy, F. et al. (1985) *Dictionary of American Regional English*, Cambridge, Belknap Press of Harvard University Press

Caute, David (1978) *The Great Fear*, New York, Simon & Schuster

Cheng, Charles W. (1973) 'The Cold War: Its Impact on the Black Liberation Struggle Within the United States, Part One,' *Freedomways*, 13, Winter, 184-203

Cheng, Charles W. (1973a) 'The Cold War: Its Impact on the Black Liberation Struggle Within the United States, Part Two,' *Freedomways*, 13, Fourth Quarter, 281-93

Chomsky, Noam (1975) *Reflections on Language*, New York, Pantheon Books

Clark, Wayne Addison (1976) 'An Analysis of the Relationship Between Anti-Communism and Segregationist Thought in the Deep South (1948-1964),' Ph.D. thesis, University of North Carolina, Chapel Hill

Clay, Nate (1983) 'Harold Washington's Campaign must become a Movement,' *Chicago Metro News*, 12 February

Cluster, Dick (ed.) (1979) *They Should Have Served That Cup of Coffee*, Boston, South End Press

Collins, Keith E. (1980) *Black Los Angeles: The Making of a Ghetto, 1940-50*, Saratoga, California, Century 21 Publishing Company

Collins, Sharon (1983) 'The making of the Black Middle Class,' *Social Problems*, 30 (4) April, 369-82

Comaroff, John (1987) 'Of Totemism and Ethnicity: Consciousness, Practice and the Signs of Inequality,' *Ethnos*, 52 (3-4)

Cornelius, Wayne, Leo Chavez and Jorge Castro (1982) 'Mexican Immigrants and Southern California: A Survey of Current Knowledge,' Centre of US-Mexican Studies, University of California, San Diego

Cox, Oliver C. (1948) *Class, Caste and Race*, New York, Doubleday

Dalby, D. (1969) *Black through White: Patterns of Communication in Africa and the New World*, Bloomington, Indiana University Press

Dalby, D. (1970) 'Jazz, Jitter and Jam,' *The New York Times*, 10 November

Daniel, J. L. (ed) (1974) *Black Communication: Dimensions of Research and Instruction*, New York, Speech Communication Association

Darby, Henry E. and Margaret N. Rowley (1986) 'King on Vietnam and Beyond,' *Phylon*, 47 (1), March, 43-50

Darity, W. (1990) 'Race, Class and Conservatism,' *Journal of Economic Literature*, 28 (1), 117-19

Davis, Mike (1986) *Prisoners of the American Dream*, London, Verso Books

de Graaf, Lawrence B (1962) 'Negro Migration to Los Angeles 1930-1950,' Unpublished Ph.D., University of California, Los Angeles

Demarco, Joseph P. (1972) 'The Concept of Race in the Social Thought of W.E.B. DuBois,' *The Philosophical Forum*, 3 (2), 227-42

Dennis, Rutledge M. and John V. Moeser (1982) 'Metropolitan Reform and the Politics of Race in the Urban South, 1960-1980,' *Western Journal of Black Studies* 6 (1), Spring, 35-43

Dillard, J. L. (1972) *Black English*, New York, Random House

Doeringer, P., Poire, M., Feldman, P., Gordon, D. and Reich, M. (1972) *Low Income Labor Markets and Urban Manpower Programs: A Critical Assessment*, Washington DC, US Department of Labor, Research and Development Findings, No. 12

DuBois, W.E.B. (1966) 'The Conservation of Races,' in Howard Brontz, *Negro Social and Political Thought, 1850-1920*, New York, Basic Books, 203-331

Dunbar, Anthony P. (1981) *Against the Grain: Southern Radicals and Prophets (1929-1959)*, Charlottesville, University Press of Virginia

Durkheim, Emile (1984) *The Division of Labor In Society*, New York, The Free Press, first published 1893

Dworkin, Ronald (1977) *Taking Rights Seriously*, Massachusetts, Harvard University Press

Eastland, Terry and William Bennett (1979) *Counting by Race,* New York, Basic Books

US Government (1983) *Economic Report of the President,* Washington DC, United States Government Printing Office

Edwards, Richard C. (1979) *Contested Terrain,* New York, Basic Books

Ehrenberg, Ronald G. and Robert Smith (1982) *Modern Labor Economics: Theory and Public Policy,* Glenview, Illinois, Scott Foresman

Elias, R. (1986) 'Nukespeak and Beyond,' *Quarterly Review of Doublespeak,* 12 (4) 9-10

Eliasoph, Nina (1987) 'Politeness, Power and Women's Language,' *Berkeley Journal of Sociology,* 32, 79-104

Ellison, Ralph (1953) *Invisible Man,* New York, New American Library

Elsinger, Peter K. (1973) 'The Conditions of Protest Behavior in American Cities,' *American Political Science Review,* 67, 11-28

Evans, Sara (1979) *Personal Politics,* New York, Alfred A. Knopf

Fainstein, Norman (1986-7) 'The Underclass/Mismatch Hypothesis as an Expanation for Black Economic Deprivation,' *Politics and Society,* 15 (4) 403-51

Featherman, David and Robert Hauser (1978) *Opportunity and Change,* New York, Academic Press

Feinberg, J. (1973) *Social Philosophy,* New Jersey, Prentice-Hall

Finkle, Lee (1973/4) 'The Conservative Aims of Militant Rhetoric,' *Journal of American History,* 60, 692-713

Flaim, P. and E. Sehgal (1985) 'Displaced Workers of 1979-84: How Well have they Fared?' *Monthly Labor Review,* 108 (6), June, 3-16

Forman, James (1972) *The Making of Black Revolutionaries: A Personal Account,* New York, The Macmillan Company

Fortney, Nancy D. (1977) 'The Anthropological Concept of Race,' *Journal of Black Studies,* 8 (1), 35-54

Foster, Lorn S. (1983) 'The Voting Rights Act and the New Southern Politics,' *Western Journal of Black Studies*, 7 (3), Autumn, 120-9

Foucault, Michel (1972) *The Archaeology of Knowledge*, London, Tavistock Books

Fowler, R. and Kress, G. (eds) (1979) *Language and Control*, London, Routledge & Kegan Paul

Fox, Roger et al. (1980) *Blacks in Policy-making Positions*, (Chicago, Chicago Urban League

Frankena, William (1970) 'Some Beliefs About Justice,' in Joel Feinberg and H. Gross (eds) *Justice*, California, Dickenson

Freeland, Richard M. (1971) *The Truman Doctrine and the Origins of McCarthyism*, New York, Schocken Books

Freeman, Jo (ed.) (1983) *Social Movements of the Sixties and Seventies*, New York, Longman

Fries, C. (1940) *American English Grammar*, New York, Appleton Century

Gardner, Lloyd C. (1976) *Imperial America: Foreign Policy Since 1898*, New York, Harcourt, Brace Jovanovich

Garraty, John A. (1978) *Unemployment in History*, New York, Harper & Row

Garrow, David J. (1981) *The FBI and Martin Luther King Jr*, Harmondsworth, Penguin Books

Geschwender, James (ed.) (1971) *The Black Revolt: The Civil Rights Movement, Ghetto Uprising and Separatism*, Englewood Cliffs, NJ, Prentice Hall

Gilroy, Paul (1989) 'One Nation Under the Groove: The Cultural Politics of "Race" and Racism in Britain,' in Goldberg, q.v.

Gintis, Herbert and Tsuneo Ishikawa (n.d.) 'Wages, Work Intensity and Unemployment,' manuscript

Ginzberg, Eli (1979) *Good Jobs, Bad Jobs, No Jobs*, Cambridge, Harvard University Press

Glazer, Nathan (1975) *Affirmative Discrimination*, New York, Basic Books

Goldberg, David (1987) 'Raking the Field of the Discourse of Racism,' *Journal of Black Studies*, 17 (1) Autumn, 58-71

Goldberg, David Theo (ed.) (1989) *Anatomy of Racism*, Minneapolis, University of Minnesota Press

Goldberg, David Theo (1989a) 'The Social Formation of Racist Discourse,' in Goldberg, q.v.

Golden, R. I. (1960) *Improving Patterns of Language Usage*, Detroit, Wayne State University Press

Goldman, Allan H. (1977) 'Justice and Hiring by Competency,' *American Philosophical Quarterly*, 14 (1), 17-28

Goldstein, Michael (1981) 'The Political Careers of Fred Roberts and Tom Bradley: Political Style and Black Politics in Los Angeles,' *Western Journal of Black Studies*, 5 (4), Winter, 139-46

Gorz, André (1971) 'Immigrant Labor,' *New Left Review*, 61

Gould, Mark (1981) 'The Devaluation of Labor Power,' *Berkeley Journal of Sociology*, 26, 139-56

Gould, Mark (1981) 'Parsons Versus Marx: "An earnest warning",' *Sociological Inquiry*, 51, 197-218

Gould, Stephen Jay (1981) *The Mismeasure of Man*, New York, W. W. Norton

Gould, Mark (1983) 'Egalitarian Values: Some Unintended Consequences, Some Equitable Remedies,' Paper delivered at the Annual Meeting of the Eastern Sociological Society, Baltimore, Maryland

Gould, Mark (1987) 'Proximate Sanctions, Institutional Structures and the Exploitation of Labor-Power,' manuscript, Haverford College

Gould, Mark (1988) 'Legitimation and Justification: The Logic of Moral and Contractual Solidarity in Weber and Durkheim,' Paper delivered at the Annual Meeting of the American Sociological Association, Atlanta, Georgia

Gould, Mark (1989) 'The Problem of Order in Hobbesian and Lockean Theory,' Paper delivered at the Annual Meeting of the American Sociological Association, San Francisco, California

Gould, Mark. and Michael M. Weinstein (1989) 'Class in a Neoclassical Theory of Competitive Markets,' manuscript, Haverford College

Gramsci, Antonio (1971) *Selections from the Prison Notebooks*, New York, International

Griffith, Robert and Anton Theoharis (eds) (1974) *The Specter*, New York, New Viewpoints

Gross, Barry R. (ed.) (1977) *Reverse Discrimination*, New York, Prometheus Books

Grove, David J. (1974) *The Race vs Ethnic Debate: A Cross National Analysis of Two Theoretical Approaches*, Denver, Center on International Race Relations, University of Denver

Hacker, Andrew (1979) 'Two "New Classes" or None?,' *Society*, 16 (2), 49-54

Haines, Herbert H. (1984) 'Black Radicalization and the Funding of Civil Rights: 1957-1970,' *Social Problems*, 32 (1), October, 31-43

Halliday, M. A. K. (1976) 'Anti-Languages,' UEA Papers in Linguistics, 15-45

Hanke, Lewis (1959) *Aristotle and the American Indians*, Chicago, Regnery

Harrison, B. (1972) *Education, Training and the Urban Ghetto*, Baltimore, Johns Hopkins University Press

Hauser, Arnold (1951) *The Social History of Art*, I, New York, Vintage

Hechter, Michael (1987) *Principles of Group Solidarity*, Berkeley, University of CAlifornia Press

Hegel, G. W. F. (1952) *The Philosophy of Right*, Oxford, Oxford University Press, first published 1821

Hill, Richard Child and Cynthia Negrey (1989) 'De-industrialization and Racial Minorities in the Great Lakes Region,' Urban Affairs Program, Discussion Paper 12 (1) Winter, Michigan State University

Hill, Robert A. and Barbara Bair (eds) (1987), *Marcus Garvey: Life and Lessons*, Berkeley, University of California Press

Hirshberg, J. (1982) 'Towards a Dictionary of Black American English on Historical Principles,' *American Speech*, 57, 163-82

Holt, G. (1972) '"Inversion" in Black Communication,' in T. Kochman (ed.) *Rappin' and Stylin' Out: Communication in Urban Black America*, Urbana, University of Illinois Press

Hook, Sidney (1977) 'Discrimination, Colour Blindness, and the Quota System,' in Gross, q.v., 88-96

Horne, Gerald (1986) *Black and Red: W.E.B. DuBois and the Afro-American Response to the Cold War (1944-1973)*, Albany, SUNY Press

Huges, Graham (1975) 'Reparations for Blacks?' in Tom L. Beauchamp, *Ethics and Public Policy*, New Jersey, Prentice Hall

Hume, David (1964) 'Of National Character,' *Philosophical Works*, 3, Germany, Scientia Verlag

Hume, David (1985) *An Inquiry Concerning the Principles of Morals*, Indianapolis, Bobbs Merrill

Jordan, Winthrop (1969) *White Over Black*, Chapel Hill, University of North Carolina Press

Kamin, L., R. Lewontin and S. Rose (1984) *Not in Our Genes*, New York, Pantheon Books

Kant, Immanuel (1960) *Observations on the Feelings of the Beautiful and the Sublime*, Berkeley, University of California Press

Karnig, Albert and Susan Welch (1980) *Black Representation and Urban Policy*, Chicago, University of Chicago Press

Killian, Lewis (1965) 'Community Structure and the Role of the Negro Leader Agent,' *Sociological Inquiry*, 35, 69-70

Killian, Lewis M. (1981) 'Black Power and White Reactions: The Revitalization of Race-Thinking in the United States,' *The Annals of the American Academy of Political and Social Sciences*, 454, March

Kluegel, James. R. and Eliot R. Smith (1986) *Beliefs About Inequality: Americans' Views of What Is and What Ought to Be*, New York, Aldine de Gruyter

Knight, Frank (1965) *Risk, Uncertainty and Profit*, New York, Harper Torchbooks, first published 1921

Kochman, T. (ed) (1972) *Rappin' and Stylin' Out: Community in Urban Black America*, Urbana, University of Illinois Press

Kochman, T. (1981) *Black and White Styles in Conflict*, Chicago, University of Chicago Press

Kolko, Gabriel (1968) *The Politics of War: The World and United States Foreign Policy (1943-1945)*, New York, Vintage Books

Kovel, Joel (1970) *White Racism: A Psychohistory*, New York, Pantheon Books

Kozol, J. (1975) 'The Politics of Syntax,' *English Journal*, December, 22-27

Kress, G. and Hodge, R. (1979) *Language as Ideology*, London, Routledge & Kegan Paul

Kushnick, Louis (1981) 'Racism and Class Consciousness in Modern Capitalism,' in Benjamin P. Bowser and Raymond G. Hunt (eds), *Impacts of Racism on White Americans*, Beverly Hills and London, Sage Publications

Kushnick, Louis (1981/2) 'The Parameters of British and North American Racism,' *Race and Class*, 23 (2/3), Autumn/Winter, 187-206

Labov, William (1972) *Language in the Inner City*, Philadelphia, University of Pennsylvania Press

Labov, W. (1982) 'Objectivity and Commitment in Linguistic Science: The Case of the Black English Trial in Ann Arbor,' *Language in Society*, 11, 165-201

Landry, Bart (1987) *The New Black Middle Class*, Berkeley, University of California Press

Leggett, J. C. (1968) *Class, Race and LABOUR: Working-class Consciousness in Detroit*, Oxford, Oxford University Press

Lewis, W. Arthur (1985) *Racial Conflict and Economic Development*, Cambridge, Mass., Harvard University Press

Liebow, Elliot (1967) *Tally's Corner*, Boston, Little, Brown & Co.

Lipietz, Alain (1986) 'Behind the Crisis: The Exhaustion of a Regime of Accumulation: A "Regulation School" Perspective on some French Empirical Works,' *Review of Radical Political Economics*, 18 (1+2) 13-32

Light, Ivan (1972) *Ethnic Enterprise in America*, Berkeley, University of California Press

Littler, Craig R. and Graeme Salaman (1984) *Class at Work: The Design, Allocation and Control of Jobs*, London, Batsford

Locke, John (1963) *Two Treatises of Government*, New York, Mentor, first published 1690

Lowenstein, Gaither (1981) 'Black Mayors and the Urban Underclass,' *Western Journal of Black Studies*, 1 (1), Spring, 18-23

Lowry, Glenn (1984) 'The Need for Moral Leadership in the Black Community,' *New Perspectives*, 16, Summer

Lowry, Glenn (1985) 'The Moral Quandry of the Black Community,' *The Public Interest*, 79, Spring

Lowth, R. (1762]) *A Short Introduction to English Grammar*, Delmar, New York, Scholars' Fascimiles and Reprints (reprint 1979)

Luhmann, Niklas (1979) *Trust and Power*, New York, John Wiley

Lukács, George (1971) *History and Class Consciousness*, Cambridge, MIT Press

Lutz, W. (1987) 'Notes toward a Description of Doublespeak (Revised),' *Quarterly Review of Doublespeak*, 13 (2) 10-12

MacDonald, J. Fred (1985) *Television and the Red Menace: The Video to Vietnam*, New York, Praeger

Malvaeaux, Julienne (1985) 'The Economic Interests of Black and White Women: Are They Similar?,' *The Review of Black Political Economy*, 14 (1), Summer, 5-28

Marable, Manning (1983) Race, *Reform and Rebellion: The Second Reconstruction*, London, Macmillan

Marable, Manning (1985) Black American Politics, London, Verso

Marable, Manning (1986) *W.E.B. DuBois: Black Radical Democrat*, Boston, Twayne Publishers

Marglin, Stephen (1974) 'What Do Bosses?' *Review of Radical Political Economics*, 6, 60-112

Marshall, Arthur (1890) *Principles of Economics*, London, Macmillan

Marx, K. (1968) 'Economic and Philosophical Manuscripts of 1844,' in K. Marx and F. Engels, *Selected Works*, New York, International Publishers, first published 1844

Marx, Karl (1976) 'On the Jewish Question,' in L. Easton and K. Guddhat (eds) *Writings of the Young Marx on Philosophy*, Garden City, New York, Doubleday Publishers

McAdam, Doug (1982) Political Process and the Development of Black Insurgency, 1930-1970, Chicago, University of Chicago Press

McAdam, Doug (1983) 'Tactical Innovation and the Pace of Insurgency,' *American Sociological Review*, 48, 735-54

McClory, Robert (1977) *The Man Who Beat Clout City*, (Chicago, The Swallow Press

McGary, Howard Jr (1977/8) 'Justice and Reparations,' *The Philosophical Forum*, 9 (2-3), 250-63

McGary, Howard Jr (1984) 'Reparations, Self-Respect and Public Policy,' *The Journal*, 1 (1), 15-26

Mead, Lawrence (1986) *Beyond Entitlement: The Social Obligations of Citizenship*, New York, Free Press

Meitzen, Mark (1986) 'Differences in Male and Female Job-quitting Behavior,' *Journal of Labor Economics*, 4, 151-67

Melden, Abraham I. (ed.) (1970) *Human Rights*, Belmont, Calif., Wadsworth Publishing Company

Milbrath, Lester W. and M.L. Goel (1977) *Political Participation*, Chicago, Rand McNally

Mitchell-Kernan, C. (1969) 'Language Behaviour in a Black Urban Community,' Unpublished doctoral dissertation, Berkeley, University of California

Montagu, Ashley (1969) 'The Concept of Race,' in A. Montagu (ed.) (1969a) q.v.

Montagu, Ashley (ed.) (1969a) *The Concept of Race*, London, Collier-Macmillan

Montagu, Ashley (1980) *Sociobiology Reexamined*, New Jersey, Oxford University Press

Morales Rebecca (1983) 'Transitional Labor: Undocumented Workers in the Los Angeles Automobile Industry,' *International Migration Review*, 17, 570-96

Morales R., T. Azores, R. Purkey and S. Ulgen (1982) *The Use of Shift-Share Analysis in Studying the Los Angeles Economy*, UCLA Graduate School in Architecture and Planning Publications Report 58

Morrison, T. (1984) 'Epigraph,' as quoted in Giddings, P., *When and where I Enter... The Impact of Black Women on Race and Sex in America*, New York, William Morrow

Mosse, George (1979) *Toward the Final Solution*, New York, Howard Fertig

Mouffe, Chantal and Ernesto Laclau (1985) *Hegemony and Socialist Strategy: Towards a Radical Democratic Politics*, London, Verso

Muller Thomas (1984) *The Fourth Wave*, Washington DC, Urban Institute Report

Murray, L. (1795) *English Grammar*, New York, Collins and Company (reprinted 1819)

Murray, Nancy (1986) 'Anti-Racists and Other Demons: The Press and Ideology in Thatcher's Britain,' *Race and Class*, 27 (3), Winter, 1-20

Murray, Nancy (1986a), 'Reporting the Riots,' *Race and Class*, 27 (3), Winter, 86-90

Murray, Richard L. and Arnold Vedlitz (1982) 'The Historical Dynamics of Black Political Organization in the Urban South,' *Western Journal of Black Studies*, 7 (2), Spring

Myrdal, Gunnar (1962) *An American Dilemma: The Negro Problem and Modern Democracy*, New York, Harper & Row

Naison, Mark (1983) *Communists in Harlem During the Depression*, Urbana, University of Illinois Press

National Organization for an American Revolution (1982) *Manifesto for an American Revolutionary Party*

Nei, M. and A. K. Roychoudhury (1972) 'Gene Differences between Caucasian, Negro and Japanese Populations,' *Science*, 177, August, 434-5

Nei, M. and A. K. Roychoudhury (1983) 'Genetic Relationship and Evolution of Human Races,' *Evolutionary Biology*, 14, 1-59

Newton, Lisa H. (1973) 'Reverse Discrimination as Unjustified,' *Ethics*, 83 (4), 308-12

Noel, Donald L. (1972) *The Origins of American Slavery and Racism*, Ohio, Charles E. Merrill

Nozick, Robert (1975) *Anarchy, State and Utopia*, New York, Basic Books

Oberschall, Anthony (1973) *Social Conflict and Social Movements*, Englewood Cliffs, NJ, Prentice Hall

Offe, Claus (1985) *Disorganized Capitalism*, Cambridge, MIT Press

Ogbu, John (1978) *Minority Education and Caste*, New York, Academic

Omi, Michael and Howard Winant (1986) *Racial Formation in the United States: From the 1960s to the 1980s*, London, Routledge & Kegan Paul

Palmer, Lu (1984) 'Black Leadership in Crisis: The Case of Chicago,' (speech at University of Illinois-Urbana)

Parker Richard (1981) 'Winning Through Inflation,' *Mother Jones*, July

Parkin, F. (1979) *Marxism and Class theory: A Bourgeois Critique*, New York, Columbia University Press

Parsons, Talcott (1949) *The Structure of Social Action*, New York, Free Press

Pettigrew, Thomas (1965) 'Complexity and Change,' in T. Parsons and K. Clarke (eds) *The Negro American*, Boston, Beacon Press

Phelps, Edmund (1972) 'The Statistical Theory of Discrimination,' *American Economic Review*, 62, 659-61

Pinkney, Alfonso (1984) *The Myth of Black Progress*, New York, Cambridge University Press

Piore, M. J. (1969) 'On the Job Training in the Dual Market,' in A. Weber, F. Cassell and W. Ginsberg (eds) *Public-Private Manpower Policies*, Madison, Wisconsin, Industrial Relations Research Association, 101-32

Plato, (1972) *Philebus*, Cambridge, Cambridge University Press

Pollenberg, Richard (1980) *One Nation Divisible*, New York, Pelican

Pomerantz, Charlotte (ed.) (1963) *A Quarter Century of Un-Americana*, New York, Marzani & Munsell Publishers

Popkin, Richard (1977/8) 'Hume's Racism,' *The Philosophical Forum*, 9

Popkin, Richard (1984) 'Hume's Racism Reconsidered,' *The Journal*, 1

Portes, A. and R. Bach (1980) 'Immigrants Earnings: Cuban and Mexican Immigrants in the United States,' *International Migration Review*, 14, 315-41

Pouissant, A. (1967) 'A Negro Psychiatrist Explains the Negro Psyche,' *The New York Times Magazine*, 20 August

Poulantzas, N. (1973) 'On Social Classes,' *New Left Review*, 78, 27-54

Poulantzas, N. (1975) *Political Power and Social Classes*, London, New Left Books

Prager, J. (1972/3) 'White Racial Privilege and Social Change: An Examination of Theories of Racism,' *Berkeley Journal of Sociology*, 17, 117-50

Preston, Michael (1982) 'Black Politics in the Post-Daley Era,' in Gove and Masotti (eds.), *After Daley: Chicago Politics in Transition*, Urbana, University of Illinois Press

Pryor, F. (1981) 'The "New Class": Analysis of the Concept, the Hypothesis and the Idea as a Research Tool,' *American Journal of Economics and Sociology*, 40 (4) 367-80

Rivera, R., G. McWorter and E. Lillienstein (1964) 'Freedom Day II in Chicago,' *Integrated Education*, 2 (4) 34-43

Robeson, Paul Jr (1971) 'Paul Robeson: Black Warrior,' *Freedomways*, 11, *First Quarter*, 22-33

Roemer, John (1979) 'Divide and Conquer: Microfoundations of the Marxian Theory of Discrimination,' *Bell Journal of Economics*, 10, 695-705

Roemer, John (1982) *A General Theory of Exploitation and Class*, Cambridge, Harvard University Press

Roemer, John (1986) 'New Directions in the Marxian Theory of Exploitation and Class,' in John Roemer (ed.) *Analytical Marxism*, Cambridge, Cambridge University Press, 81-113

Rorty, Richard (1980) *Philosophy and the Mirror of Nature*, Princeton, Princeton University Press

Rosen, Sumner (1969) 'The CIO Era (1935-55),' in Julius W. Jacobson (ed.), *The Negro and the American Labor Movement*, Garden City, Anchor Books

Rytira, Nancy (1982) 'Earnings of Men and Women,' *Monthly Labor Review*, April, 105 (9)

Samuelson, Paul (1957) 'Wage and Interest: A Modern Dissection of Marxian Economic Models,' *American Economic Review*, 47, 884-912

Sassen, S. (1988) *The Mobility of Labor and Capital*, Cambridge, Cambridge University Press

Sassen-Koob, S. (1984) 'The New Labor Demand in Global Cities,' in M. P. Smith (ed.) *Cities in Transformation*, Beverly Hills, Sage

SCAG (Southern California Association of Governments) (1984) *Profile of an Economic Transition: A Statistical Report on the Southern California Economy*, Los Angeles, SCAG, April

SCAG (1984a) 'Southern California; A Region in Transition', *Impact of Present and Future Immigration*, 11, Los Angeles, SCAG

Schuman, Howard et al. (1985) *Racial Attitudes in America*, Cambridge, Harvard University Press

Searle, Chris (1987) 'Your Daily Dose: Racism and the Sun,' *Race and Class*, 29 (1), Summer, 55-72

Shapiro (trans.) (1972) *Knowledge and Human Interests*, London

Shapiro, Carl and Joseph E. Stiglitz (1986) 'Equilibrium Unemployment as a Worker Discipline Device,' in George A. Akerlof and Janet L. Yellen (eds.) *Efficiency Wage Models of the Labor Market*, Cambridge, Cambridge University Press, 45-56

Simpson, Lorenzo C. (1987) 'Values, Respect and Recognition: On Race and Culture in the Neo-Conservative Debate,' *Praxis*, 7 (2), July

Singer, Marcus G. (1978) 'Some Thoughts on Race and Racism,' *Philosophia*, 8 (2-3) 153-83

Smith, Adam (1978) *The Wealth of Nations*, London, Pelican, first published 1776

Smitherman, G. (1976) 'The Language of Black Workers,' unpublished research report

Smitherman, G. (1986) *Talkin and Testifyin: The Language of Black America*, Detroit, Wayne State University Press

Smitherman, G., Daniel, J. and Jeremiah, M. (1991) 'Black-White Linguistic Solidarity,' unpublished manuscript

Soja, E. (1989) *Post Modern Geographies*, London, Verso Books

Soja, E., R. Morales and G. Wolff (1983) 'Urban Restructuring: An Analysis of Social and Spatial Change in Los Angeles,' *Economic Geography*, 59, 195-230

Sowell, Thomas (1971) 'Economics and Blacks,' *Review of Black Political Economy*, Winter-Spring

Sowell, Thomas (1975) *Race and Economics*, New York, David McKay

Sowell, Thomas (1977) 'Affirmative Action Reconsidered,' in Gross, q.v., 113-31

Sowell, T. (1981) *Markets and Minorities*, New York, Basic Books

Sowell, Thomas (1981a) *Ethnic America: A History*, New York, Basic Books

Sowell, T. (1984) *Civil Rights: Rhetoric of Reality?*, New York, William Morrow

Stafford, Walter (1985) *Closed Labor Markets*, New York, Community Services Society of New York

Stalin, J. (1951) *Marxism in Linguistics*, New York, International Publishers

Stanback, Thomas and Thierry Noyelle (1982) *Cities in Transition*, Totowa NJ, Allanheld, Osmun Publishers

Stiglitz, Joseph E (1973) 'Approaches to the Economics of Discrimination,' *American Economic Review*, 63, 287-95

Strickland, Arvarh (1966) History of the Chicago Urban League, Urbana, University of Illinois Press

Sweezy, Paul (1953) *The Present as History: Essays and Reviews on Capitalism and Socialism*, New York, Monthly Review Press

Sykes, M. (1988) 'From "Rights" to "Needs": Official Discourse and the "Welfarisation" of Race,' in G. Smitherman-Donaldson and T. A. van Dijk (eds) *Discourse and Discrimination*, Detroit, Wayne State University Press

Thompson, John B. (1984) *Studies in the Theory of Ideology*, Berkeley, University of California Press

Thrift, Nigel and Peter Williams (1987) 'The Geography of Class Formation,' in Thrift and Williams (eds) *Class and Space: The Making of Urban Society*, London, Routledge & Kegan Paul

Thurow, Lester (1969) *Poverty and Discrimination*, Washington DC, Brookings Institute

Thurow, Lester (1975) *Generating Inequality*, New York, Basic Books

Thurow, Lester (1980) *The Zero Sum Society*, New York, Basic Books

Toll, William (1979) *The Resurgence of Race*, Philadelphia, Temple University Press

Tryman, Donald L. (1977) 'A Typology of Black Leadership,' *Western Journal of Black Studies*, 1 (1), Spring, 18-23

Tucker, Robert (1969) *The Marxian Revolutionary Idea*, New York, Norton Publishing Company

Turner, L. D. (1949) *Africanisms in the Gullah Dialect*, Chicago, University of Chicago Press

Tyler, Gus (1987) 'A Tale of Three Cities: Upper Economy, Lower and Under,' *Dissent*, Fall

Uzzell, Odell (1981) 'Role Perception of Black Decision-Makers: A Case Study,' *Western Journal of Black Studies*, 5 (4), Winter, 285-99

van den Berghe, Pierre (1981) *The Ethnic Phenomenon*, New York, Elsevier

van Dijk, T. A. (1988) 'How 'They' Hit the Headlines: Ethnic Minorities in the Press, in G. Smitherman-Donaldson and T. A. van Dijk (eds) *Discourse and Discrimination*, Detroit, Wayne State University Press

Vincent, Theodore G. (1971) *Black Power and the Garvey Movement*, Berkeley, Ramparts Press

Viscusi, W. Kip (1980) 'Sex Differences in Worker Quitting,' *Review of Economics and Statistics*, 62, 388-98

Vlastos, Gregory (1970) 'Justice and Equality,' in Melden, q.v.

Volosinov, V. N. (1929), *Marxism and the Philosophy of Language*, New York, Seminar Press (reprint 1973)

von Humboldt, W. (1810) 'Man's Intrinsic Humanity: His Language,' in M. Cowan (ed.), *Humanist without Portfolio*, Detroit, Wayne State University Press (reprint 1963)

Vygotsky, L. S. (1962) *Thought and Language*, Cambridge, Massachusetts Institute of Technology

Walker, A. (1982) *The Colour Purple*, New York, Harcourt Brace

Walton, Hanes (1972) *Black Politics*, Philadelphia, Lippincott

Warren, Mary Ann (1985) 'On the Moral and Legal Status of Abortion,' in R. Wasserstrom (ed.) *Today's Moral Problem*, New York, McMillan

Wasserstrom, Richard (1970) 'Rights, Human Rights, and Racial Discrimination,' in Melden, q.v.

Wasserstrom, Richard (1977) 'Racism, Sexism, and Preferential Treatment: An Approach to the Topics,' *UCLA Law Review*, 24

Wasserstrom, Richard A. (1980) 'Racism and Sexism,' in Wasserstrom (ed.), *Philosophy and Social Issues*, Indiana, University of Notre Dame Press

Weber, Max (1968) *Economy and Society*, Kansas, Bedminster Press

Webster, N. (1784) *A Grammatical Institute of the English Language*, Part II, Delmar, New York, Scholars' Fascimiles Reprints (reprinted 1980) SMITHERMAN

Weiss, Andrew (1984) 'Determinants of Quit Behavior,' *Journal of Labor Economics*, 2, 371-87

West, Cornel (1982) *Prophesy Deliverance! An Afro-American Revolutionary Christianity*, Philadelphia, Westminster (McGary)

Whorf, B. (1941) *Language, Thought and Reality: Selected Writings of Benjamin Lee Whorf*. Edited by J. B. Caroll, Cambridge, Massachusetts Institute of Technology (reprint 1965)

Williams, Bernard (1962) 'The Idea of Equality,' in P. Laslett and W.G. Runciman (eds) *Philosophy, Politics and Society*, 2, Oxford, Basil Blackwells

Williams, Walter (1982a) *The State Against Blacks*, New York, McGraw Hill

Williams, Walter (1982b) 'On Discrimination, Prejudice, Racial Income Differentials and Affirmative Action,' in Block and Walker (1982), q.v., 69-99

Williams, William A. (1972) *The Tragedy of American Diplomacy*, New York, Delta

Williamson, Oliver (1975) *Markets and Hierarchies*, New York, The Free Press

Williamson, Oliver (1985) *The Economic Institutions of Capitalism*, New York, The Free Press

Wilson, Edward (1975) *Sociobiology*, Cambridge MA, Belknap Press

Wilson, James Q. (1960) *Negro Politicians*, Chicago, University of Chicago Press

Wilson, W. J. (1978) *The Declining Significance of Race*, Chicago, University of Chicago Press

Wilson, William Julius (1987) *The Truly Disadvantaged: The Inner City, The Underclass, and Public Policy*, Chicago, University of Chicago Press

Winant, Howard and Michael Omi (1986) *Racial Formation in the United States*, New York, Routledge & Kegan Paul

Wood, Allen (1972) 'The Marxian Critique of Justice,' *Philosophy and Public Affairs*, 1

Wright, Erik Olin (1985) *Classes*, London, Verso

Wright, Gavin (1987) 'Segregation and Racial Wage Differentials in the South Before World War II,' Paper presented at a University of Pennsylvania Mellon Seminar on Work and Population

Zald, Mayer and John McCarthy (eds.) (1979) *The Dynamics of Social Movements*, Cambridge, MA, Winthrop Publishers

Zax, Jeffrey (1989) 'Quits and Race,' *Journal of Human Resources*, 24, 469-93

Zinn, Howard (1980) *A People's History of the United States*, London, Longman

Index

269